Aging and Adaptation

Aging and Adaptation

Chinese in Hong Kong and the United States

Charlotte Ikels

ARCHON BOOKS
1983

Printed in the United States of America

The paper in this book meets the guidelines for permanence and durability of the Committee on Production Guidelines for Book Longevity of the Council on Library Resources.

Library of Congress Cataloging in Publication Data

Ikels, Charlotte.
  Aging and adaptation.
  Bibliography: p.
  Includes index.
  1. Chinese American aged—Massachusetts—Boston
Region. 2. Aged—Hong Kong. 3. Boston Region (Mass.)
—Social conditions. 4. Hong Kong—Social conditions.
5. Aging—Case studies. I. Title.
F73.9.C5I36 1983   305.2′6′089951074461   83-7130
ISBN 0-208-01999-5

For my parents

Contents

Tables   *ix*
Preface   *xi*

PART I   BACKGROUND   1

1   Images of Aging   3
2   Aging in China   13

PART II   AGING IN HONG KONG   37

3   Hong Kong—The Challenge   39
4   Hong Kong—The Variation   52
5   The Family   73
6   Community Support Systems   102

PART III   AGING IN GREATER BOSTON   135

7   Greater Boston—The Context of Immigration   137
8   Greater Boston—The Variation   157
9   The Family   180
10   Community Support Systems   216

PART IV   CONCLUSIONS   239

11   Aging and Adaptation   241

Glossary of Cantonese Terms   *247*
Bibliography   *249*
Index   *261*

Tables

1   Living Arrangements of Elderly Chinese
    by Marital Status and Presence of Children   75
2   Closest Kin in Hong Kong and Prior Living
    Arrangements of Those Living in Homes or
    Hostels for the Elderly   97
3   Sex and Generation Status of Out-Marrying Chinese   196
4   Living Arrangements of Noninstitutionalized
    Elderly Chinese   198

Preface

The data on which this work is based derive from my research among Chinese families in Hong Kong and in Greater Boston. For a period of 20 months between 1973 and 1976 I gathered data in Hong Kong for my dissertation. (This research was sponsored by the National Institute of Mental Health 5 TOI MH 10469). At that time, very little qualitative information about the life circumstances of the elderly in Hong Kong was available. Thus, a central goal of the research was to determine the range of variation in the life circumstances of the elderly.

I spent three months in Hong Kong during the summer of 1973, at which time I attempted to learn as much as I could about the general state of affairs of the elderly. This was a fortuitous time to embark on such an investigation because the Hong Kong Government and the private social service sector were simultaneously investigating the topic. Because of the general interest, I was very well-received by both government departments and private (voluntary) agencies, who shared with me all their statistical data and program information. As part of this investigation, homes for the aged were being visited, and I was invited to go to several homes with one of the committees. Subsequently, I visited 19 of the 21 homes then in existence and selected 6 for return visits, at which I interviewed (through an interpreter) 78 residents in all. The residents were not selected on the basis of any more rigorous criteria than accessibility, willingness to communicate, and mental intactness. The results of that summer's research are contained in Ikels (1975).

The following summer, I spent another three months in Hong Kong, by which time my research goals had become more clear—I wanted to focus on the development of adaptational skills in the older population. Because of the limited amount of time at my disposal, I had to gain access to older people quickly, and I returned to the officials

xi

who had been helpful to me the previous year. Two of the issues which I wanted to explore were the impact of relocation on the social networks of the elderly and the relative advantages or disadvantages of age-homogeneous environments for the elderly. Accordingly, I attempted to locate individuals with at least one of the following characteristics: (1) a likelihood of moving in the near future, (2) current residence in a neighborhood with a high density of older people, and (3) residence in age-segregated housing (other than conventional homes for the aged).

In order to locate people with the first characteristic I went to the Housing Department and requested their assistance in locating elderly people likely to move in the near future. Public housing is a very popular alternative to private housing in Hong Kong and does not suffer the stereotype that public housing in the United States often does. The Housing Department provided me with a list of older people who were applicants (along with their families) to low cost housing. The names were taken in order from the top of the waiting list until 130 names had been reached. These applicant families were scattered all over the Kowloon Peninsula and the northern fringe of Hong Kong Island. Their housing included rooftop shacks, "cubicles," private apartments, and resettlement estates. Many of the families had been on the list for more than five years and had already moved elsewhere.

I was able to interview 60 potential movers. The 70 not interviewed were omitted for the following reasons:

11—Their spouse was interviewed instead (both names were on the list)

13—No such address or moved from address and not locatable

12—Declined to be interviewed

15—Away from home for extended period (usually visiting relatives in China)

10—Working long hours and unreachable

9—Other (language difficulties, illness, etc.)

In addition, I was allowed access to a "licensed area," a site occupied by families and individuals who had been "cleared" from their squatter huts by the government, but who had not yet been assigned new housing. I interviewed 5 individuals at the licensed area.

I suspected (correctly) that the Housing Department list would consist primarily of individuals in their 60s (the age of the bulk of the older population), and I wanted to locate more of the "old old"— those aged 75 and over who were more likely to have already had to deal with problems of widowhood and disability. In 1973, the De-

partment of Social Welfare had introduced a non-means tested allotment known as the Infirmity Allowance. Any individual regardless
of financial circumstances was eligible for this modest sum provided
he or she had reached the age of 75. In the summer of 1974 the
Department was planning an evaluation of the impact of the Allowance
on older people and their families by drawing a random sample of
recipients. In response to my request, they drew a larger sample than
needed and allowed me to contact 60 recipients. I had specially requested that the sample include particular districts on Hong Kong
Island noted for the density of their elderly population and their being
slated for urban renewal.

The cooperation of government officials was essential to the im-
plementing of my research. It would have been extremely difficult to
locate older people meeting my design requirements in any other way.
Needless to say, the cooperation of the older people to whom I was
allowed access was also essential. The two departments required different strategies in my contacting the older people whose names they
had located for me. The Social Welfare Department conducted a pre-
screening of the list of names. I prepared a letter in Chinese, which
was sent to the prospective interview subjects along with their monthly
allotment. On the bottom of the letter, which introduced me and
explained my objectives, was a stamped portion which could be removed and returned to the DSW. The person simply checked whether
he or she was interested in being interviewed, and if interested, was
asked to check the time of day that was convenient and to supply a
phone number where they could be reached (many had no phones).
The DSW then gave me the names and addresses of the 34 individuals
who indicated a willingness to be interviewed.

The Housing Department allowed me to contact the individuals
on their list on my own, provided I made clear that their willingness
to be interviewed by me would have no effect on their pending application. My initial contact with these people was also by mail. I sent
a letter explaining the nature of the research and that I would be visiting
people in that particular neighborhood during the following week and
hoped that it would be possible to speak with them. Accompanied by
a research assistant, I then knocked on doors. A one to two hour
interview schedule was utilized to gather information on genealogy,
household composition, health, employment status, activities, and
residential histories. This data served as the baseline data.

When I returned in the fall of 1975, I planned to reinterview the
same set of informants, and added 24 residents of a hostel for the

elderly in order to provide comparative data with those in special housing. The former individuals are referred to as the "community sample." Residents of the hostel were selected on the basis of one from each room, varying the target individual systematically. The youngest occupant of the first room, the second youngest in the second room, the next to oldest in the third room, and the oldest in the fourth room (each room had four residents). Of the original 99 community dwellers I was able to relocate and to reinterview 75. All the tables which appear in the Hong Kong sections of the book are based on data derived from the community sample unless otherwise specified. Informants for whom information is lacking are not included in the N of the tables. Following my revisits I selected 15 older people for intensive life histories (12 from the community sample and three from the hostel). By this time my competence in Cantonese made accompaniment by a research assistant optional.

Summary of Hong Kong Sample

1973	Homes for aged	78
1974	Applicant for Public Housing	60
	Resident of Licensed Area	5	Community Sample
	Infirmity Allowance Recipient	34
1975-76	Reinterviews	75
	Residents of Hostel	24

During my stay from September 1975 to November 1976 I lived with a Chinese family in a modest private apartment building in Kowloon. Several of the 12 or so families in the building including the family with which I lived were originally from Sze Yap, especially from Taishan (Toisan) County. These families were my first introduction to families whose property had been acquired primarily through remittances of relatives living in the United States and Canada. These particular families had been living in Hong Kong for many years, spoke standard Cantonese, and except for the presence of family members abroad, did not seem superficially different from the non-Sze Yap families in Hong Kong. Conversations with neighbors, friends, and research assistants all supplemented the information I was acquiring through the survey strategy.

In the fall of 1978, I joined a research project conducted through the Laboratory of Human Development at the Harvard Graduate School of Education. The goals of this project entitled Cultural Factors in Family Support for the Elderly (National Institute on Aging 5 R01 AGO 1095 Robert A. LeVine, Principal Investigator) included assessing the relative impact of cultural values, kinship, and extra-familial resources on the adaptation of elderly first and second generation Americans. The project eventually focused on families of Chinese or Irish ancestry in Greater Boston. In the first year of the project, key informants (individuals deemed especially knowledgeable about the communities and their populations) were interviewed to ascertain the degree of consensus about attitudes and practices relevant to the elderly of these two ethnic groups. In the second year, older people and their family members were brought into the study directly, primarily by a recruiting strategy designed to assure representation of the three major subgroups of Chinese families in the Greater Boston area. Chinese from Southeast Asia, however, have not been included in this study.

My own research was conducted among English-speaking or Cantonese-speaking elderly within the Chinese community. An undergraduate who immigrated from Hong Kong with her family several years earlier and who was well-known within the Chinatown-South End community assisted me in locating and interviewing Toisan-speaking families. A locally reared Chinese-American doctoral student interviewed the Mandarin-speaking population and located most of the suburban dwellers through her own network. As in Hong Kong, a key goal of the research was to determine not a statistical generalization about Chinese families but a documentation of the variability of Chinese families in the American context. Efforts were directed at including elderly individuals or families typical of the following populations: Chinatown Chinese, meaning people from the Sze Yap area of Guangdong Province whose ancestors first came to the United States to work in mines or in railroad construction and subsequently in laundries and restaurants (this population is primarily China-born though there are a few elderly who are American-born); older people who came to the United States in their 20s and 30s for advanced degrees (these people are primarily from well-to-do families, spoke English prior to arrival, and are from provinces other than Guangdong); and older people who came to the United States in old age from China directly or after a ten or twenty year sojourn in Hong Kong or Taiwan. This last category is perhaps the most diverse, including illiterate country women who speak no English to former high officials in the Nationalist Government who have retired in the United States.

There are two fundamental differences in the kinds of data collected in the United States compared to Hong Kong. First, in Hong Kong, the elderly per se were the objects of attention and the primary source of information. There is no systematic primary data from the young or middle generations explaining their views about aging or aged parents. In Greater Boston, in contrast, the focus was on the family unit, and great effort was expended to assure that the views of individuals of different generations were included. Since many of these families were fairly recent arrivals from Hong Kong, it is not unreasonable to assume that the views they express are not very different from the views that younger family members in Hong Kong would have expressed. Second, the data gathering strategies were different. Rather than fixed interview schedules, researchers attempted to carry out guided interviews and to allow informants to express themselves at whatever length they chose on related though not prescribed topics. In both Hong Kong and Boston extensive notes were taken during interviews, and informants' remarks were recorded as accurately as possible. Participant observation also provided a substantial proportion of the data on the significance of peer relationships to the elderly.

As a result, it is difficult to put a precise figure to the number of informants included in the Boston study. Some data about older people was supplied by younger family members who described not only their own parents' situations but also those of in-laws, grandparents, aunts and uncles. Older people talked not only about themselves but also about siblings, siblings-in-law, acquaintances, and about particular situations such as remarriage. Therefore, the discussions on mate selection, living arrangements, property transactions, and so on are based on more than the actual number of households interviewed.

For statistical purposes, tables are based on 119 elderly who are members of 53 families or are relatives of members of the key 53 families in the study. Nevertheless, because there are gaps in the data, not all tables have a usable N of 119. Of the 119 people over the age of 60 included in our data, 70 percent lived in Massachusetts, almost all in the Greater Boston area. Twelve individuals lived elsewhere in the Eastern United States, while 22 lived in the western part of the country, primarily California and Hawaii. One individual's location was not clear. Of the 84 Massachusetts residents, 42 lived in the

Chinatown-South End districts of Boston. Most of these individuals were of Sze Yap origin. Thirteen elderly lived in the Brighton-Allston and Brookline sections, and 3 lived in other parts of Boston. This population is quite diverse and includes both Toisan immigrants as well as Hong Kong immigrants who have come over fairly recently. Twenty-six elderly live in the suburbs west of the city. Few live to the north and even fewer to the south of Boston. These families are primarily Mandarin speakers from the mainland of China though frequently via Hong Kong or Taiwan. The exact proportions of the Chinese community these subpopulations compose is not known, but the diversity is represented by our sample.

A work such as this could not have been completed without the assistance and encouragement of several institutions and many individuals. The National Institute of Mental Health and the National Institute on Aging provided the funds which made possible the fieldwork and the analysis of the data. In Hong Kong, the Housing Department, the Research and Evaluation Unit of the Department of Social Welfare, the Census and Statistics Department, and the Hong Kong Council of Social Service all made available to me the resources of their offices including reports, contacts, and guidance. Without the research facilities and staff support of the Universities Service Centre I probably could not have endured the climate, pace, and cultural conflicts inherent in living in Hong Kong.

In terms of individuals, I am especially indebted to Kenneth Topley, Marjorie Topley, James L. Watson, and Bernard V. Williams for their help in laying the foundations of my Hong Kong research. For interviewing and translation assistance I am grateful to: Alfred Ho, Winnie Ip, Catherine Ko, Cindy Lau, Jennifer Wun, and Teresa Yim.

The Boston project would never have taken place except for the inspiration of Robert A. LeVine of the Laboratory of Human Development at the Harvard Graduate School of Education. For an introduction to the Boston Chinatown community I am especially indebted to the South Cove Community Health Center. Interviewing in Greater Boston could not have been carried out without the initiative and skills of Julia Shiang and Bet-har Wong. Coding and analysis of the Chinese data were carried out by Mei-huey Liu and Shao-hua Yang. From the office Seth Sweet assisted the project in all of its phases. For comments on this and earlier drafts of this manuscript I would like to acknowledge: C. Fred Blake, Alice G. Dewey, Alan Howard, Jennie Keith, Anthony Lenzer, Richard W. Lieban, Ezra F. Vogel, and James L. Watson.

PART I
Background

1 Images of Aging

In his philosophical work on American and Chinese differences, anthropologist Francis L. K. Hsu (1953:328-29) presented an enviable picture of old age in traditional China.

> Long before he is physically unable to work (the elderly Chinese) is likely to have retired to live thenceforth on the fruits of his youngsters' labor. An older man who does seek employment not only is unhandicapped by age, but, if equally qualified otherwise, is preferred to a younger person. The relative economic security of the Chinese elder is surpassed by his social importance. Instead of restricting their associations to persons of their own age level, Chinese men and women seek the counsel and company of their elders. Furthermore, the elders enjoy a degree of authority over the young unheard of in the West. When living under the same roof, the former tend to exercise full control. If sons live separately from their elders, the authoritative position of the old is somewhat modified, but not surrendered, and their advice is sought on every conceivable matter.

The realities behind this description are difficult to know. The traditional China that Hsu describes is no more, and no social historians have yet attempted to determine the extent to which these ideals were translated into reality or whether, if realized, they depended upon a specific combination of other unstated factors for their implementation. Yet this image continues to influence the thinking of both Chinese and Americans, who contrast the image of the respected older Chinese with that of the discarded older American.

It was, therefore, with some surprise that I read the following stories in the daily newspapers of Hong Kong, a city-state with a population nearly 99 percent Chinese.

3

The charred body of a 53-year-old woman was found inside the bathtub of her flat in Shaukiwan yesterday.

No foul play was suspected and the police have classified the case as a suicide.

The dead woman, Lau Chui-gay, was believed to have set fire on herself early yesterday. There was a strong smell of kerosene inside the bathroom when her body was discovered by her son at about 10:30 a.m.

Neighbors of the dead woman said loneliness might have been a major cause for her suicide.

Lau had been a widow for some years. Her sons and grand-children used to live with her at her Shaukiwan Road flat.

But she was recently left alone as her sons and grandchildren had moved into the Stanley Prison staff quarters and into another newly purchased flat.

Lau's charred body was discovered when one of her sons came back to her flat for something he left behind. (*Hong Kong Standard* 31 May 1976).

The suicide of Mrs. Lau is indicative of the rising incidence of suicide in the older age groups. Traditionally suicides among Chinese peaked in young adulthood (Wolf 1975:122), but in contemporary Hong Kong the elderly are overrepresented in the statistics on suicide. According to the Director of Medical and Health Services (Hong Kong 1976) people over 65 accounted for only 5.6 percent of the population but for 21.7 percent of the suicides in 1975-76.

And from the *South China Morning Post* of 17 June 1976 was this article entitled "Stranded Woman Back":

A 65-year-old woman who spent four days on the Macau hydrofoil wharf waiting for her son to return with her travel documents finally got back to Hong Kong yesterday with the help of friends. Lee Ho Min-ching was taken to Macau two weeks ago by her son and daughter-in-law for medical treatment. Once there, her son, whom she identified as Lee Kwong-wah (38), put her in a boarding house and gave her $200HK. The couple then took her identity card and travel documents and told her to wait "three or four days" for their return. She stayed at the boarding house for ten days until her money ran out and then took up her vigil at the hydrofoil wharf.

This story also received extensive radio and television news coverage and had been heard by many of my informants, who not only acknowledged that such things do happen nowadays in Hong Kong but went on to relate cases of neglect with which they were familiar. Such cases of abandonment may be few, but the fact that they can happen at all leads to the conclusion that the fate of the elderly in Hong Kong does not always accord with traditional expectations.

One of the major reasons for the media exposure of the negative aspects of aging in Hong Kong is the desire of young advocates to stir the government to action. While this may seem a laudable aim, it has the unintended consequence of frightening people. In Hong Kong it is not possible to "write a letter to a Congressman" in an effort to influence government policies. Hong Kong has a restricted franchise, and prior to the fall of 1982 elections were held only for positions on the Urban Council, which presides over such matters as trash collection, street cleaning, and cultural events. In Hong Kong the functional equivalent of a letter to a Congressman is a letter to the editor of the *South China Morning Post*, one of the major English language dailies. Thus, one sees letters complaining of long lines at public clinics, of inadequate attention to patients in government-assisted hospitals, or of abuses of power by the police or housing officials. Such letters are usually answered publicly within a few days by an official spokesman for the offending department; the department's policies are patiently reviewed and the letter-writer is informed that his problem is being investigated. Therefore, people hoping to influence the government on behalf of the elderly are naturally inclined to concentrate on tales of woe.

Perhaps another reason for the campaign on behalf of the neglected elderly is the belief among advocates that strong cultural prejudices make it difficult for those in power to understand that more than an emphasis on the restoration of filial piety is required to meet the needs of some elderly. The monied elite are less likely to perceive the problems of older people because their residences are large enough to allow for privacy should there be friction between the generations, because sick parents are sent to private hospitals and returned to their homes to be cared for by servants, and because their experience of the generation gap is different, since the elderly elite themselves are often graduates of Western-style colleges. Thus, the Chinese elite are shielded from knowledge that old people lacking financial resources can encounter considerable difficulties.

The incongruity between Hsu's statement and these stories of abandonment and neglect requires some explanation. Is the situation of the elderly in Hong Kong really as bad as it appears? Have the twin forces of Westernization and modernization totally undermined the position of the elderly or are we only witnessing the public's awakening to the needs of a poor minority? Similar questions have been raised concerning the circumstances of the elderly in the United States. In the 1950s and 1960s advocates for the elderly emphasized their problems in an effort to bring about major policy and program changes which would alleviate these problems. By the time these efforts culminated in Butler's (1975) documentary *Why Survive? Being Old in America*, the public was convinced of the reality of the problems of impoverishment, loneliness, and ill health among the elderly. According to surveys carried out by Louis Harris in 1975 and 1981 for the National Council on the Aging, most Americans believed that a wide range of serious health, housing, transportation, and social problems afflicted the elderly. Yet when asked whether these were serious problems for them personally, most older Americans responded in the negative.

Indeed, a strong countercurrent affirming the strength and value of America's older population has arisen. Maggie Kuhn, the outspoken founder of the Gray Panthers, an activist association of the elderly and their young allies, has decried the tendency of policymakers and service providers to treat the elderly as "wrinkled babies" in need of "playpens"—that is, senior centers focused on entertainment. She feels that many of the programs developed *for* the elderly undermine their self-esteem and deny them the opportunity to articulate their own needs or to play a major role in policy determination. Some service providers have countered by arguing that the active, decision-making, socially-concerned person is the exception among the elderly (as among the population at large) and that prescribing such a role is to set unrealistic expectations.

Of these various currents and countercurrents, it is the problems of the elderly that continue to dominate the public mind. When foreigners, including potential Chinese immigrants, contemplate life in America, they express fears that in their old age they may face separation from their children, financial hardship, and abandonment in nursing homes. To what extent are these fears justified by the actual living situations of the American elderly?

With respect to separation from children, the figures are clear and unambiguous. Although most parents have children living within 30 minutes of the parental home, census data and studies (e.g. Hareven

1976; Mindel 1979) all indicate that the incidence of elderly parents living with adult children has steadily decreased during this century while the incidence of elderly parents living alone has steadily increased. Mindel (1979) points out, for example, that the proportion of "single" (never married, divorced, separated, or widowed) women over the age of 75 living with children has dropped from almost 45 percent in 1950 to 25 percent by 1977. Younger singles—those between 65 and 74 years of age—are even more likely to live alone.

Furthermore, the proportion of multigenerational households in which the older person is not the head has increased. Historically, much intergenerational living took the form of the adult child remaining in the parental home, but now such arrangements are more likely the result of a parent's move into a child's home. Mindel (1979) and Robinson and Thurnher (1979) note that the proportion of the single very old living with children seems to have stabilized and interpret this phenomenon as a new life-cycle stage. As long as couples or individuals are able to manage independently they will struggle to maintain their own households. When frailty, disability, or financial hardship make this impossible, they will move in with a child. This solution is much preferred and much more frequent than a move into a nursing home.

In the past, multigenerational households were usually a result of the linkage of family and workplace. Family enterprises, particularly in rural areas, provided employment for most family members, and the young eventually succeeded to the parental property. When adult children were forced to leave the farm to seek employment, separation of households became common, and when forced retirement removed older people from the labor force, elderly dependency became a major social problem. Demographic changes have also played a role in the increase of young independent households. A study by Ikels (1983) revealed that among Chinese and Irish American families in Greater Boston early widowhood of a parent was a powerful determinant of continued co-residence. Due to advances in public health and medical care, widowhood is now more likely to occur at a later stage of the life cycle when children are already out of the home. Compression of childbearing into the earliest years of a marriage and improved life expectancies mean that children are often married and settled outside of the parental home when the parents are only in their 50s.

American values also emphasize the establishing of a separate residence by young couples. Hareven (1976) and Schorr (1980) point out that many writers often take for granted that multigenerational households will cause problems and so counsel against them with little analysis of the facts. Kivett and Learner (1982) investigated morale and living arrangements of the older adults in a rural area and found that, when controlling for health and income, the morale of older people did not differ by residence status (living with or without children). In their sample, three-fourths of the parents lived in their own homes or were the responsible tenants while one-fourth lived in a child's home. The former arrangement is much preferred by parents.

Financial contributions from children are neither substantial nor regular particularly when the children live away from home. Schorr (1980:12) cites studies indicating that the proportion of the aged population receiving financial contributions from children is only about 2 or 3 percent of the total, down from 5 to 10 percent just two decades earlier. Seelbach (1977:423) found that over three-fourths of his sample of predominantly low income minority elderly believed that financial support of the aged was the responsibility of the government and not of children (their children frequently had very limited financial resources); nearly two-thirds of his sample rejected the notion that an important reason for having children was to insure support and care in old age. As Bulatao (1980) points out, this attitude is relatively new, and he notes that nothing seems to lead to declines in fertility quite as strongly as the decreasing economic utility of children.

Of course, in most Western countries, the elderly are now provided for under various social security or pension schemes. Whether these programs have undermined filial incentives to provide for elderly parents is a subject of debate. Filial responsibility laws were normally applied only when a parent applied for public assistance. According to Schorr (1980), when filial responsibility was no longer required as a result of replacing Old Age Assistance with the Supplemental Security Income (SSI) program, there was little change in the caseload. In other words, parents had not declined to participate in the program for fear of burdening their children. On the other hand, when lien laws were eliminated in some states, there were significant increases in caseloads. The lien laws allowed the state to take possession of a public assistance recipient's belongings, usually a house, upon his or her death to recover the amount paid in assistance. The increased caseload upon the elimination of the lien laws suggests that parents did not want to deny children their inheritance and therefore had previously refrained from applying for assistance.

Hareven (1976:23) argues:

The major changes that have led to the isolation of older

people in society today were rooted not so much in changes in family structure or residential arrangements, as has generally been argued, as in the transformation and redefinition of family functions. Changes in functions and values—especially the erosion of the instrumental view of family relationships—and the resulting shift to sentimentality and intimacy as the major cohesive forces in the family have led to the weakening of the role and function of extended family members. Affective relationships have gradually replaced instrumental relationships in middle class families in particular.

This analysis sheds light on the often-stated reluctance of older people to become "burdens" to their children, but it should not obscure the fact that older people do receive substantial care from their children. The resumption of multigenerational living referred to by Mindel (1979) and Robinson and Thurnher (1979) is one example of this care. Another is that provided by Shanas (1979:171), who states there are nearly twice as many bedfast or housebound elderly living in the community as in institutions; most of their care is provided by a spouse (if a male) or child (if a female). Among the institutionalized elderly there are three times as many persons who have never married as are found in the community and almost twice as high a proportion of widowed persons. In short, family ties in America do protect against institutionalization, and over the past ten years the number of elderly in institutions has increased only slightly, from 4 to 5 percent. According to Schorr (1980), all of this increase can be attributed to the changing nature of the elderly population; that is, the old old, those over the age of 75 have increased more rapidly than the young old, those between 65 and 75.

Recognition of the tremendous role played by the informal support system of the family, and sometimes of neighbors, has given rise to a search for new programs that will lessen the burden on the family care-givers who are primarily middle-aged or older women. Skyrocketing health costs and manpower shortages in the health fields make it essential that services to back up the family be developed. Many researchers (Fengler and Goodrich 1979; Robinson and Thurnher 1979; Shanas 1979; Brody 1981; and Crossman et al. 1981) have recognized the competing demands facing most care-givers and the strain that their efforts put on them. Sussman (1979) found that families without a dependent elderly member tended to regard financial assistance as desirable whereas families actually providing care to a dependent member believed service programs to be more important. What constitutes the ideal balance between bureaucratic and family responsibilities for the elderly needs to be constantly reassessed (see Shanas and Sussman 1977).

The statistics cited above describing the situation of the "typical" older American fail to reveal the enormous variations in life circumstances experienced because of differences in income, race, or ethnicity. The effects of income on adjustment to old age are fairly well-known; those of race and ethnicity are less so. Many so-called ethnics—first and second generation Americans of European ancestry—and minority group members make ethnocentric judgments about the meaning of separate residences or the proliferation of services. Many ethnics and members of minority groups are not far removed from an agricultural economy that emphasized coresidence and instrumentality in family relationships. They do not know what to make of what is apparently standard American practice and hope only that they will not end up separated from their children and dependent on public institutions. The impact of ethnicity on adaptation to old age has become a central focus of social science research (e.g. Kiefer 1974; Myerhoff 1978; Woehrer 1978; Guttmann 1979; Osako 1979; Weeks and Cuellar 1981; and Holzberg 1982). These and other studies (e.g. Biegel and Sherman 1979; Trela and Sokolovsky 1979) have raised the issue of whether there are ethnic-specific styles of adaptation and how or whether public policy makers should take ethnicity into account when designing programs.

In analyzing how America was transformed from an agricultural society in which the elderly are often assumed to have had a high status to an industrial society in which they are assumed to have a relatively low status, theorists have usually turned to the modernization hypothesis. This hypothesis links certain demographic and social changes—the increasing proportion of the elderly, a decline in the proportion of the labor force engaged in agricultural work, and the spread of literacy, industrialization, and urbanization—with the changed status of the elderly.

In the past few years, however, some social historians have called into question the recency of this changed status while others have questioned the preexestence in the eighteenth and nineteenth centuries of a relatively golden age for the elderly. Laslett (1972) and Hareven (1976) have pointed out that the respected patriarch surrounded by his descendants was an anomaly even in the past. Most households were small, and even those larger than today's mean household size were enlarged not necessarily by kin but by boarders young and old and by servants. Achenbaum (1978) argues that it is very difficult to untangle the relative influence of industrialization, urbanization, and bureaucratization and that the use of "modernization" as an explanatory variable frequently overlooks the socio-cultural context in which these three factors were originally linked. Perhaps modernization need not inevitably lead to a loss of status for the elderly.

Fischer (1978) points out that public symbols expressing respect for age were threatened as early as the 1780s in America, long before the demographic and other changes associated with modernization had gotten under way. He regards these challenges to the veneration of age as a consequence of ideological changes and, in particular, of the idea of equality associated with the French Revolution. Thus in the West an ideological package composed of notions about liberty, equality, and individualism preceded and paved the way for the emergence of new social and economic forms following the advent of modernization. Cultures operating under other ideological constraints may be able to modify what Western scholars frequently assume to be an inevitable, if unfortunate, correlation between modernization and the worsened position of the elderly.

In trying to understand the changes that have led to an apparent devaluation of the aged, social scientists in Europe and America have been hampered by searching for causes too narrowly in time and in space—in the twentieth century and in Western societies. In the last few years historians have broadened our time perspective. It is the primary task now of anthropologists to broaden our spatial perspective by helping us to examine societies whose underlying assumptions and structural features differ from our own. For many years researchers seeking information about the comparative status of the elderly in non-Western societies were restricted to the findings of Simmons (1945), who, using the Human Relations Area Files, studied the role of the aged in 71 "tribes." Drawing on the work of Simmons and other studies, Rosow (1965:21-22) goes beyond the earlier works to conclude that the position of the aged is stronger when:

1. They own private property (or control it) on which younger people are dependent.
2. Their experience gives them a vital command or monopoly of strategic knowledge of the culture, especially in preliterate societies.
3. They are links to the past in tradition-oriented societies,

especially when they are crucial links to the gods in cultures with ancestor worship.

4. Kinship and the extended family are central to the social organization of the society.

5. The population clusters in relatively small, stable communities (gemeinschaft societies).

6. The productivity of the economy is low and approaches the ragged edge of starvation.

7. There is high mutual dependence among the members of a group.

Evaluating the position of the elderly with reference to these seven statements allows us to break free of the modernization hypothesis. All seven of these conditions were met in traditional China and, at least theoretically, would have operated to ensure a secure old age for most Chinese. The primary task of this book is to demonstrate how the Chinese adapt to very different situations in which most of these conditions no longer exist. How does the micro-environment of the family interact with the macro-environment characteristic of various socio-political systems to produce particular outcomes for the elderly? Each older person and each family make decisions about acceptable or necessary alternatives to traditional solutions. The multitude of these decisions gradually leads to a new consensus about legitimate alternatives, and these in turn become part of the array of alternatives presented to the next aged generation. The stories with which this chapter opened are documents in this process of change.

2 *Aging in China*

Aging in Traditional China

Most descriptions of the position of the elderly in non-Western societies fail to take sufficient account of the diverse circumstances of the elderly. Furthermore, the elderly as a status group usually command more limited privileges than they do as parents. Deference to old people may be officially required, but obligations to support may be due only to parents. While fairly generalized pictures of the status of the elderly as a group within the community and as parents are presented below, it must be emphasized that other variables, such as education, wealth, sex, and personality, also played major roles in determining the relative position of any particular older person.

Age and Status

Traditionally the 60th birthday was an occasion for special celebration because, in a sense, the individual was reborn on this birthday. The traditional Chinese calendar consisted of sixty year cycles; thus, the 60th birthday marked the beginning of a new calendrical cycle. very tenth subsequent birthday was also regarded as a "big birthday" and was ideally marked with a banquet or festive meal with family and friends. The 60th birthday also signified elevation to the status of elder.

The Chinese language has institutionalized the recognition of age, both relative and absolute, in social interaction through a complex system of address terms. Most of my informants indicated that at least in so far as address terms were concerned, they were elevated to the category of senior some years before the 60th birthday. The common address terms* for older people are in the case of men *abaak*, which

---

*Chinese terms are transliterations of Cantonese following the system employed by Parker Po-fei Huang 1970.

in its most restricted sense refers to one's father's older brother, and in the case of women *apoh*, which similarly restricted refers to one's mother's mother. Most of my informants were so addressed when they were in their 50s and sometimes even in their 40s, and they usually attributed their new address status to physical changes such as gray hair.

Traditionally, and even today in Hong Kong, strangers would be frequently addressed with a kin term appropriate to their sex and age relative to the speaker. Thus a child would be told to address a female of his mother's age as "Aunt" or a male of his older brother's age as "Big Brother." The socially accomplished individual knew it was better to err by addressing a newcomer as too old rather than too young because this demonstrated greater respect. When two unrelated individuals of the same surname are members of the same group, the younger will usually be called "Little X" and the older "Old X." The 35 year old addressed as "Old X" is more honored than the 30 year old addressed as "Little X," and this is equally true of men and women. Some of the more Westernized Chinese have become ambivalent about using these address forms. One young woman who came to the United States from Hong Kong at the age of 12 wanted to demonstrate proper respect in her dealings with a group of elderly women in an American Chinatown. When she asked how she should address them, they all said in Cantonese "Just call me Old Mrs. X." The young woman confessed to me that she felt very disrespectful prefixing "old" to their names since in America one usually avoids calling attention to someone's age. No young person would have felt this way in traditional China.

When describing the social position of the elderly in general, most writers on traditional Chinese society emphasize the prestige associated with old age (e.g. Hsu 1953; Doolittle [1865] 1966). Becoming a village elder entitled one not only to an extra share of meat at all ritual feasts but also to the unqualified respect of one's juniors. However, if we can extrapolate at all from contemporary village life in Taiwan, it appears that there was considerable variance in how closely reality approximated this ideal. According to Diamond (1969:44),

> because of the emphasis on work, there is a falling off of prestige as the person moves into old age. K'un Shen gives lip service to the Confucian ideas of respect for age, but in actuality there are few people of advanced years who can attract respect and maintain authority, unless they belong to

the small group of educated property owners. They then continue to have a voice as village leaders and mediators.

Similarly, Harrell (1981:199) points out that in his Taiwan village juniors respect and care for their elders but also make sure that they do not interfere too much in their economic and political affairs. In other words respect is not an unqualified award, and it should not be equated with the possession of actual power.

Another interesting feature of the attitudes towards the older members of the village was the comparative license they were given to indulge themselves. For example, according to Doolittle ([1865] 1966 2: 253-54), the village elders,

> if of active habits and good health . . . usually interest themselves in the affairs of their neighborhood, and crowd themselves into other people's society much oftener than is agreeable. . . . It has become allowable for the elders to invite themselves (if they please to do so, and if they do not receive an invitation) to attend any festive occasion which may occur in their own neighborhoods. . . . On account of their venerable age, they are permitted to take liberties in their own community, and to enjoy privileges which would not be tolerated in young men.

Referring to contemporary Taiwan, Gallin (1966:215-16) reported:

> Unlike younger people, the old are not under pressure to adhere to the proprieties of life. Old women smoke in public, appear at public dinners normally attended by men only, and are generally outspoken. Old men frequent banquets and festivals held in Hsin Hsing and even surrounding villages. On such occasions they care little how much they eat and frequently gorge themselves with the good food. Their juniors watch and say nothing, and in fact seem to enjoy watching the old men behaving in ways that they cannot. . . . When old people talk, even though the younger people may consider their words pure nonsense, they merely smile and agree. When the evening is over there is usually some young grandchild waiting to lead the old man back over the dark paths to his house.

Apparently at this stage of the life cycle, the restraints normally applied earlier were lifted. Having married off the children and greeted the arrival of the third generation, the older person had fulfilled his obligations as a family and societal member. After the marriage of their youngest child, a couple were said to *sai geuk seuhng syuhn* ("wash the feet and get into the boat")—that is, to be freed of the burdens of labor and to be borne along by the labors of others. This image of relaxation and indulgence exerted a powerful hold on many of the men who migrated from Guangdong in search of work in Hong Kong and even in the United States. They hoped that after years of deprivation they could return to their ancestral villages to live in the homes their remittances had constructed and to pass their time smoking and drinking in the nearest tea house with their friends.

In a society with high mortality rates, the mere fact of being old suggested that the individual was in some way special or at least quite different from those many others who had not survived. Theoretically, the attainment of a long life implied virtue as well as possession of specialized knowledge about the appropriate diet to preserve the body, techniques to promote the circulation of the body's *hei* (breath or air), and medicinal herbs. Mote (1977:227) cites the case of the founder of the Ming Dynasty who invited a centenarian to court to honor him for his longevity. When asked the secret of his long life, old Chia Ming replied that the esssential thing was to be most cautious about what one ate and drank. He subsequently submitted to the throne a book which he had written on the subject and which was widely reprinted in the centuries which followed. Gruman (1977), in his study of the early Taoist beliefs, describes their focus on dietary, respiratory, gymnastic, and sexual techniques, though he notes a great gulf between the adepts who attempted to practice these techniques and the mass of the population who could not give time to them.

When I asked my own informants in Hong Kong why they have had such long lives and what, if anything, can be done to lengthen one's life, I received a wide variety of responses. One woman volunteered that perhaps her long life was due to the fact that her two daughters who died in early childhood had given their allotted time to her. This belief is in accordance with a popular folk tale in which a son, on learning that his parent's life was about to end, rushed to the god in charge of these matters and offered up the remainder of his lifespan on behalf of his parent. The god agreed and took the child instead. Another woman stated that there is really nothing one can do as one's death is predetermined. One elderly gentleman, perhaps because of his greater participation in literate society and his membership in a Taoist association, espoused the classical as well as some magico-religious ideas. He stressed moderation in both diet and emotions. While he does not restrict himself in terms of the variety of foods he eats, he emphasized that the critical thing is to avoid overeating, to eat only "70 percent full." He said that one should not worry about things because worry leads to illness and described himself as always optimistic. He also does Taoist breathing exercises and drinks a special tea which, while made from ordinary tea leaves, has had the Taoist scriptures recited over it.

There is also a basically Buddhist belief that doing good deeds will bring good, including long life, to the doer. While a few informants were familiar with this idea, they thought it more likely that bad deeds will bring bad consequences. One man stated that, particularly in one's last few years, one should scrupulously avoid evil, as evil deeds can cancel the death that destiny had planned and bring about an earlier death.

In traditional China, literacy was the luxury of a few. Most families did not have the resources necessary to spare even one son from labor in the fields. Under these circumstances, most people acquired knowledge either from direct experience or through others with direct experience. The longer one had lived, the greater one's wealth of experience—at least in relatively stable societies. Thus, the elderly were considered the repositories of wisdom or, at the very least, experts in some areas of knowledge such as medicinal herbs or ritual. A host of Chinese proverbs testify to this view of the elderly (see Lai 1970; and Chen 1973); "Employ a young carpenter, but an old physician"; "It's the old horse that knows the road"; "If you wish to succeed, consult three old people"; and "He who will not accept an old man's advice will some day be a beggar." All my informants were familiar with the expression "An old person in the family is like a precious stone" and readily explained it in terms of the value—that is, knowledge—of the old person. Several added that this expression is not applicable in present-day Hong Kong.

The depiction of the old person as the indulged free spirit and the reservoir of traditional knowledge has convinced many contemporary Chinese—and non-Chinese—that, in the old days, parents had no fears of abandonment, and old people in general received the respect of the community. However, a number of proverbs and folk characters suggest another side of the picture: "With nine sons and twenty-three grandchildren, a man may still have to dig a grave for himself"; "Grown-up sons run things their way, and grown-up daughters stroll on their own"; "There are only affectionate fathers and mothers, but no affectionate sons and daughters"; "Long disease wears away a child's filial devotion"; and "Old men and yellow pearls are not worth much."

As pointed out by Smith ([1914]1965:272-74), a common figure of ridicule was the Old Lady: "An old lady trying to bite with her teeth forgets that she has none" said of those who make purchases and then find that they have no money; or "An old lady wearing spectacles—all for show" meaning that since she cannot read, the glasses are useless and thus said of useless things or people. Smith also reports on the figure of the Old Man or the Old Villager whose ignorance of the world is so great that he is constantly being surprised or making foolish errors: "The old countryman having an interview with the Emperor—very little talking and a great deal of head-knocking" used to ridicule people who are slow of speech and who merely assent to what others say; or "The old villager having never seen a peacock—what a big-tailed hawk!" used to ridicule people of great pretensions. These two figures, the Old Lady and the Old Villager, suggest that while there may indeed have been respect for the wisdom of the old, it was tempered by recognition of their limitations. Furthermore, the situation of any particular older person was highly dependent on his social circumstances and, first and foremost, on his relationships with his family.

The Elderly in the Family and the Village

A common Chinese saying states that "of all the teachings in the Classics, filial piety comes first." The tremendous sense of gratitude that a child was supposed to feel toward his parents ideally (we know little about the actuality) found its expression in the three years of mourning which followed a parent's death—the three years corresponding to the three years the child had spent in its parents' arms. But one did not need formal instruction in the classics to appreciate the emphasis Chinese culture placed upon responsiblity to one's parents. Even the child of an unlettered family knew the inspirational stories of the *Twenty-Four Examples of Filial Piety*.

One such story was about a young boy whose mother loved to eat carp. He was unable to obtain any because it was the dead of winter, and the carp lay under several inches of ice. When he discovered that he could not chop a hole in the ice to get to them, the young boy decided to remove his shirt and lie down on the ice. Thus the heat of his body melted a hole in the ice through which he was enabled to catch the fish for his mother.

Another such story tells of a family so poor that they could not afford mosquito netting. Every summer at night the mosquitoes descended. Little Wu Mang who went to bed early allowed the mosquitoes to feast on his blood until they were sated. Then, when his parents went to bed, the mosquitoes had no desire to bite them.

An important key to understanding intergenerational or interpersonal relations is the element of reciprocity. There is both long-term and short-term reciprocity. In the early years of the parent–child relationship, the parents are clearly the providers of care; later, ideally, when parents are elderly, they are cared for by their children. On the other hand, short-term reciprocity is expressed through behavior on discrete occasions. For example, if today one party borrows from the other, then tomorrow or next week the other borrows from the first. If one party helps the other find a job or a place to live, then the other will do so later should the occasion arise. Thus, the dynamic operating between the generations is based on the expectation of an ultimate payoff on the initial investment of care whereas between peers it is based on a much more immediate expectation of reciprocity. One can determine very quickly whether a peer takes reciprocity seriously and, if he doesn't, can take steps to replace him with someone more reliable. With children the situation is different. Although one may find out that they are unreliable, they are irreplaceable. Therefore, it is extremely important to make it clear to children very early that support of parents is not easily shirked.

As Doolittle ([1865] 1966 1:140) points out, the entire community was expected to play a role in ensuring that children fulfill their obligations.

> If a son should murder his parent, either father or mother, and be convicted of the crime, he would not only be beheaded, but his body would be mutilated by being cut into small pieces; his house would be razed to the ground, and the earth under it would be dug up for several feet deep; his neighbors living on the right and left would be severely punished; his principal teacher would suffer capital punishment; the district magistrate of the place would be deprived of his office and disgraced; the prefect, the governor of the province, and the viceroy would all be degraded three degrees in rank. All this is done and suffered to mark the enormity of the crime of a parricide.

That these sentences were ever carried out is doubtful, but they illustrate that such a crime was viewed so seriously and that a community had the responsibility to check unfilial conduct long before it reached the point of parricide. Village parents did not hesitate to strike their children to get a point across. Striking them in public was desirable as it demonstrated that the parent took his role as disciplinarian and moral guide seriously. A parent who failed to discipline a wayward child was regarded as fainthearted or uncaring. In extreme cases the older men of the village might take disciplinary action themselves. Two of my informants described the ultimate punishment in their village. A true incorrigible would be taken from his parents, placed in a basket, such as those used to transport pigs or ducks to market, and dunked in the nearest pond or stream. Any young man with a notorious reputation would have difficulty obtaining a wife or maintaining his business relationships. In public discussions his opinions would be ignored, and he would have little choice but to reform or leave the village.

Ideally then, children, particularly male children, were the basis of security in old age. But what of people lacking male descendants? Where could they turn for support? One obvious alternative was to rely on daughters and sons-in-law. Parents hoped to persuade one daughter to remain at home by bringing in a son-in-law, either an orphan or someone with many brothers, who, freed of the responsibility of providing for his own parents, could devote himself to his wife's parents. In the absence of any descendants, one could adopt a child, preferably a fraternal nephew if one's brothers had several sons of their own (Levy 1949:127). This strategy minimized dispersal of the ancestral estate.

Another alternative, especially for those few who remained unmarried or were widowed without children, was to bind themselves to their natal or spouses' natal families as dependent aunts or uncles. During their productive years, they would share the fruits of their labor with these natal units. In old age they would then be sheltered by their nephews.

Other special relationships, beyond the family, could also be drawn on in times of need or old age. There are at least two forms of fictive kinship in Chinese society. The first, "sworn" sibling relationships, are characteristic of age peers. The model for "sworn" relationships is the oath taken by the three principle figures in the novel *The Romance of the Three Kingdoms* whereby the three heroes swear eternal brotherhood. The model is not restricted to males; "sworn" sisterhoods appear to have been common in the silkweaving districts of Guangdong province during

the first few decades of this century. Women usually joined these sisterhoods at an early age. Ideally, they lasted until the partners died but,
according to some observers (e.g. Sankar 1978), they were frequently
unstable unless institutionalized by co-residence and economic interdependence. In any case, since they were associations of peers, the needs
of the last survivor fell outside their scope.

The second form of fictive kinship is the *kai* relationship, characteristic of partners of different generations. There were a variety of
kai relationships in which the common theme was that of need on the
part of one and nurturance on the part of the other. A sickly child,
for example, might have been kaied to a god or to an adult who had
been conspicuously fortunate in the rearing of his own children. In
neither case did the natural parents give up the child, but on significant
occasions such as rites of passage the attentions of the patron god or
kai parent would be sought. The kai relationship of greatest significance for the elderly was that in which an older person kaied a young
adult, preferably a young adult without parents of his own. The two
would exchange gifts publicly; in the early years of the relationship,
the senior would provide services to the junior, and, in the later years,
the junior to the senior. Supernational sanctions and the strength of
public opinion encouraged the participants to fulfill their obligations.

Less personalized means of gaining support included relying on
community organizations. In villages with strong lineage systems, a
person could appeal to the lineage head for some suppport, if only
for the right to live in the ancestral hall. A wealthy lineage might even
have provided additional support through the proceeds of ancestral
land held in common by the lineage (Chen 1936:27). Monasteries or
nunneries, less common than ancestral halls, also provided some accommodations for destitute elderly. Less regularized support might
be obtained from neighbors or through begging in public areas or
around temples during festivals or the new year. But in harsh times,
which were frequent, community support would be curtailed first,
fictive ties next, and in the end only family members could be trusted.

Conspicuously absent from the possible sources of support in old
age was self-support. In the traditional rural villages of Guangdong,
few people were able to amass sufficient capital or property to live
off its interest (Chen 1936:103). Those who were able to do so generally made their wealth available to their descendants, and the wealthy
had no difficulty in acquiring descendants. A concubine could readily
compensate for an infertile wife, and there were no shortages of adopt-
able children. Generally speaking. those who had wealth in old age

also had descendants. Those who had no descendants were generally poor, and what little money they could put together went towards their funerals. Thus, social relationships were the main basis of support in old age, and villagers of all ages shared the ideology of interdependence.

The dues of filial piety continued to be paid even after the ending of the three year mourning period (which, in fact, was usually considerably shorter) in the form of ancestor worship. While Chinese ancestors were believed on occasion to harass their descendants, they were usually perceived as benign and helpful though concerned with the morals of their juniors (Freedman 1967). Good behavior was owed to the ancestors; bad behavior brought shame to them and caused a loss of face in the spirit world. To bring shame to the ancestors or to living parents was to brand oneself a truly inferior person.

In ceremonies paying respect to the ancestors, the senior male of the senior generation was the ritual leader. Since he himself would soon become an ancestor, this role was especially fitting, although a person fit by age and relative rank to lead these rites might be unfit by other criteria. The father of one of my informants still cringed thirty years later when relating how twice a year a shiftless beggar was brought in off the streets to lead his extensive lineage in the ancestral rites. It is also important to note that there were socioeconomic differences in ancestor worship (e.g. Hsu 1940:130; Ahern 1973). A wealthy family would be particularly attentive to the ancestors, for the family's present wealth was presumed to be due in part to the influence of these ancestors. A poor family, by its very poverty, had reason to doubt the abilities of its ancestors to aid their descendants, and a poor family had neither the time nor the money to indulge in relatively unproductive ceremonies. Large ancestral halls and branch halls were symptomatic of wealthy lineages. Jordan (1972:101) found that in contemporary village Taiwan, ancestor worship beyond the dead of the immediate family was either uncommon or perfunctory.

The filial piety and generalized respect which most elderly felt were their due were not the simple consequence of a random cultural choice made thousands of years ago and followed by countless generations of conservative peasants. Rather the realities of family and village life in China served to reinforce a high position for the elderly despite the fact that many aged individuals, for one reason or another, failed to receive either familial or communal regard. The nature of this reinforcement can best be understood by returning to the seven factors that Rosow (chap. 1) found relevant in understanding the welfare of the aged and relating them to the conditions of village China.

Rosow's first variable is an economic one—the extent to which the old own or control private property on which the young are dependent. In village China, the economic relationship between fathers and sons contributed greatly to the sense of obligation to parents. A son usually owed his occupation to his father or other close kinsman. In the case of a peasant, he inherited land or tenancy rights from his father; in the case of a craftsman, he usually owed his training to his father or other male relative (e.g. Lee 1953:274; Fei 1946:141, 143; Chan 1953:208). His tools, his skills, his clientele, his trading partnerships—all were owed to his senior kinsmen. Furthermore, so long as the father remained alive, he usually retained legal right to the land. Ideally, family property was not divided up among the sons until after his death. If divison did occur earlier, it was normally with a stipulation regarding the care of the parents. The son assigned this particular responsibility could expect to receive a larger share of the estate than his brothers (Levy 1949:137). Thus, sentiment aside, Chinese sons had very practical reasons to fulfill their filial obligations.

The residential family and the economic family were not necessarily coextensive, and caring for parents did not always mean coresidence. In land-poor villages, a son frequently had to migrate to the city and send money back to his parents. In other cases where responsibility was rotated among a number of sons, the parents might live alone or with one of them, in their shop for example, but take meals on a regular basis with the others (Hsu 1971:114; Cohen 1976:74-75). The significant point was the provision of care not the coresidence.

The second variable, monopoly or control of strategic knowledge, operated as we have said, to ensure the elderly a needed place even when their physical strength had declined. Although traditional China was by no means a preliterate society, the relative scarcity of formally-educated people meant that personal experience and the very fact of having survived into old age made elders valuable resources.

Rosow's third variable, the extent to which the elderly are links with the past, is of particular significance since pre-modern China is well-known for its focus on the past. From the time of Confucius onward, philosophers preached that peace and harmony would reign only when the people returned to the ways of their ancestors. The Chinese took special pride in noting their links with the past in the form of genealogies stretching back twenty or more generations, and strong supernatural sanctions reinforced the practical reasons behind filial piety.

Fourth, kinship and the extended family were central to the social organization of the Chinese village. Most Chinese villages were composed of the members of a few lineages, the founders of which had migrated to the area many years before. Some villages, especially those in the southern provinces such as Guangdong, consisted of the male members of a single lineage plus their wives and unmarried daughters (e.g. Freedman 1970:1). In such circumstances, one's neighbors were also very likely to be one's kin. In this context, the misbehavior of any one person was an insult to the ancestors of everyone else and could jeopardize the relations of the entire community with the supernatural. Furthermore, the neglect of elderly lineage members, the last survivors perhaps of a nonproductive branch, reflected on the morality of the entire group. Therefore, there was a major incentive for the lineage to provide for at least some of their needs.

Fifth, Chinese villages varied in size from several hundred to several thousand members. In most cases, it was possible to know something about everyone in the village or, at the least, to be able to get such information at will. Anonymity was impossible, and serious delinquencies followed one for life. In addition, while some members left the village for employment in the cities, their families usually remained behind. Village growth came about as the result of reproduction and not as the result of in-migration. This stability meant that debts and favors were long remembered, and that over the course of a lifetime an individual probably developed personal ties with nearly every family through one of its members. In times of need such as a luckless old age, these personal ties could make the critical difference.

Rosow's sixth variable, the inverse correlation between local productivity and care of the aged, seems at first glance paradoxical, but in a marginal economy the contribution of every person to the small gross product is highly valued. Elderly Chinese could gather the droppings of water buffalo or tend chickens, and they could frighten birds away from the fields. So long as productivity exceeded consumption, there was a place for the old. Under conditions of prolonged hardship, however, the elderly could be among the first sacrificed (e.g. Turnbull 1972) unless, as in China, there were additional factors operating to protect them.

The seventh variable, the degree of mutual dependence, also operated to protect the aged. In the Chinese village, for example, the irrigating and draining of the rice fields required extreme coordination and cooperation on the part of the villagers. Similarly, intensive co-operative labor was essential during the harvest particularly if the weather threatened (e.g. Pasternak 1972:20). In some parts of China, intervillage rivalries were so intense that pitched battles occurred, necessitating the formation of village patrols (Freedman 1970:105-11). The need for cooperation put high priority on such character traits as reliability and loyalty. The way in which an individual treated his parents indicated the strength of these traits in his personality. Clearly, any person who was not good to his parents was also not good for the community, and it is this linkage which partly explains the community's interest in the strength of filial piety.

In summary then, practical economic considerations, supernatural sanctions, strong cultural supports, and the force of public opinion all served to protect the villager in old age. Age was not, however, the only factor affecting an older person's status in the community. Wealth, personality, and fate were also important intervening variables, and a person whose life consisted of a string of misdeeds was not likely to fare well when he became dependent on the people he had previously victimized.

The Elderly in the City

So far, we have said little about the situation of the elderly in the cities of pre-modern China. There are two reasons for this omission: there is a relative scarcity of material on this topic; and there was a relative scarcity of the old in the cities. Clearly the first reason derives from the second. The pre-modern Chinese city was populated primarily by the young and middle-aged, most of whom were males unaccompanied by their families. According to Skinner (1977:535) in Guangzhou (Canton) in 1895, the sex ratio was 168 males per 100 females for the northeastern "gentry" districts of the city, and 224 males per 100 females for the southwestern "merchant" districts. Most men were in the city as sojourners sending their money back to the villages and returning annually for the ancestral festivals or the new year, and most men expected to retire to their villages in their old age.

Even as late as 1936, Lang (1946:82) found that in Beijing (Peking), a non-industrial city

> wage earners and members of the lower middle class have
> intimate contacts with the soil. Many workers, apprentices,
> riksha coolies, servants, and others of this class belong to

families living in the country: they send money to their rural homes, leave their wives and children with their old folks, and regard their sojourn in the city as temporary, even when they spend their entire lives there. Evidently a nonindustrial city does not induce many peasants' sons to establish their families in it, although there are exceptions.

Those who did spend their final years in the city did so because they either had family in the city or had no one willing to provide for them in the countryside. This latter category faced a problematic future (Skinner 1977:545).

Ideally, the values operating in the urban context were the same as those operating in the rural: mutual dependence, filial piety, and respect for the past and those associated with it. However, given the fact that the social organization was so very different with regard to community size, stability of residence, and familiarity of neighbors, it was impossible to know the personal histories of everyone, let alone to have personal ties to them. In this context, an anonymous older person was assumed to be someone else's responsibility. The city was not, of course, so totally atomized as to lack personal relationships and notions of mutual assistance; it was rather that one had to make more conscious efforts to develop such relationships.

Newcomers to the city usually went first to live with relatives or fellow villagers who had gone before them, and some, in old age, were able to derive considerable support from such familiars. For others, however, a larger population base was necessary to provide some measure of social welfare, and this larger base could be found in district and surname or "family" associations (e.g. Crissman 1967). In a provincial city, these district organizations usually consisted of the natives of a county or a cluster of neighboring counties. In a metropolitan city such as Beijing or Shanghai, the inclusive "district" might have been an entire province. The surname associations recruited people with the same patronym regardless of place of origin and were in essence clan associations. Even though no genealogical connections could be traced, the members were all considered descendants of a common ancestor, and families with the same surname could not intermarry.

Both district and surname associations provided a means of keeping in touch with the home community by the channeling of remittances and the dissemination of news. They also sponsored credit associations and, of great interest to the elderly, burial societies. In exchange for monthly payments up to a certain amount, the participant was guaranteed a coffin, funeral, and either transport back to the village or local burial. These organizations also introduced the newcomer to opportunities for building up his social networks; in the city just as in the countryside, enduring personal relationships were the key to security in time of need.

Some old people gained a modicum of security through their work contacts. While craft and trade guilds were primarily concerned with business matters, they would on occasion perform meritorious acts such as providing a free burial or helping out a widow (e.g. Rhoads 1974:104; Skinner 1977:533).

These formal organizations did not really offer much security for the ordinary aged worker, however, and no union contracts provided for pensions or unemployment compensation. At best, the larger firms made lump-sum payments to retiring workers and considered their obligations at an end. Instead, the ordinary worker had to depend on personal relationships built up over a long period of time (e.g. Lamson 1934:138; Fried 1953:152). For example, a shop employee who had worked for the same owner-manager for thirty or forty years was not simply discharged as his usefulness declined. Normally, his duties and remuneration were gradually reduced until perhaps he became little more than a night watchman sleeping on the floor in the front of the shop in exchange for his meals. Similarly, a woman who had faithfully served one master and his household for many years was not turned aside in her old age. For all practical purposes, such long-term servants were members of the family and as such were kept on, though their duties were greatly lessened.

In the pre-modern period, the elderly constituted a very small proportion of the urban population (and of the rural population also), and the period between the cessation of their usefulness to their employers and their deaths was usually quite short. Anyone so debilitated that he or she could perform no services about the house was an easy target for infectious diseases. Furthermore, since most of the elderly retired to their native villages, few employers had to worry about the buildup of a large group of aged employee-dependents. Since the elderly consumed considerably less food than either adolescents or working adults, providing them with meals was unlikely to have a great impact on business or household economics.

Workers could sometimes rely on each other in old age. A worker with a family in the city might shelter another older worker, particularly if they were from the same village. Temporary domestic servants sometimes maintained quarters to which they could retire between jobs or in old age. These so-called *jaai tohng* ("vegetarian halls") could be religious or secular in nature (e.g. Yap 1962:448–49; Topley 1975:79, 83; Sankar 1978). Another possibility was to establish fictive kinship ties (kai relationships) with someone younger; but the endurance of these ties in the city was more doubtful than in the countryside as the partners were not so susceptible to public scrutiny.

Those in the weakest position in the city were elderly refugees and those with irregular employment histories. Refugees from famine in the countryside were not welcomed in the cities regardless of their age, and at times the streets were crowded with desperate beggars (e.g. Skinner 1977:546). A worker lacking adequate skills, a laborer whose strength was impaired by injury, or a servant who was insufficiently accommodating found employment infrequently. As soon as their services were no longer needed, they were discharged. Under these circumstances, they were never in a position to build up the emotional dimensions of the employer-employee relationship, and thus found themselves helpless in old age. For some the only certainty in old age was a burial.

Aging in the People's Republic of China

Value Changes

Attacks on the traditional family system did not begin with the establishment of the People's Republic of China. As far back as the last decades of the nineteenth century, when facing the European challenge, Chinese reformers were already saying that "to make China strong and preserve Chinese learning, we must promote Western learning." (Chang 1898 excerpted in de Bary 1960:747). Beginning around 1919, the May Fourth Movement expressing the views of the educated vanguard of youth attacked the power and authority of the extended family, the basic unit of Chinese social organization. The power of parents to require youth to marry unknown partners for the good of the family was especially decried. But generally speaking this assault on the core values was limited to city and upper-class youth (e.g. Chow 1967).

In the meantime, major social changes were seriously disrupting Chinese society. According to Levy (1949:305), by late Republican China, the splitting of old people into two distinct categories, parents and others, was already well-advanced.

While the "traditional" family values required that one would support one's own parents, it said nothing of one's obligations to support aged persons unrelated by kinship. Therefore, if an old man's sons do not provide for him, no one else in the society feels responsible for him. Now the cases are becoming more and more common. Local charity cannot handle the burden, and the general members of the community feel no responsibility for an old person unless bound to him by personal ties. No adequate government provision is being made at present, although the problem is fast exceeding the ability of private charity to meet it.

The Communist regime inherited and intensified this chaotic situation with even broader attacks on the tyranny of tradition and faced unanticipated consequences. According to Chen and Chen (1959:176) the neglect of old people, including old parents,

> became so serious that the Communists found it necessary to inaugurate a campaign to emphasize respect and support of parents. From October 1956 to the early part of 1957, the Chinese Communist press and periodicals abounded in articles exhorting young people to love and support their parents. The articles censured the younger generation for maltreatment and cruelty toward their parents.

Nevertheless, assaults on the old values and old forms of social organization have continued. Over the past thirty years there have been several campaigns culminating in the Great Proletarian Cultural Revolution whose objectives have been the destruction of the old order politically, economically, socially, culturally. Free marriage, population control, greater equality between the sexes and the generations— all potentially undermine the traditional organization of family life (e.g. Yang 1959). The communization of land means that parents no longer control their children's access to a livelihood. At the same time the power of the lineage has been broken—lands taken away, ancestral halls converted to meeting halls and schools. As literacy among the young increases, the gap in knowledge between old and young grows, though the old are still called upon to "speak bitterness", to tell of the terrible times before Liberation. Yet despite all this Davis-Friedmann (1977) finds that the strategies of the elderly have changed scarcely at all. How can this be?

Perhaps two factors are of greatest importance: first, the traditional value of interdependence both between parents and children and among the masses as a whole has never been attacked; second, the economic conditions in China, and in rural China in particular, provide the elderly with opportunities to contribute to household income while at the same time making it impossible for them to go it alone.

Structural Continuities

According to Parish and Whyte (1978) the Chinese government has passively supported the continued existence of the patrilocal family. During the 1958-59 Great Leap Forward there was talk of building public housing for peasants and setting up homes for the aged, but most of the time the emphasis has been on letting people keep their private housing and encouraging—and in the case of sons *requiring*—familial support of elderly members. Since the government has not actively discouraged the traditional practice of out-marriage for girls but has discouraged young men from leaving their natal villages, the end result is the patrilocal stem family. Major economic incentives continue to encourage coresidence of parents and at least one adult married child. While land reform means a parent cannot pass on substantial property, he can still provide his son with living accommodations as well as a baby-sitting service. Normally he cannot control his children's access to employment since the majority of able-bodied adults are expected to work on the production teams and brigades composed of their co-villagers. The contributions these labor units provide to the commune determine the quantity of grain that the commune assigns to them. Therefore, the teams and brigades are very concerned with individual output. On the other hand, consumer items such as bicycles and radios must be purchased out of individual or household savings. These purchases encourage the pooling of family resources, and the family that stays together has more resources to pool. Furthermore the rapid spread of the alternative "household responsibility" systems in the early 1980s has again made family cooperation an important means of economic advance.

The distribution of power within the family has been altered in accordance with the Party's principles of generational and sexual equality. These alterations have not eliminated generational and sexual differences in power and responsibility, but they have moderated them. By and large, fathers yield household headship to their sons earlier than before, and mothers-in-law exercise greater restraint in their relationships with their daughters-in-law. While parents continue to play a role in the selection of spouses for their children, the children can and do refuse these matches. But given the persistence of sex-segregated social lives and restricted mobility, many youths are unable to locate spouses on their own and welcome parental or other initiatives on their behalf (Parish and Whyte 1978:173). Following a couple's betrothal, they are allowed to get acquainted before the wedding. One significant change in public attitudes has been that towards a man's primary loyalty. Parish and Whyte's informants (1978:217) indicate that while many men prefer to keep out of disputes involving their mothers and their wives, they are now just as likely to support their wives instead of, inevitably, their mothers.

The participation of women in the work force has increased their value and means that older people left at home assume some of the household chores. By and large, however, sexual equality has not made great advances in the home. Women remain responsible for almost all household chores despite their labor force involvement. Men's major domestic labor is the tending of the household's private vegetable plot.

Westerners hear of pensioned retirement at the age of 55 or 60 for men and 50 for women but do not realize that this applies primarily to workers in the industrial sector and not to the vast majority of the agricultural workers, still 80 percent of the population. In the late 1970s a few well-to-do suburban communes introduced modest pension schemes for their retired agricultural workers (Davis-Friedmann 1981:5) but these are still considered experimental in nature, and the vast majority of the rural elderly are deemed the dependents of their sons. They are, however, free to pursue potentially lucrative sidelines such as raising pigs, gathering medicinal herbs, or, most important of all, tending private vegetable plots and selling the produce on the open market. These are all cash sidelines. They may also choose to continue in the work-point tradition by working at other less physically demanding tasks such as in nurseries.

Of course, the reasons for the greater involvement of old people in the economic life of the People's Republic of China are straightforward economic reasons having little to do with the Western notion that old people must be kept active for their own peace of mind. The need of every family to utilize the labor of every individual, especially in the countryside, means that the labor of old people is also required. Furthermore, the devaluation that can occur with the loss of productivity means that old people dare not sit around in idleness (Kallgren 1968; Liu 1976:69). The relative ease with which old people can obtain exit visas from China is less a reflection of the humanitarian attitude of the government than it is of a desire to remove those no longer able to contribute to the economy. Especially during periods of economic distress, such as the late fifties and early sixties, old people, including some of my informants, were encouraged to emigrate because social welfare resources were inadequate to provide for those who were ill or otherwise unable to work.

For the same reason, few visitors to China report on the availability of medical services for the long-term ill. According to a number of visitors and refugees from China with whom I talked, when serious illness strikes an older person the individual himself or his family will take it for granted that the person should not apply for extensive medical care. Medical care in China is not universally free. While workers in state-run organizations receive subsidized treatment, Parish and Whyte (1978:88-89) report that participation in brigade level medical insurance costs a little over 3 yuan per person or 15 yuan per year for a family of five—which amounts to about 10 percent of the cash they would get from the collective. In addition, other expenses such as registration fees or food while a clinic inpatient are the responsibility of the individual. Unless they have savings of their own, the elderly are unlikely to receive long-term care from other than their own family members. Indeed, according to one of my informants, during the hard years of the early sixties, even short-term care was not provided to the elderly. When her mother-in-law injured her leg in a fall, my informant was unable to locate a doctor who would treat her because they were afraid that they would be criticized for keeping alive "useless eaters of rice." Her mother-in-law died within a week of receiving her injury.

While immediate family ties remain strong, extended ties have been greatly weakened. Lineages have been undermined by the removal of the land which formerly gave them their power. Their halls have been taken over, and intermarriage between lineage members (though usually of distant branches) is on the rise. During the Cultural Revolution, many ancestral tablets were destroyed, and ancestor worship is officially discouraged. Ritual specialists, Taoist and Buddhist alike, are largely inactive. Family members must now perform abbreviated versions of traditional rituals such as funerals in their own homes. "Big birthdays" are still customary in many villages though on a smaller scale. The decline of these institutions which previously enhanced the status of the elderly make the return to the home village a less attractive option than in the past.

Support of most of the elderly is *not* communal support but familial support. Only those lacking kin are eligible for some form of public support. Though the Constitution of the PRC proclaims equality of the sexes in terms of obligations to parents, daughters are rarely held responsible for such support. Thus only old people without sons and of "good" class background (e.g. *not* former political pariahs) are eligible for the rural welfare programs known as the Five Guarantees, which originally consisted of food, fuel, clothing, education, and burial guarantees, but which now include medical and housing assistance. However, depending on the size of the surplus available for welfare purposes, a commune or brigade sometimes has to redefine its program to make four or even just three of the guarantees. Parish and Whyte (1978:76) found only a small number of people in Guangdong villages receiving this aid. The average number of persons per production team of 150-200 persons was 1.24, or about 6 percent of all people over age 60. Clearly it is best to remain with the family.

Generally old people without families are not content to rely on the bare subsistence provisions of the Five Guarantees. Women, in particular, attempt to make use of the traditional strategy of fictive kinship by recruiting allies from among the "sent down youth" (Davis-Friedmann 1977). During the 1960s and much of the 1970s the Chinese government was actively resettling ("sending down") urban youth in the countryside. Ostensibly this practice enriched the villages by providing them with higher skilled labor than was locally available, but it also removed a potential source of instability from the cities which, in fact, were unable to absorb all of their middle school graduates (Chen 1972). In the villages, then, these youths are the functional equivalent of orphans and as such are suitable partners for childless old people. Men may be more reluctant than women to initiate these ties since their motives in *kai*ing a young woman may be suspect, and *kai*ing a young man has overtones of homosexuality (Anderson and Anderson 1973:88). Unfortunately, the duration of these alliances is unpredictable as most of these young people are anxious to return to the cities. While some have accepted and, indeed, even volunteered for a lifetime of service in the countryside, others hope to be recalled after a three or four year tour of duty. The decision by the government to push for industrial development now provides many of them the necessary opportunities to return to work in the cities (e.g. Gold 1980).

Another source of informal assistance comes from distant kin, friends, and neighbors,—that is, from the traditional extrafamilial sources. Parish and Whyte (1978:76) found frequent examples of "individual compassion" in their interviewing. Neighbors might lend a spare room to someone whose house is beyond repair, tend a private plot for someone who is weak or lame, or lend cash or grain to someone whose supplies have run short.

The situation of the elderly in the cities is somewhat different. On the one hand, if employed in a large-scale state enterprise, they are entitled to some form of pension when they retire, and under the policy of *dingti* which was formally implemented in January 1979 (Gold 1980:763) they are able to pass on their places (though not their exact jobs) to their children when they retire. On the other hand, there are fewer opportunities to engage in lucrative sidelines. Although the kind of economic interdependence which binds a village together is lacking in the city, there are two circumstances that serve to bind urban neighborhoods together which did not exist in the pre-modern Chinese city and which do not exist in Hong Kong today (Salaff 1971). First, the Chinese government does not encourage residential mobility. Migration from the countryside is officially, if not always successfully, opposed, and even migration within the city is restricted. Second, the neighborhood through its residents' committee is the unit responsible for the adjudication of disputes and the determination of eligibility for welfare services. The relative stability of the neighborhoods plus the increased involvement of local cadres in the lives of the residents provide a greater sense of community than existed under previous regimes.

Urban old people without families also utilize fictive kin ties, but they have additional resources as well: neighbors and institutional facilities. The costs to neighbors of casual attention to the elderly are not as great as in the village. First, since urban people have fewer opportunities for cash sidelines, they are giving up less when they spend time tending a sick neighbor. Second, the greater affluence of the cities means more extensive backup services such as hospitals and cadres specializing in welfare work. Thus, neighbors need not fear being locked-in to providing care should a temporary illness turn into a long-term one.

Despite the problems encountered by old people in Hong Kong, most of my informants considered themselves better off than their counterparts in China. They did not have to worry about rationing and shortages in Hong Kong such as they knew in China. While a number of my informants return to China on annual or biennial visits, few wanted to return there to live. Some informants saw ways in which China was superior to Hong Kong, such as in the relative absence of crime and of interpersonal violence, but none of these features was considered sufficient to counterbalance China's low standard of living.

PART II
Aging in Hong Kong

3   Hong Kong—The Challenge

The demographic, social, economic, and political characteristics of Hong Kong create an environment quite unlike either the pre- or post-liberation China familiar to most of Hong Kong's elderly. We shall examine here those features which have the greatest impact on the lives of Hong Kong's older residents.

Demographic Features

The British Crown Colony of Hong Kong contains approximately 5,207,000 people (Government Information Service 1982:227) and lies less than 100 miles southeast of Guangzhou, the largest city in the adjoining Chinese province of Guangdong. The Chinese government ceded parts of Hong Kong to the British government in the middle of the nineteenth century following military action by British soldiers and merchants. The remaining predominately rural and suburban parts of Hong Kong, known as the New Territories, were leased from China in 1898. This lease is due to expire in 1997.

The present population of Hong Kong is nearly 99 percent Chinese, but the size of this population has varied greatly over the past forty years. According to Lethbridge (1969:78), the population in 1940 numbered approximately 1,846,000 of whom about 750,000 were refugees from the Sino-Japanese conflict. After nearly four years of occupation by the Japanese, the population had been reduced to about 600,000. While some of Hong Kong's inhabitants starved to death and others died for lack of medical attention, migration back to China accounted for the major loss in population during those years. As soon as the war was over in 1945, Chinese civilians began returning at the rate of almost 100,000 a month rising to the 1.8 million pre-war high by the end of 1947.

While the years surrounding the war were characterized by great migrations in and out of Hong Kong, migration itself was not an unusual phenomenon in Hong Kong's history. Prior to the war, the majority of Chinese in Hong Kong did not consider themselves permanent residents even though they might have spent most of their adult lives working there. Hong Kong, like administrative, commercial, or industrial centers in China proper, provided employment opportunities for laborers and domestic servants from the rural hinterland. Most of these workers had families left behind in Guangdong whom they visited on at least an annual basis and with whom they expected to spend their later years. Craftsmen and small businessmen were more likely to be accompanied by their families. Passage from China to Hong Kong or from Hong Kong to China did not require any special arrangements and meant no more separation from family than did employment in Guangzhou or Shanghai.

Beginning in the late 1940s, as the forces of the Chinese Nationalist Government faced defeat, Hong Kong experienced for the first time in its history the start of what was to be a wave of one-way migration. The people who left China during and immediately after the Communist takeover had no plans to return even though family members may have remained behind. These new migrants were fleeing not only economic but political chaos and in many cases feared for their lives. About three quarters of a million people, mainly from Guangdong province, Shanghai, and other commercial centers, entered during 1949 and the spring of 1950. The population continued to grow: to 3.2 million by 1961, 4.0 million by 1971, and 5.2 million by the end of 1981.

The age structure of this population has changed greatly over the past twenty years. The proportion of young people under the age of 15 fell from 40.8 percent in 1961 to 35.8 percent in 1971 to 24.8 percent in 1981 (Government Information Service 1982:228). This drop is at least partly the result of the efforts of family planners to encourage fewer births, as well as of the rising age of couples entering their first marriages. At the same time, improved medical services reduced the mortality due to infectious diseases and resulted in increased life expectancies. The life expectancy of males born in 1981 is 71.7 years and of females 77.5 years (Government Information Service 1982:15). Data from the 1976 by-census as reported in *Services for the Elderly* (Hong Kong 1977:2; hereinafter referred to as the Green Paper) reveal that the proportion of persons aged 60 or older rose from 4.9 percent in 1961 to 7.4 percent in 1971 to 9 percent in 1976. Between 1961 and 1976 the total population increased by 41 percent, but the elderly population increased by 163 percent. By 1982 the elderly constituted 9.8 percent of the population. About 57 percent of the population is of Hong Kong birth, but the vast majority of the elderly were born in China, largely in Guangdong.

According to the census (Hong Kong 1972:16), 92.1 percent of the age-group 14 and under speak Cantonese as their usual language, but this is true of only 78.8 percent of the age-group 55 and over, and there are at least three other distinctive languages spoken by immigrants from Guangdong alone. Hoklo, a dialect characteristic of northeastern Guangdong and closely related to the language families of neighboring Fujian province, is spoken by 6.0 percent of the older people. This language, known locally as Chiu Chow, is actually spoken by a slightly larger proportion of the next age-group (those 40-54) because more Chiu Chow were among the more recent migrants to Hong Kong. Hakka, a language spoken by the descendants of northerners who migrated to Guangdong hundreds of years ago, is spoken by 4.5 percent of the older people. Sze Yap (referred to as Toisan or Toisanese in the United States), a variety of Cantonese distinctive of four counties in the south coastal region of Guangdong, is spoken by 4.4 percent. Other Chinese languages, such as Mandarin and Shanghainese, are spoken by 5.6 percent of the older people, and 0.7 percent speak a language other than Chinese dialects. Thus a substantial minority of the elderly speak a language other than Cantonese though many of these can understand Cantonese because their descendants speak it.

These language differences can severely restrict the social lives of the minority speakers who prefer to settle in areas inhabited by members of the same dialect group. In recent years, however, families have found it increasingly difficult to select housing on the basis of the language spoken by the area residents. This difficulty is a direct result of the increased role of the Hong Kong government in providing housing.

Hong Kong's public housing program began in early 1954 following a disastrous fire on Christmas Day which left 50,000 people in the Shek Kip Mei squatter area homeless. In the mid-1950s almost one-quarter of the population of Hong Kong "squatted" in flimsy huts of wood, tin, and cardboard, while those who settled in more permanent structures frequently found themselves jammed into spaces not originally intended for long-term habitation. As late as 1971, the census (Hong Kong 1972:213-14) listed 36,812 households living in bedspaces, verandas, cocklofts, corridors, storerooms, basements, roof-shacks, and derelict boats. Rooms or cubicles housed the largest number of households, 356,317 or 42 percent of all households. (By 1981 only 19 percent of all households lived in rooms or cubicles (Census and Statistics Department 1982:37)).

Up until the early 1970s, the major housing priority of the Hong Kong government was to clear sites of squatter settlement and to relocate the inhabitants to "housing estates" newly constructed on the periphery of the urban nuclei of Kowloon and Hong Kong Island. Such cleared sites were frequently designated for industrial or commercial purposes.

The steady increase in population had led by 1971 to truly staggering densities in the core urban areas. Hong Kong's approximately 400 square miles consists of numerous islands, including Hong Kong Island, as well as a large portion of the mainland. The rugged nature of much of the terrain leaves only 20 percent of the land area suitable for agriculture or occupation. Podmore (1971:22) stated that about 80 percent of the population lived in the metropolitan area—three million people crowded into 20 square miles. According to the census (Hong Kong 1972:28), the three most densely populated districts on Hong Kong Island were Wan Chai with 293,283 persons per square mile, Sheung Wan with 254,814, and Western with 248,675. In Kowloon, however, these figures were easily exceeded by Mong Kok with 400,612 and Yau Ma Tei with 336,222 persons per square mile.

In an effort to alleviate this overcrowding, the government committed itself in 1973 to erecting most of the future housing estates in the relatively rural New Territories. By 1978, thousands of people each month were moving to housing in the three new towns of Tsuen Wan, Tuen Mun, and Sha Tin. The vast majority of these movers were voluntary applicants for public housing, though location in the new towns was not necessarily their preference. As the government annual for 1978 (Hong Kong 1979:2) put it:

> The New Territories building programme means that significant numbers of people from the cramped conurbations of Hong Kong Island and Kowloon are exchanging their former homes—in older resettlement blocks, tenements and squatter areas—for contemporary flats in public housing estates. For many this means a complete change in lifestyle. However, Hong Kong people have demonstrated repeatedly during the territory's 137 years of history their ability to adjust to the new and unexpected.

Historically, squatter relocation entailed the movement of geographically discrete entities. The fact that the residents were moved en masse to new settlements sometimes meant that former neighbors found themselves living near one another in the new setting. Old social ties could reassert themselves. Other residents of low-income housing, however, did not and do not share a common origin. They originated from outside of squatter areas, applied as individual households, and were recruited from waiting lists several years long as openings in new estates became available. In the past, many families turned down the Housing Authority's first offer of an apartment because they preferred to relocate within the urban area, near relatives and work places. As new public housing is now largely available in the New Territories, families realize they have no choice but to "adjust to the new and unexpected."

The elderly are hit particularly hard by these massive relocations. As members of applying households, they find on relocation that they are in an unfamiliar environment and must rely on younger family members for orientation. Elderly who live alone are not eligible to apply for public housing unless they agree to share an apartment with two other old people. Many, therefore, continue to live in some of the most decrepit, private-sector housing. Such housing, however, is frequently slated for urban renewal, and these single elderly who rely very heavily on a complex local network for support and assistance are very concerned about the consequences of such programs on their daily lives. Forced relocation creates special hardships for minority language speakers. Those who prefer not to move and have no family to assist them worry endlessly about the impermanence of their highly localized microcommunities. They all risk facing their later years surrounded by strangers—a very different situation from aging in a small, stable, and familiar village setting.

Social Features

The social climate in Hong Kong has also created difficulties for many elderly. The community consensus on values which usually characterized the stable village is absent in Hong Kong. Traditional values, Western values, and hybrid values have resulted in a fragmented public opinion. The elderly find the actions and ideas of the young unpredictable and frequently disturbing. They grew up in an environment which limited close contact between the sexes to relatives, and even these contacts were tinged with reserve and formality. Many of the older couples were partners in blind marriages, in which the partners met for the first time at their wedding. They probably played or attempted to play some role in helping to arrange the marriages of their own children. Few realistically expect to influence the mate selection of grandchildren, and the increased intimacy between unmarried young people fills them with apprehension. The music, movies, and magazines of Western pop culture are audible and visible in nearly every corner of Hong Kong, and the challenge they pose to traditional thinking is recognized by everyone.

More subtle and perhaps more difficult to deal with for that very reason is the impact on traditional values of Western-style education. According to the *Working Party Report* (1973:5), 57 percent of those aged 60 or over had received no formal education, and 90 percent of all older people had not reached the level of secondary school. Old women are six times more likely than old men to be illiterate. The vast majority of educated older people received traditional Chinese educations. They practiced writing the elaborate Chinese characters which were used to instruct them in Chinese literature, philosophy, and history. Few learned more than rudimentary mathematics. Some individuals received Western-style educations in missionary-run schools and subsequently studied abroad to acquire the skills "to help build a strong China." This minority can share in the education of its young people as experienced guides. Most parents and, in particular, grandparents can only applaud the academic achievements of the young even as they realize the distance they create between them.

In 1981, according to the Hong Kong Government Information Services (1982:74-83), over one million students were enrolled in primary and secondary schools. Over 7,500 were enrolled in three post-secondary "colleges" and nearly 8,000 were enrolled full-time in the Hong Kong Polytechnic. The two universities enrolled a total of 9,241 undergraduates and competition for entry was keen. In addition in 1981, over 11,000 students went abroad for their education, largely to Britain, Canada, and the United States.

Economic Features

The arena of employment has increasingly become one in which the young adult in Hong Kong plays out his own individual destiny. In the traditional village, one followed one's father or other male relative into the fields or into the family business. If population pressure forced a young man to go far afield for employment, he was still very likely to be under the guidance of an older male relative or former village resident. Even individuals who migrated out of the country—to Hong Kong, Thailand, or the United States—usually went to join relatives in their endeavors. Dependence on senior kinsmen for access to farm land, training, or job introductions is minimal in Hong Kong. According to the 1981 Census (Census and Statistics Dept. 1982:25) only 2.0 percent of the population is employed in agriculture or fishing. Training, except for those who join small family enterprises, is acquired outside of the family in school and on the job. According to Mitchell (1972b:172), the youngest men in his sample (those aged 18-24) were the most likely to have relied on relatives for obtaining their current job; even so, this amounted to only 20 percent, in contrast to the 46 percent who obtained the job through friends, and the 25 percent who obtained the job through direct application.

Prior to 1940 Hong Kong was a commercial center serving as a major link in China's foreign trade network. There were only 800 factories employing about 30,000 workers. The war and continuing political upheaval in China necessitated a reorientation of economic priorities. The Western embargo imposed on Chinese goods following the outbreak of the Korean War meant an end to the China trade. At the same time, as pointed out by Agassi (1969:66), capital, connections, and labor flowed into Hong Kong from China. Shanghai industrialists with their international trading networks, Western-educated professionals, and hundreds of thousands of potential workers flooded into Hong Kong during the late forties and early fifties. This potent combination propelled Hong Kong into the industrial arena. The 1981 Census reveals that by 1981, out of a total workforce of 2,404,067, over 41 percent or 990,365, were employed in manufacturing. The other major employment sectors were trade, restaurants, and hotels with 461,489 employees; community, social, and personal service with 375,703 employees; construction with 185,999, and transport, storage, and communication with 181,368. The incidence of separation of residence and workplace is high. Co-workers, except in company housing, are unlikely to be neighbors. One's family life has little direct bearing on one's work life. Specifically, strained family relationships do not mean that one's job security is in doubt. Senior kinsmen have little economic leverage over disobedient or otherwise wayward juniors.

The employment situation of older workers is, as in most industrializing settings, unenviable. Their lack of education in comparison with the young is a great disadvantage. Even when highly trained, their skills are utilized in slowly fading traditional handicraft industries, which they do not expect even their own children to enter (e.g. Cooper 1980). Prior to 1973 and the introduction of the Infirmity Allowance (now called the "old age allowance" and a part of the Special Needs Allowance Scheme) there was no public program which assured the elderly a reliable source of income other than a minimal public assistance program for elderly not living with kin. Pensions were and remain the exception and not the rule, except for those elderly in government service or high status posts in the private sector. Some long-term workers—and these are likely to be few given the high rate of business turnover—receive a lump sum payment on retirement. Most older people have no alternative but to rely on their families for economic support in old age. Those without families or from families of minimal income hover on the edge of the labor market.

The Green Paper (Hong Kong 1977:2) reported that 60 percent of the males and 27 percent of the females aged 60-64 were still employed and that 35 percent of the males and 12 percent of the females aged 65 or over were still employed. Of these working people, 21 percent worked 15-44 hours a week, and 79 percent worked more than 44 hours. Three-quarters of the working elderly earned less than $800 HK a month (at that time $5 HK = $1 US) though this figure includes those who worked part-time.

At the time of my first contact with them in 1974, a significant minority of my elderly informants, 21 of 99, were still members of the work force. Of these, 11 were employed full-time, 6 part-time, and 4 doing piecework in their homes. When I returned in 1976, a similar number, 20 of 74, were employed—6 full-time, 10 part-time, and 4 doing piecework in their homes. What these figures conceal, however, is the instability of the older worker's participation in the labor force. For example, I was able to follow up only 16 of the original 21 workers. Of these only 9 were involved in the same job as a year and a half earlier. Of the others, 4 had withdrawn from the labor force, 2 had changed job location, and 1 had reduced his hours of work. Another 8 who had not been employed at the time of the first visit were employed at the time of the second. (And one man though recorded as unemployed at the times of both visits had, in fact, held a job for several months in the interim.) Therefore, over the course of my two years of research, 30 of my 99 informants had some involvement in the labor force. Even these figures depress the actual extent of the employment of older people as several potential informants declined to be interviewed because of their jobs.

My figures are not significantly different from those of the *Work-*

ing Party Report (1973:6) which found 31 percent of older people to be employed. According to this report:

> while the general response from members of the public has indicated that the elderly are interested in finding suitable work, this has not been followed through in pressure on the employment services provided by the Labour Department and the Hong Kong Council of Social Service. This may be due to the fact that the elderly prefer to find employment through relatives or other personal contacts, rather than through an employment agency; or it may be because the elderly do not consider making use of the services of the Labour Department or the Hong Kong Council of Social Service. But taking into account the lack of pressure, and the Labour Department's view that many suitable job vacancies exist for the aged (e.g., vacancies for restaurant workers and packers), it is difficult to regard the creation of special employment facilities for the aged as a matter of priority. This is the more so in view of the employment needs of other groups, such as former mental patients, discharged prisoners and former drug addicts, whose requirements in this respect we should regard as more pressing. (1973:31-32)

The extent to which this status quo attitude of the Working Party affected employment opportunities for the elderly is not clear, but it is interesting to note that only a few years later the Social Service Needs Study (1977:47) reported only 25 percent of the elderly to be employed. Another 15 percent of the elderly not working full-time expressed interest in employment. The major reasons given for working were to contribute to family income (37 percent), to be self-reliant (36 percent), and to have something to do (16 percent).

The elderly are concentrated in traditional sectors of the economy. The Social Service Needs Study (1977:47) found that of those old people currently employed, 29.5 percent were unskilled workers, 23 percent service personnel, and 22 percent "technicians"—only 2.5 percent were "professional". When I asked my own informants the nature of their present or most recent job, I found that the largest employment category for women was domestic servant (36 percent) and for men, unskilled laborer (39 percent). Unskilled laborer ranked second among women at 26 percent.

Many of my informants were clearly operating on the fringes of the working world, filling niches that no one else would or that no one else perceived. One 85-year-old woman (my oldest full-time employed informant) served as a domestic servant in the household of a paralyzed woman. In addition to caring for the physical needs of the employer, she also had to do cooking, washing, and cleaning for the woman's husband and son. She was, however, so weak herself that she could scarcely carry out these tasks and received notice that as of the 1976 Lunar New Year, she would not be employed any longer. Another 79-year-old man had worked as a casual laborer up until the age of 75. Then he shifted to collecting used cardboard and wooden boxes, which he sold for scrap. Since this was not a particularly lucrative activity, he eventually went back to casual employment, obtaining a day job several times a month. Another 78-year-old man peddled toys in the morning and rented out his room for gambling (mah jong) in the afternoon! All three of these people received an infirmity allowance, and the two men also received financial assistance from family members.

Other informants worked sporadically or when convenient opportunities presented themselves. One old woman took up piecework for the denim industry when she moved to a more spacious and expensive unit in public housing. Another ceased doing similar piecework because her relocation had taken her away from the metal works factory for which she had previously worked. One 65-year-old woman who had retired as a fruit peddler more than ten years previously continued to make rice cakes, which she sold every ten days to a restaurant. In short, older workers face serious obstacles when seeking employment. Their agricultural and craft skills are increasingly devalued. Their lack of Western-style education and of fluency in English bar them from most professional and administrative posts. Strong young men—illegal emigrants from China—compete with aged unskilled laborers, and Westernized young women brought in on contracts from the Philippines compete for the best domestic positions. These numerous obstacles have forced a substantial minority of the elderly to be the scavengers of the job market.

Political Features

Political insecurity is a problem touching all residents of Hong Kong. In less than fifteen years, the lease under which the British administer Hong Kong will expire. Will the People's Republic of China then take over the Colony? If so, what will be the consequences? Will the Hong Kong Government develop an adequate social security scheme given its uncertain tenure? Will more firms adopt pension schemes and will employment conditions stabilize so that more workers will become eligible for them? Or will firms take their money and flee the Colony leaving vast unemployment in their wake? Should the younger people emigrate while they still have the chance? Technically the lease expiration does not apply to Hong Kong Island or to most of the Kowloon peninsula which were ceded "in perpetuity" to the British. The Colony, however, is an integrated economy, and the severance of New Kowloon and the New Territories from the rest of the territory would mean an impossible economic situation.

At the beginning of the 1980s the People's Republic of China gave several indications of its interest in retaining and expanding foreign investment in the regional economy, meaning the county adjacent to Hong Kong. Plans were underway to build an airport on the China side of the border which would serve both Guangzhou and Hong Kong. The Chinese government was in the process of encouraging joint ventures in export-oriented zones, such as the Shenzhen and Zhuhai in which foreign firms could conduct their business. The Hong Kong Government, for its part, gave no indications of a loss of interest in the well-being of its economy. The development of the New Towns and the construction of a rapid transit system bisecting Kowloon required enormous investments. The expectations of both governments seemed to be that their two economies would gradually become one regional economy.

The political conditions under which this regional integration would occur remain obscure. As early as the mid-1970s, the Colonial Administration began to experience problems when attempting to staff government posts with recruits from Britain. Potential recruits were aware that they had no guarantee of completing the 20 year term of service which ensured them their pensions. Then too, many of Hong Kong's residents had come to Hong Kong to escape persecution because of political, religious, or other intellectual differences. The People's Republic of China authorities presented Hong Kong as a capitalistic outpost in which only those incorrigibly resistant to socialist thought could find comfort. Such "incorrigibles" wonder what treatment they might face in the not-too-distant future. Others who had come to Hong Kong for straightforward economic motives wonder what might happen to their standard of living should the poverty-ridden China of their memory become linked with Hong Kong.

Many of the older people I visited in the mid-1970s stated emphatically that they had no desire to spend their later years in China because of the serious shortages of goods. Some insisted that even if their Hong Kong descendants sent them money, they had no assurance that there would be goods available for purchase. Indeed some of these individuals or members of their families return to their ancestral homes on an annual basis, carrying on each trip items specially requested by their kin. In the mid-1970s requests were for items of immediate obvious utility, such as plastic buckets, yards of dark blue cotton cloth, canned foods. By 1980, requests had expanded to include electric fans, cassette recorders, and color televisions. Relatives do not hesitate to specify the brand names and models preferred. Such indications of increased prosperity in the Guangzhou area come too late to convince most older people that a return to the land of their birth does not mean a return to shortages. By 1980, most older people had been absent for so long that most of their peers in the village were dead, while most of their descendents were in Hong Kong. They know that many of the valued traditions of their earlier years have been destroyed as feudalistic vestiges of the old society.

The long-term political uncertainty in Hong Kong also affects the plans of the middle and youngest generations. While some view themselves as admirers of China's progress, few are prepared to move to China and give up the personal freedoms which they enjoy in Hong Kong. For them the question is not whether to remain in Hong Kong or return to China but whether to remain in Hong Kong or emigrate to the United States or to other hospitable lands. Thousands of Hong Kong students are abroad every year ostensibly to receive an education, but in fact, in many cases, to pursue the precious cards which grant them permanent resident status. From permanent resident to citizen to sponsor of relatives is a progression familiar to most Chinese in the United States. Single women students from Taiwan speak of marrying a man with the "three P's"—permanent resident status, a Ph.D. and property. United States Immigration and Naturalization Service records reveal that in the mid-1970s over 2,000 Chinese parents were brought into the country annually through the sponsorship of their children. Thus, another option for the elderly in Hong Kong is to follow their children to a foreign land, or else be left behind if unwilling to go. Those who do come to the United States face major adjustment problems as their children frequently settle in suburban neighborhoods in which there are few other Chinese language speakers.

Aging in Hong Kong, then, requires that the individual adapt to an environment very different from the one in which he or she grew up. If mere differentness were the only issue, perhaps years of living in Hong Kong would ease the sense of being in an alien environment. Rather, it is the instability, the unpredictability of the environment, which poses the real challenge—instability of residence, instability of neighborhood, and instability of social networks. And looming in the not-too-distant future is the uncertainty of Hong Kong's economic and political stability.

4   Hong Kong—The Variation

Differences in income, education, and family resources are only a few of the variables that shape the options available to older people in Hong Kong today. Together with health status, however, they probably have the greatest impact on the daily lives and long-range prospects of older people. By introducing two individuals who are at opposite ends of the socioeconomic spectrum, I hope to convey a sense of the different contexts in which they live. (The events described occurred in the middle and late 1970s.)

Daily Life—Mr. Go

At just past six every morning Mr. Go rolls over on his wooden bed and glances through the bars of his window to determine the likelihood of rain. Every morning he rides to a market town in the New Territories to meditate. An overcast day means that he must carry his umbrella with him on the minibus. Twice this summer he left the umbrella on the bus when he got off only to be called back by the driver. Although no one has yet pointed out to him that he is becoming increasingly forgetful, Mr. Go himself is painfully aware of the fact. Several times he has paused in his conversations in the tea house only to discover that he could not recall what he had just said, but his table mates have politely overlooked his stumbling. Fortunately, a distinguished gentleman of 82 is still given respect in his circles.

Mr. Go is not alone. His daughter-in-law is usually up before him preparing formula for his newest grandson. Though she is, in his opinion, a decent and obedient girl, she has not accepted his recommendation that she breast-feed the baby. Mr. Go is not especially concerned with the issue of nutrition; rather, he believes that nursing the baby would help to alleviate his daughter-in-law's unfortunate disability. She cannot fully control the movement of her limbs, and while she gets about with no serious difficulty, her movements are not at all graceful. Mr. Go believes that nursing the baby would release the blocked air (*hei*) within her body which is probably responsible for her disability. He has also suggested that she receive *hei gung* treatment, a therapeutic technique performed by Taoist practitioners, which could enhance the flow of air through her body. However, these methods do not appeal to her.

Mr. Go's youngest son, a driving teacher, delayed his marriage until well into his 30s. Previously he had lived in this Mong Kok apartment for several years with his mother, while his father, Mr. Go, lived with the fourth son. When the fourth son and his family emigrated to London to enter the restaurant business, Mr. Go joined his wife and youngest son. Mrs. Go died seven years ago at the age of 75, and father and son were left to do all the household chores. For Mr. Go, the greatest inconvenience imposed by his wife's death had been the restriction on his freedom to come and go. Fear of crime, particularly of burglary and robbery, is widespread in Hong Kong. Most buildings not only have barred windows, but also heavy barred doors at the entry to the building and to every individual apartment as well. Mr. Go had to assume his wife's role as a "door-watcher" within the apartment and found his normally active life restricted. Five years later, when the youngest son married, the new daughter-in-law took over the household responsibilities and liberated Mr. Go.

Her arrival, however, put additional strain on the family resources, so Mr. Go and his son decided to rent out one of their rooms. Previously, Mr. Go had had his own bedroom as well as a small room which he used as a studio to teach painting. His students had gradually become fewer and fewer, and Mr. Go finally ceased to take on new students as his eyes were failing. His bedroom and studio are now merged, and paintings and scrolls are lodged here and there among his books leading the untrained eye to see nothing but chaos. Some of his favorite works are still displayed in the living-dining area.

Relations between tenants in Hong Kong are a very delicate matter, for it is difficult to know in advance how everyone will get along. The Gos rented the room to a young couple in their 20s, and Mr. Go feels that they are working out satisfactorily. They recognize that they have rented only the bedroom and have rights to use the kitchen and bathroom. They do not spill over into the living-dining area, and they do not bring people to visit. At one time Mr. Go and his son had considered buying the apartment outright, but the asking price of

$80,000 HK had been too high. Instead, they had decided to continue paying the rent of more than $500 HK a month and to save up enough money to buy a house in the rural market town where they had lived when they first came to Hong Kong. During the mid-1970s prices skyrocketed, and now even market town properties are beyond their range. They will probably stay where they are.

Smoothing the wrinkles from his traditionally cut suit, Mr. Go steps into the dining area and reaches for the large thermos on top of the refrigerator. Every morning he pours himself a glass of dark tea. Though all of the adults in the family drink this tea, only Mr. Go drinks it full strength. Though the tea appears completely unremarkable, it is no ordinary tea. The tea leaves have undergone a special rite at the Taoist hall in the market town. On the feast day of one of the Taoist gods, the leaves were placed in the worshipping area while believers recited the scriptures. The god then changed the leaves into a medicine effective against many ailments including fever, flu, and stomach ache. Mr. Go knows one man, the father of four mute children, who obtained some of the tea from the hall. After drinking the tea, all his children regained the power of speech.

Mr. Go does not drink the tea in the expectation of similar miracles. For him it is simply a necessary daily preventive, and it seems to work. He has not been ill in over ten years. He takes good care of himself otherwise too. He tries to do everything in moderation, because he knows that excess damages one's health. When he eats, he never stuffs himself. When he has a problem, he remains optimistic. He always tries to laugh and talk pleasantly with others. Perhaps because of this his company is often sought.

In the old days as a lawyer in Guangzhou, he had attended many restaurant parties, and his friends had always asked his advice when seeking concubines. Mr. Go himself had never taken a concubine into his household, for he had promised his wife he would not. She had provided him with fifteen children including seven sons so he had no complaints. His wife had also been very skillful socially. Mr. Go had encouraged her to play mah-jong with the wives of other prominent men, and through her, he had acquired a greater understanding of these men. But he never really liked the gambling aspect of mah-jong, and he rarely plays it himself and does not permit his daughter-in-law to play it.

Up until the past year, Mr. Go usually headed for the Mong Kok railroad station to catch a train for the New Territories. There he would stop in the market town for tea before proceeding to the Taoist hall for meditation. One morning while on his way to the station, he had encountered a robber, and though he had successfully resisted the man, he feared that the robber might recognize him and try again. So he changed his route. He now eats breakfast in a restaurant near his home and then catches a minibus out to the New Territories.

Some mornings the restaurant is crowded, and he finds himself sharing a table with several strangers. When unable to strike up a conversation with any of them, he quietly orders two dishes of the meat stuffed pastries he likes so much and a pot of tea. Although he retired some sixteen years ago from a teaching post and does not receive a pension of any kind, Mr. Go does not lack spending money. While he is not a rich man, he does receive money from his children and his grandchildren. These gifts are not received on any regular basis, but they are sufficiently frequent that nearly any month finds him at a table waving a one-hundred-dollar bill and insisting on paying for the meals of several guests. He also receives the $100 HK a month (now $225 HK) from the government Infirmity Allowance program which is available to all people over 70. When the Infirmity Allowance program was introduced several years ago, Mr. Go had not at first applied for it, but after a couple of years and discussions with his friends, he came to feel that he too was entitled to it. In any case, he reasons that he can use the money to do good by passing it on to some person in greater need than himself.

After completing his breakfast, Mr. Go walks a short two blocks to a major road where he catches his minibus. When he steps into a crosswalk he raises one arm as a halt signal to the oncoming traffic. He does this even when he sees no traffic coming because his vision is so poor he can never be sure. Most people his age avoid riding minibuses because they have no fixed stops, but simply come to a sudden halt whenever a passenger yells that he wishes to get off or someone flags the bus down. Flagging the bus means being able to read the destination card in the front window so, since many of the elderly are illiterate or have poor vision (or both), it is not surprising that they are infrequently seen on minibuses. Mr. Go, however, is a familiar passenger to the drivers who ply the route to the New Territories.

At this hour of the morning, few passengers travel in Mr. Go's direction. The drivers are anxious to get to the New Territories as quickly as possible because the bulk of their passengers are waiting there to be brought to their places of employment in the industrial and commercial centers of Kowloon and Hong Kong Island. The minibus rapidly ascends Taipo Road and within just a few minutes leaves congested Kowloon behind and enters the peaceful forests of the New Territories. Mr. Go particularly enjoys the ride past the reservoir because there is a good chance of observing Hong Kong's only troop of wild monkeys along the roadside. The bus continues down the hillside and through one of the New Towns which is rapidly becoming an extension of the urban area on the other side of the mountain. Mr. Go knows this growth is necessary and inevitable, but he is glad that development has not yet engulfed the market town which was his home when he first came to Hong Kong.

Mr. Go and his family left Guangzhou in 1938. He had watched the approach of the Japanese from north China with trepidation and finally decided to move some of his assets and his family to the safety of British Hong Kong. He had not expected the Japanese to move to Hong Kong also. During the war, the Japanese appointed him principal of a secondary school, and he has ever since been addressed as Go *Louhsi*, Teacher Go, by the townspeople. After the war he did not return to China for any extended stay. As a former official under the Nationalists and a landowner in the Guangzhou region, he knew that he would have been a target of the Communists. It still amazes and hurts him that one of his daughters remained in China and became a Communist. During land reform, his family lost all its property, so they had no choice but to make their lives in Hong Kong. Two of his daughters continue to live in the region of the market town, and Mr. Go drops in on them whenever he wishes on his way to or from the Taoist hall.

Originally the hall had been located in a district capital near Guangzhou, but fifty or sixty years ago it was moved to the present New Territories site. In its early years in Hong Kong, the hall owned 100,000 square feet of land but has since sold some of it. On the remaining land, the Taoists rent out apartments and maintain one of the buildings as a residence for female Taoists. Plans are underway to erect a twelve-story apartment building to provide additional revenues for the activities of the hall. Mr. Go is especially proud of his participation in the Taoist organization. He has always believed that one of man's most important duties is to promote harmony. In his days as a lawyer, he sought to achieve this aim by resolving disputes. As a teacher, he attempted to inculcate this idea in his students. It serves as a guiding principle of his own behavior in everything from health practices to social intercourse. Now that he is retired and has time to devote to religious and charitable activities, the association has come to claim his major allegiance. Though he tends to explain his participation in abstract principles, he obviously enjoys the companionship and respect that he continues to receive from his fellow members.

There are numerous other Taoist halls and associations in Hong Kong. Perhaps the most famous one of all is the temple at Wong Tai Sin to which thousands of people go during the New Year festival to learn their fortunes for the coming year. The members of these associations pay frequent visits to each other's halls and participate in each other's activities. Mr. Go's hall probably has a regular membership of about 400, but few are as active on as regular a basis as Mr. Go who comes every morning. On a typical morning only twenty or thirty worshippers visit the hall, but a special occasion can draw well over one thousand. On the birthday of the association's special deity, nearly twelve hundred people came for the vegetarian banquet.

The association also tries to meet nonspiritual needs. Recently it raised nearly $12,000 HK, which it donated to the Red Cross to help those in need in other countries, but the Taoists are also concerned with charity in Hong Kong. The association attempts to meet a variety of needs, and the services with which Mr. Go is most involved are medical in nature. Once a week he practices the art of *hei gung* treatment in a Taoist hall in Kowloon. He is anxious to teach female Taoists the proper techniques of the art because it is more appropriate for women to touch women patients.

Healing by hei gung is not a skill which can be acquired simply by instruction. Certain people who have long studied Taoism gradually acquire control of their own *hei*, breath. When such a person touches the troubled part of the patient's body, his own hei has such strength that it can stimulate the movement of the patient's hei. Essentially, the cure is a laying on of the hands though sometimes it is accompanied by massage or by herbal medication. A good friend of Mr. Go, 81-year-old Mr. Lai, carries out hei gung treatment three times a week, and he and his assistants treat scores of patients at every afternoon session. One of the purposes of Mr. Go's daily meditation is to gain greater control over his own hei.

The Taoists are also concerned with the needs of the dead. For example, during the Hungry Ghosts festival, the association offered more than 100 tables of food to those ghosts so unfortunate as to have no kin to make offerings to them. Providing such ghosts with food, clothing, and vast sums of paper money assures their good will. A few years ago, because of the great earthquake in Tang Shan in northern China, many more ghosts than usual needed the Taoists' attentions. Had they not been provided for, they might have vented their frustrations on the people of Hong Kong.

When he finishes meditating, Mr. Go likes to return to the minibus terminus via the vegetable market where he chats with the vegetable sellers whose stalls are closest to the sidewalk. He usually returns to Mong Kok in time to catch his son setting off for a driving lesson. Mr. Go is very pleased with this son as he has followed his father's interest in Taoism and painting. When he is free, he drives his father to the hall himself and makes every effort to participate in the great occasions of the association. Mr. Go is well aware that today young people as a whole evince little interest in Taoism. In China itself Taoism is officially regarded as pernicious superstition, but in Hong Kong it has been officially ignored and left to face competition from Western education and ideas.

Following his afternoon nap, Mr. Go looks over the day's mail. On some days he receives nothing, but over the course of a week he usually receives one or more invitations to attend a meeting or banquet. The Benevolent Society of which he has long been a member recently announced its plans for a banquet on the birthday of Confucius. He quickly sent off $100 HK as his contribution. He has many friends (who are also his schoolmates) in the society and has not seen them since the early summer when his secondary school held its annual meeting. Although he graduated from a secondary school in Guangdong, so many of its alumni have found their way to Hong Kong that he sometimes finds it hard to believe that he is not still in China. An academic association has invited him to attend a banquet on October 10 (Double Ten), the anniversary of the founding of the Republic of China in 1911. October is a sensitive time politically in Hong Kong, for all the wounds of the Chinese civil war are reopened. The refugees who identify most closely with the Republic of China (Taiwan) celebrate their national day on October 10th with banquets, speeches, and the display of the Nationalist flag. Those who identify most closely with the People's Republic of China display their flags on October 1, the anniversary of its founding in 1949. In most cases, the displays of these flags do not overlap, but at this time of year, the political coloration of a neighborhood or village is readily visible.

Years ago in the 1920s, Mr. Go actually met Mao Zedong in Guangzhou when the Communists and the Nationalists had been temporarily allied. Experience, however, has long since taught him that the topic of politics is inflammatory, and he studiously avoids it. He personally feels that the Communists have betrayed their own ideals.

In his view, they say they are concerned with the welfare of the people, but in fact the people at the top seem to be concerned only with gaining power for themselves. Mr. Go also believes that the philosophies of Taoism and Communism are not completely opposed; both share the theme of teaching people to help each other to contribute to the common good, but Mao dismissed religion as superstition.

Mr. Go is not involved in the activities of his lineage or clan. He had only one brother, a few years younger, who died in his 70s; his brother's son is in Hong Kong. Mr. Go has never joined the Go surname association as he already has many friends chosen on the basis of criteria other than a shared surname. Most of his family interaction is among his own numerous descendants. Though not all of his fifteen children survive or remain in touch, several of them are in Hong Kong. He has more than thirty grandchildren many of whom he cannot recognize. These grandchildren, even though living in such remote places as Canada and England, continue to honor his birthday and to send him presents or money on special occasions.

Many of his former students regard him as a father in some respects and send him postcards or gifts when they travel abroad. Mr. Go looks after their interests too. Even though he does not have quite so many contacts as he once did, he still keeps his eyes open for a marriageable girl for his bachelor students and inquires about job possibilities for his children and grandchildren.

When he reflects on his life, he concludes that fate has been good to him. Despite a few reversals, he has many descendants, the respect of his peers, and the satisfaction of having lived a long and useful life of service to others. He has sought to maintain his own inner state in a harmonious condition, and also to restore harmony to the outside world. These are noble objectives and pursuing them has no doubt added years to his life.

Daily Life—Mrs. Wong

A half mile to the northwest of Mr. Go in the more industrial section of New Kowloon known as Sham Shui Po, Mrs. Wong slips quietly out of bed each morning. She does not wish to awaken any of the twenty or so co-tenants with whom she shares this subdivided apartment. Most of her co-tenants are single men who spend little time there, returning only to eat or sleep. There is only one family in the apartment, the Fungs, consisting of husband, wife, and five children; they occupy a cubicle facing onto the street as well as the upper bunk of Mrs. Wong's bedspace. Because three of the younger Fung children sleep immediately above her, Mrs. Wong must rummage quietly through her belongings in the dark to find her packet of incense sticks. She pays $60 HK a month for this bedspace and uses the side of it against the wall as well as the area under her bed for storage. Her possessions are wrapped in a variety of plastic and paper bags, tied with string, and stuffed into larger plastic and paper bags or into boxes. When she locates the incense sticks, she takes out enough to burn for the sky, door, and earth gods. Although there is also a kitchen god, Mrs. Wong knows that one of her co-tenants will attend to him so she does not burn any incense for him.

She combs her short hair straight back and fastens it with a metal headband in the fashion of many older women. Among her peers, nearly everyone has cut her hair in this style, though there are still a few older women who choose to wear their hair long and tied up in a bun at the nape of the neck. Mrs. Wong even knows a couple of women who claim to have had their hair cut only once in their lives. Mrs. Wong finds the short hair much more convenient, and while she regrets the passing of some customs, she does not regret the passing of others including this one. All the changes she has encountered in her lifetime sometimes make it seem that the whole world is in flux and beyond anyone's control. She doesn't worry about such changes as she has certainly seen enough of them, but occasionally she feels that they have cheated her of her rights. These feelings are strongest when she contemplates her own sufferings as a daughter-in-law.

She had married in the traditional fashion at the age of 18 when a matchmaker had asked her mother for the eight characters specifying the time of her birth. Comparing the eight characters of the prospective bride and groom was considered essential in determining the likelihood of a compatible match. In their case, there had been no obvious indications of incompatibility, so they had been married.

The distance between their two villages was somewhat greater than usual, but Mrs. Wong's mother, who had only reluctantly agreed to marry her off, had made a clever choice. Though Mrs. Wong's natal family lived in the district of Nan Hai, her husband's family lived across the river in the district of Shunde. As the center of the silk-reeling industry in the Guangzhou region, Shunde had a very special economic situation, which led to the development of some practices peculiar to the district. (For a fuller treatment of this topic see Sanker 1978 and Topley 1975.) Women workers were important, and so a family found that its daughters, normally regarded as drains on the family resources, had become major providers of resources. Parents became reluctant to marry off their daughters, and the girls themselves enjoyed their economic power. Some girls refused to consider matrimony at all, whereas others agreed to marriage in name only. The girl went through a wedding ceremony, but declined to consummate the marriage, and after the wedding returned to her natal home or to a "girls' house" in the village. The husband of such a woman was free to take a concubine to bear him children. The motivation for a marriage in name only was to provide a family tree upon which to graft the woman, for after her death, she had to receive offerings from her husband's descendants. An unmarried woman could not receive the offerings of her brother's children. Some unmarried women adopted children to provide for their spirits while others contributed substantial sums to Buddhist or Taoist temples to meet this need.

In any case, a large number of women unwilling to marry meant a shortage of potential daughters-in-law and forced Shunde parents to look further afield for spouses for their sons. On the other hand, it gave families with daughters additional leverage in arranging marriages to men from Shunde. For example, a girl traditionally passed at marriage from her natal family to her husband's family, but in parts of Shunde this was not an immediate transfer. Instead, it sometimes happened that after the wedding, the girl returned to her natal family and visited her in-laws in Shunde only two or three times a year. She would not permanently transfer to her in-laws' home until she was pregnant with or safely delivered of her first child. Mrs. Wong's mother took advantage of this situation. She had been widowed when Mrs. Wong was a baby and Mrs. Wong's brother was still in her womb. Although hers was not a silk family, but a petty trading one, she did not want to lose the labor of her daughter. Immediately after the wedding, Mrs. Wong returned to live with her mother. Since Mrs. Wong's husband was employed in Hong Kong and returned to his Shunde home on the same two or three annual occasions that Mrs. Wong did, they did not have their first child until three years after the wedding.

Mrs. Wong had dreaded the trips to her in-laws. She had been expected to stay out of sight, keep quiet, and work like a servant girl. She had gotten up before dawn to heat water for tea and to light incense before the household shrines. When the rest of the family awakened, they would look at the incense sticks to see how far down they had burned. An incense stick which had burned down only slightly was considered compelling evidence of a late-rising daughter-in-law. In addition, she knew that her mother-in-law did not trust her and suspected that she stole food to take back to her own mother and brother. Yet she had patiently borne all this. A daughter-in-law had really had no choice in those days.

But now the situation has altered completely. According to Mrs. Wong, the daughter-in-law has become the ruler of the house. She becomes indignant whenever she recalls the experience of a co-villager living in Hong Kong. This woman's daughter-in-law objects to her constant presence around the house and insists that she spend her time outside. The old woman finds this both boring and tiring and tries to return home, but the daughter-in-law has had the lock changed and refuses to let her in. Even though the family lives in incredibly crowded quarters, Mrs. Wong can not help feeling that such treatment is going too far.

Although she herself has three daughters-in-law, they are in China, and she is in Hong Kong. She has, however, given some thought to the matter and has decided that were she to live with a son's family, she would treat the daughter-in-law as a co-tenant rather than a daughter-in-law. Although sharing the same accommodations, they would cook independently. Traditionally the division of a Chinese household was symbolized by the use of separate hearths. In Hong Kong, separate cooking burners serve the same function among co-tenants.

Mrs. Wong takes her breakfast at the restaurant where she works. If she misses the morning meal, she has to wait until 11:45 for the midday meal. The stone stairs and wall of her old building are clammy and slippery from the high humidity. She must climb slowly and carefully down the four flights to the street. Though it is usually still dark when she sets out, Mrs. Wong does not fear the possibility of robbery. She dresses in the white shirt of a restaurant worker and knows that this makes it obvious to everyone that she is unlikely to be carrying any money. When she first started this job two and a half months ago, she was so proud of her uniform that she would not allow the restaurant to wash it. She brought it home to launder it herself explaining that she was taller than the other workers and that if her shirt got mixed up with theirs, she might wind up wearing a shirt that was too small. Her real reason was somewhat different. She knows that the restaurant washes the shirts and tablecloths together, and when she thought about the fat, oil, and chicken bones that were daily rubbed into the tablecloths, she could not submit her new shirt to the ordeal. Now, however, she is not so squeamish and only occasionally brings the shirt home.

Sometimes Mrs. Wong suffers from rheumatism (*fung sap*; "wind and wet") brought on, she believes, by the fact that she had often gotten her feet wet while working in the fields too soon after delivering her children. She has never gone to see a doctor about this, but treats herself by using ointments designed to "drive out the wind" responsible for her symptoms. A few months ago, shortly after moving to her present address, she had been out on an early morning walk, slipped, and fractured her wrist. At that time she had had to receive medical treatment daily and had been unable to perform such basic tasks as cooking and washing. For nearly six weeks her co-tenant, Mrs. Fung, had performed these tasks for her, and afterwards Mrs. Wong had paid her $200 HK.

Twenty minutes after leaving home, Mrs. Wong reaches the restaurant. She works the ground floor, which is the first floor to fill up with customers. She pushes a cart around the floor laden with small, stuffed pastries, *dim sam*, and occasionally calls out her wares. The cart is quite light and not any strain on her still sensitive wrist, and because of her age, she is not required to go up or down the stairs. At the age of 69, Mrs. Wong is one of the oldest of the *dim sam* workers at her restaurant. Mrs. Wong believes that younger people prefer to work in the factories where they can make more money, but she finds that a half day's work, even if every day, is more to her liking and her ability.

When she first started working here, she earned $10 HK a day, but after a month her wages went up to $14 HK a day. If she doesn't miss a single day, she can earn just over $400 HK a month. In addition, the restaurant also provides the workers with two meals a day, and Mrs. Wong rates these meals highly. Usually each table of workers receives limitless rice and three side dishes. Since she actually has to pay for only one meal a day, she has found that she can live on $200 HK a month—but with absolutely no frills. Mrs. Wong does not gamble or attend movies and very rarely travels. Since she can not read, she very easily gets lost any time she finds herself in an unfamiliar place. For example, she knows which bus she has to take to get to a friend's place, but she always has to ask someone where to get off, and then she has to ask her way along the street. Consequently, she does not relish traveling and avoids it whenever possible.

Mrs. Wong returns home in the early afternoon when Mrs. Fung goes over homework with her children. Fortunately, they recite in a small room that lets on to the kitchen, so their voices do not really disturb her when she takes her afternoon nap. Her bedspace along the apartment corridor is quite cool and dark even on bright sunny days. She frequently pulls a thin blanket over her legs before she feels completely comfortable. These quiet moments after work and before sleep are among the few available to her for daydreaming and reminiscing. Mrs. Wong has seen many harsh things in her day and has often wondered where her next meal would come from, but somehow she has always managed to pull through. Perhaps, as a proverb says, she will have good fortune since she has survived so many difficulties.

At the time of Mrs. Wong's first period of residence in Hong Kong, during the Japanese occupation, it had been very difficult to get food. Her husband was working in the dockyards for the Japanese, but his rice payment was not sufficient to feed them all and to allow for the purchase of additional vegetables. Finally, she decided to take her youngest child, an infant of eight months, leave the older boys with their father and grandmother, and return to China to work in the fields. In 1950 her husband died of cancer in Hong Kong, and his employer had arranged his burial near the border. Then she had to live through the terrible period of land reform when nearly a third of her husband's village had either committed suicide or run away as a result of the struggle sessions.

Though she herself had not been criticized, she felt that the Communists had done wrong in taking the means of livelihood away from people. Even the Japanese had not done that. But what most rankles her is their hypocrisy. Supposedly they have made the poor man the master of China, but so far as she has seen, it has not worked out that way in practice. She recalls that when her mother-in-law was injured in a fall during the calamitous years following the failure of the Great Leap Forward, no doctor had been prepared to treat her, for at that time, the Communists felt that useless old people should not be given medical attention. All they were said to be good for was eating the short supply of rice, so if they died, it was no loss. Then, when her mother-in-law did die, Mrs. Wong had wanted to bury her in the village instead of where the Communists insisted. After all, another family had been allowed to bury one of its members in the village. But Mrs. Wong had not been given permission. Since the other family received large remittances from overseas, Mrs. Wong concluded that, as usual, money talked, and that the Communists were just as prepared as anyone else to listen to the rich. She borrowed a large sum of money from neighbors and friends and buried her mother-in-law in proper style.

The cadres were furious and threatened her with arrest, but Mrs. Wong had already obtained an exit visa for Hong Kong. When applying for the visa, she told the officials she wanted to go to Hong Kong to marry and had shortly thereafter received permission to leave. In fact, it is unlikely that the officials believed her story. It was not the custom for widows with young adult children to remarry, but it was clear that Mrs. Wong was a potential troublemaker. Her insistence on burying her mother-in-law in extravagant style, even in a time of near famine, was offensive and disobedient, but her courage in defying official policies and the filial piety which she demonstrated had won local admiration. To punish her would probably have caused the cadres more grief than granting her an exit visa. Besides, she was already in her early 50s and would not be productive much longer. Thus, in the early 1960s, Mrs. Wong became one of the fifty people a day to receive legal exit papers (Vogel 1971:293) from China.

Upon arrival in Hong Kong, she went immediately to Wan Chai, the area of Hong Kong Island where she had lived during the Japanese occupation and where several of her co-villagers still lived. She moved in with them, and they gradually introduced her to various employment opportunities. At one time or another, she has been a helper in a beauty shop, a household servant, and a seller of bread. She saved every penny that she could and eventually repaid the debt she had incurred when burying her mother-in-law.

A couple of years after her return to Hong Kong, the government declared the building in which she lived to be dangerous, and the residents were forced to scatter. Luckily Mrs. Wong and one of her co-villagers found a tiny room in Shek Kip Mei Resettlement Estate. They moved in with the knowledge and permission of the legal occupants, other co-villagers who had moved to larger accommodations but had not officially relinquished their Shek Kip Mei room because they did not want to lose their eligibility for a larger unit in a more modern resettlement estate. Mrs. Wong and her friend could live there only so long as no one took official notice of them. For more than ten years they went undetected.

The rent for the tiny room amounted to a mere $5 HK a month, but it meant little more than having a roof over their heads. The plumbing for each floor was concentrated in one area of the building, and the water tap served almost the same function as a village well. In the morning housewives washed their clothes together. In the evening they would gather and discuss the events of the day. Neighbors were immediately aware of strangers and unusual activities and looked out for each other. When Mrs. Wong had been ill, they fetched water for her.

Then a few years ago, her luck began to run out. First, her roommate died, and Mrs. Wong lived on in the room all alone. Next, a few months later, the restaurant in which she had worked for several years let her go due to financial difficulties. Finally, the authorities discovered that she was an illegal occupant. The building in which she had been living was one of several scheduled for renovation. All legal residents were to be temporarily put up in a nearby housing estate, but Mrs. Wong was not a legal resident and received no consideration. In great distress, she had gone to a welfare agency asking them to help her find a place to live, but they had said this was not their responsibility. Eventually she found her present bedspace several streets away from Shek Kip Mei.

Until obtaining her present job, she struggled to make a living. Fortunately she had some savings which she supplemented with occasional part-time jobs such as substituting for a sick restaurant worker or baby-sitting for a mother who had to run an errand. Sometimes a co-villager's daughter or her own kai daughter had given her small sums of money. Mrs. Wong had kaied a young woman and a man in his 30s at the same time. A neighbor at Shek Kip Mei had introduced them to her; neither had parents, and they seemed "good" to her so she kaied them. Ideally, the assumption of the tie is marked by a banquet, but in Mrs. Wong's case there had not been enough funds to do this. They had just had a simple meal together and exchanged gifts.

One of the major responsibilities of the kai children is to see that Mrs. Wong receives a decent funeral. Since her descendants are in China, they will not be able to perform this duty for her. Mrs. Wong has already taken steps to ensure that her death will not become a source of embarrassment to her spirit. She has purchased shares in two funeral societies to cover the costs of her funeral, and she has also purchased a memorial tablet at a Taoist temple for $350 HK. This means that the Taoists will assume responsibility for tending to the needs of her spirit; she need not become a "hungry ghost."

Lately, however, Mrs. Wong has been wondering about switching the authorization for her funeral from her kai children to her co-tenant, Mrs. Fung. When she lived in Shek Kip Mei, she had taken the evening meal with her kai son who lived in a bedspace elsewhere in the neighborhood, and she had also done his laundry. Now that she has moved, she sees him less frequently. He is in his 40s and unmarried, and she is just not certain what his intentions really are. Her kai daughter is married with two children and seems to have a good heart as evidenced by the money she contributed when Mrs. Wong was unemployed, but since her family moved to Oi Man Estate, their relationship has been somewhat strained. Originally Mrs. Wong had been listed as her kai daughter's mother on her family's application for public housing. There is a general belief among applicants that the larger the number of names on a given application, the greater the likelihood of being awarded public housing. There is, in fact, some truth to this as applicants are admitted partly on the basis of the density of their present accommodations and partly on the per capita income of their families. However, when the family moved to Oi Man, Mrs. Wong had been told that she could not go along as she was not a real family member. It is not clear to Mrs. Wong who made that decision.

By late afternoon, the apartment begins to fill up again. Mrs. Wong starts preparing her evening meal before the kitchen area becomes too crowded. She makes it a point to stay out of everyone's way since she has all day (or at least all afternoon) to take care of her household affairs, whereas the workers have only the evening. From about six to nine o'clock, the apartment is in a state of chaos. Several different households jockey for space among the burners and carry their food and dishes back and forth along the corridor in front of Mrs. Wong's bedspace. She tries to sit with her feet up out of the way. While some eat, others watch television or listen to the radio. Evening is also the time when the only telephone in the apartment is likely to be in heavy use. By nine o'clock on school nights, the children usually begin to slow down; conversations become a bit softer, and Mrs. Wong, who has great tolerance for noise anyway, is able to drift off to sleep.

These days before drifting off to sleep, she is likely to reflect that her bad luck of the past several years seems to be over—her wrist is nearly healed, and her funeral is taken care of. Her job is steady and has enabled her to bring her savings back up to $1000 HK. Her co-workers enjoy her jokes and stories, and her new co-tenants, with one or two exceptions, are nearly as considerate as the neighbors she left behind. So long as she retains her vitality and her job, there will be no problems. Perhaps in her next letter to China, she will include some money for her sons and daughters-in-law.

The Older Generation

By describing a typical day in the lives of two elderly residents of Hong Kong, my intention has been to touch on some of the problems and historical experiences which distinguish the older generation. For all of its diversity, almost all members of the present generation of older people in Hong Kong had to face the challenges posed by migration, the invasion of the Japanese, and the consequences of the Chinese civil war. While not every older person has directly faced all three of these problems, all older people have been affected by them in some way.

According to the 1971 Census (Hong Kong 1972:16) only 13.7 percent of those aged 40 or above were born in Hong Kong compared with over 95 percent of those under the age of 15. The vast majority of the older population was, like Mr. Go and Mrs. Wong, born and brought up in Guangdong. For some, the transition from life in China to life in Hong Kong was gradual and relatively easy; for others, it was a traumatic, sudden shift. As a young man, Mr. Go had visited Hong Kong several times, but he did not actually live there until 1938. At that time, he did not know that he would be spending the rest of his life in Hong Kong. By the time he realized that the Communist victory in 1949 made his return to China impossible, he had already sunk deep roots into Hong Kong. When Mrs. Wong came to Hong Kong in the early 1960s, she knew that she was leaving China for good. However, as a younger woman, she had lived in Hong Kong for some ten years, and on her return went immediately to her old neighborhood and former acquaintances.

Other migrants, especially political refugees who fled as the Communist military forces took over Guangzhou and found themselves in Hong Kong, destitute and separated from their families, have had more difficult transitions, as did those who came to Hong Kong in late-middle or old age with no previous experience there. Some of these are parents who found that their adult children in China could not adequately support them, and who were encouraged by relatives and friends on both sides of the border to apply for exit visas. Those in Hong Kong at the time of the border closing are regarded by the Chinese government as Chinese citizens resident in Hong Kong and as such may enter and exit from China with little restriction. Those who left China with legal emigrant visas may also return.

What of life in Hong Kong? Are these mostly rural migrants comfortable in a densely populated urban environment with all its attendant insecurities? Such variables as rural or urban origins in China, length of time in Hong Kong, level of education, language ability, and the presence or absence of mediating kin or friends all affect the kind of adjustment the individual can make.

Probably the two historical events with the greatest impact on this generation are the Sino-Japanese War and the Communist restructuring of Chinese society. Several of my informants simply could not discuss their circumstances during the Japanese occupation of Hong Kong. The harbor areas were heavily bombed for days, and many living in the vicinity lost members of their families. There were subsequent shortages of food and medicine. The Japanese urged the population to return to China, and a great many did so, but others, already too weakened or lacking relatives in China, starved to death or succumbed to illness.

The Communist restructuring of Chinese society has been a severe blow to many of the elderly. Land reform and reclassification of families in terms of their "class origins" have nearly turned the old order upside down. The overthrowing of Confucius, the conversion of ancestral halls into schools and public meeting halls, and the condemning of religion have destroyed Mr. Go's world. The ban on ostentatious display on such occasions as funerals draws Mrs. Wong's hostility. While many younger residents of Hong Kong, such as university students and left-wing trade-union members, are proud to identify themselves as "patriotic Chinese,"—ideological supporters of the People's Republic of China—the older residents are much more ambivalent.

Many old people fled to Hong Kong precisely because of disagreement with the Communist philosophy. Others, though they came to Hong Kong for straightforward economic reasons, still shudder when they recall the humiliation and violence which accompanied the "struggle sessions" associated with land reform and the Cultural Revolution. They find the enthusiasm of the young for a system that they have never seen in operation disconcerting, but most have learned to express their opinions cautiously. One of my informants, 66-year-old Mrs. Ngai, who lives down the street from a left-wing trade union, has learned, like Mr. Go, to avoid political discussions. When asked what she thought about Mao, then still alive, she said only that it is wise to say that Mao is "Number One" because you never know whether the people who ask you are left-wing or not. She did, however, volunteer a disrespectful though silent imitation of Mao, head lolling and limp, in the advanced stages of a debilitating disease.

Most of the elderly are now living in a world very different from the one in which they grew up. Mr. Go is fortunate in being able to carry out the role of the wise, retired scholar, supported by his descendants, and spending his time in charitable pursuits. He is in some ways the epitome of the retired Confucian gentleman of traditional China, but he does not deceive himself. He knows that the traditional world is not coming back. Mrs. Wong rails at the Communists, but she too is realistic, and, in fact, wants no return to the days of "blind marriage" and mistreated daughters-in-law. In the course of their lifetimes, most of the elderly have had to accommodate many changes, and while some of the changes are unwelcome, few old people seem to be disabled by them. Others have been able to find corners relatively untouched by change, limiting their contacts to old people from the same districts as themselves, living in tenements or bedspaces in crumbling parts of Hong Kong, and eking out a marginal existence.

The everyday lives of Mr. Go and Mrs. Wong also point out some of the differences which exist among the elderly due to gender, educational attainments, availability of kin, and economic resources. Perhaps gender is the most important of these variables because in traditional China sexual status influenced opportunities for educational attainment and for family life, and both of these, in turn, affected one's economic resources.

While Mr. Go is exceptional, even for a male, in being a university graduate, Mrs. Wong, with no formal education whatsoever, is typical of old women. In a village, illiteracy did not greatly hinder people, but in urban Hong Kong it is a serious handicap in several ways. Being literate, Mr. Go can ride buses, know where to get off, and follow street signs to an unfamiliar destination. Being illiterate, Mrs. Wong cannot, and she hesitates, consequently, to move out of familiar territory. The constant tearing down of old structures and the erecting of new ones make it difficult to identify places since the surroundings are always changing. When Mrs. Wong was forced to move, she had to depend on others to read the red papers posted in public places announcing the availability of cubicles and bedspaces. When friends recommend new ointments or pills to her, she is never sure how much medication to take since she cannot read the label.

Mr. Go receives mail and reads newspapers daily. Mrs. Wong does neither. Whenever she receives an infrequent letter, she has to rely on an educated co-tenant to read it for her. Any letters that she writes go through a professional letter writer at the cost of $3 HK a letter. Mr. Go keeps up with current events through the paper. He is part of the teahouse scene of men drinking, smoking, and reading. Mrs. Wong must depend on radio and television or word of mouth for news of current events. These differences in literacy also affect the utilization of leisure time. Whereas old women are quite content to sit around and rest after their household tasks are done, old men find this very boring and prefer to read or walk around outside.

The availability of kin also makes a great difference. The support of his numerous descendants permits Mr. Go to spend his postretirement life in the pursuit of meditation and the performance of meritorious acts. The absence of descendants in Hong Kong means that Mrs. Wong can never really retire. In time of need, Mr. Go knows that his family will provide for him, but Mrs. Wong must rely on her kai children, about whom she has already expressed serious doubts, or pay a neighbor for services as she has already paid Mrs. Fung. Elderly men are far more likely than elderly women to have a family life. According to the Working Party Report (1973:4), only 9 percent of elderly males are widowed, whereas 36 percent of elderly females are; and more than twice as many women (7 percent) as men (3 percent) have never married. One percent of both sexes is divorced or separated. Nevertheless, the majority of both sexes are married (though not necessarily living together)—87 percent of the men and 57 percent of the women. The differences in widowhood by sex are due to a variety of factors including higher age-specific mortality rates among males, the tendency of women to marry older men, and the fact that traditional values sanction the remarriage of males but not that of females. Widowhood means not only a lack of a marital partner, but, in some cases such as very early widowhood, a lack of descendants as well. When I interviewed 68 widowed informants, I found that 56 percent had been widowed for more than 25 years including 10 percent who had lost their spouses 50 or more years earlier.

The reason Mr. Go and Mrs. Wong—and many other old people like them—continue to rely on traditional support mechanisms despite the disruptive influences of industrialization and value changes is, very simply, that contemporary Hong Kong does not provide adequate alternatives. Writing more than twenty years ago about social change in six Western European countries, Burgess (1960:378) stated that industrialization had forced all of those countries to develop new ways of meeting the needs of the elderly. Regardless of their particular cultural traditions, all had had to address problems of income, housing, health, and deprivation of status, in roughly that order.

The industrialization which undermined traditional support

mechanisms in Western Europe has also undermined those in Hong Kong, but Hong Kong lacks the leadership and the consensus to guarantee alternative mechanisms (e.g. Hodge 1981). Given this lack of concensus the individual is increasingly compelled to assess his own circumstances and to rely on his own judgment in making decisions as to which paths are most likely to lead to security in old age. This is a heavy burden for those who did not anticipate having to carry it.

5   The Family

Studies of the family relationships of older people in Western societies suggest several interesting questions about family relationships in Hong Kong. Has the nuclear family concept come to predominate? How are power and authority distributed within the family? Do parents continue to live with adult married children? What is the nature of the relationship between parents and the children who no longer reside with them? Now that girls need not disperse upon marriage, have they kept up or increased their ties with their natal families? What of relations with kin beyond immediate relatives? Are Hong Kong residents still involved in patrilineage activities or have the traditional lineages vanished in the urban setting? In answering these questions, this chapter examines four aspects of family life: household composition and residence patterns; intergenerational relations; family interaction and mobilization; and extended kin relations.

Household Composition and Residence Patterns

Although several studies (e.g. Wong 1969, 1979; Hong 1970; and Mitchell 1972a) as well as the census provide data on household composition and residence, these data all suffer the same limitation; they show what a given person is doing at a given time, but nothing about previous living situations. It is one thing to know that a certain percentage of elderly parents are living with a married son; but whether they moved in with that son after a substantial period of separate residence, or have lived continuously with that son, has significant implications for such relational variables as power and authority. A 65-year-old man who still contributes financially to the family and lets his newly married son bring a daughter-in-law into his household is in a position very different from that of a 75-year-old man who, upon losing financial independence, has been invited by his son and

73

daughter-in-law to move into their household. In order to understand parent-child ties, a history of the residence pattern is critical.

In 1974, I contacted 99 individuals over the age of 60 from whom I was able to obtain extensive information on residence patterns. (See preface for a description of the Hong Kong and Boston samples). This information is summarized in table 1. From the table it is clear that the majority of parents who have children in Hong Kong share a residence with them—71 of 84 parents. I will defer discussion of the 13 parents who live apart from their children until later in this section.

This population of 71 parents falls into three categories: 21 parents living with unmarried children; 13 parents living with unmarried and married children together; and 37 parents living with the family of a married child. The 21 cases of parents living with unmarried children are typical of families experiencing the gradual reduction of family size characteristic of the middle stage of the family life cycle. In 20 of these 21 cases, the parents have lived continuously with these children since giving birth to them. In 17 of these cases, the married couple itself is still intact. Of these 21 families, 11 have children who have already married out.

In the United States, it is customary to think of this phase of the family life cycle as the experience of parents in their 40s or 50s. In Hong Kong, however, this is not currently the case for several reasons. First, few children move out to pursue higher education. While some do move out because of work or possibly of conflict, most do not move out for reasons other than matrimony. The present average age at first marriage for males is in the late 20s. Secondly, in many cases, these are not families of two or three children but rather of five or six. As one woman said, "Women are expected to bear children until they can bear no more." In the past fifteen years, the Family Planning Association has been promoting the small family ideal with considerable success, but this cannot have an impact on those families already completed. Therefore, many people are in their 60s and even 70s with unmarried children at home.

Another factor contributing especially to older men having unmarried children at home is that of remarriage. Six of the 21 families still having umarried children at home are in fact second families for the husbands. In some cases these are a widower's second family. In others, they are part of a polygynous union, though in none of the cases is the primary wife co-resident. Since 1971, it has been illegal in Hong Kong to acquire a secondary wife, but the legality of previous unions has not been affected, and many Hong Kong residents are

TABLE 1.
Living Arrangements of Elderly Chinese
by Marital Status and Presence of Children (N = 99)

| | MARITAL STATUS | | | |
LIVING ARRANGEMENT	Married and Living with Spouse, Children Living in Hong Kong	Widowed or Separated, Children Living in Hong Kong	Widowed or Separated, No Children Living in Hong Kong	Single	Total
Spouse Only	4	-	-	-	4
Unmarried Child(ren)	17	4	-	-	21
Unmarried and Married Children Together	7	6	-	-	13
Married Child(ren)	8	29	-	-	37
Alone	-	6	9	2	17
Employer	-	3	-	-	3
Other	-	-	4	-	4
Total	36	48	13	2	99

convinced the practice continues, only less openly. On the other hand, traditional values frowned on remarriage of a widow, though among the poor such remarriages did occur. None of my female informants admitted to being a remarried widow, though they freely acknowledged being secondary wives. However, some of the secondary wives of my male informants appear to have been previously married. At least 2 women brought along children of their own by a previous union. This differential remarriage pattern means, of course, that there are considerably more childless old women than childless old men.

The second category, families containing both unmarried and married children, are presumably those in the process of reorganization; that is, daughters are going out, and daughters-in-law are coming in. However, closer observation reveals that this is definitely a minority pattern and an unstable one as well. Of the 13 families in this category, 6 have what might be called special circumstances, and 3 others were unstable situations; that is, in the less than two years that I knew the families, the living arrangements changed. The special circumstances tended to be of two types: either the parental residence was very large, or the spouse of the co-resident married child was absent by reason of employment or separation. The sons in 3 of the remaining 4 cases had been married for less than two years and would probably move out later when their families' size increased. In the final case, a widow and her younger son had been brought to Hong Kong after the war by the married elder son.

The third category, that of 37 informants living with a married child's family, consists of 22 parents who live with sons and 15 who live with daughters. For a society traditionally based on patrilineal ties, these figures are startling, at first glance, and lead one to speculate that the absence in Hong Kong of any territorially defined exogamous units means that daughters do not now necessarily live in areas far removed from their natal families. In the city, a move into a daughter's household does not have the same social implications it would have had traditionally, since a daughter's parents are not leaving their own territory and moving into a village in which they have few contacts. However, the absence of the exogamous patrilineal village does not seem to be the factor behind the high proportion of daughter-related families. These figures do not represent a new preference, but are the result of a simple demographic fact. Of these 15 daughter-related families, 12 have no sons, and 2 of the remaining 3 cases are easily explained. One woman's only son has been in a mental institution for several years. Another woman had previously lived with one of her sons, but due to a space problem was living with a daughter when I first encountered her. Later, when the space problem was resolved, she returned to live with her son. The unusual case is that of a couple with 2 sons and 4 daughters, who parcelled themselves out among the daughters, and my informant would not discuss the matter further. Of the 22 people living with sons, 13 live with their only son. Of those who have more than one son living in Hong Kong, 3 live with the oldest son, 1 with a middle, and 5 with the youngest. In all of these latter cases, the parents seem to have lived with the youngest son all along. He seems either to have delayed marriage or to have married and remained with the parents as in the case of Mr. Go's son.

It is also instructive to look at the residence pattern of the parent with a married child from the angle of whether the parent and child have always been together or came together only after some period of separate residence. Of the 37 cases, 14 represent continuous co-residence, while 23 represent discontinuous co-residence. *All* cases of discontinuous co-residence meant the moving of the parent to the household of the child, and in the vast majority of these cases meant a dependent older person (usually a widowed mother) moving in with an adult child accustomed to running his or her own home. In 12 cases, resumption of co-residence occurred when the older person was "rescued" from what was regarded as an abysmal situation in China, though in at least 3 of these rescues, the older person was also seen as a major source of household help. Of the 11 parents who had been in Hong Kong all along, the reasons for resuming co-residence were, in 4 cases, a specific residence problem, such as destruction of the previous dwelling; in 3 cases, prolonged unemployment; in another 3 cases, physical infirmity; and in 1 case, widowhood.

Non-co-residence of sons and daughters-in-law is not a new phenomenon in Hong Kong. As Mitchell (1972a:230-31) demonstrates, many married women did not move in with their parents-in-law even as long as thirty years ago.

> For example. . . . 57 percent of the wives age 55 and over, 45 percent of those age 45-54, 32 percent age 35-44, and 24 percent age 34 and under moved in with their parents-in-law after marriage. If only the women married in Hong Kong are considered, then there has been no historical trend in residence patterns within the past 15 years . . . Since Hong Kong has so many migrants, it is quite likely that many people who married in the Colony could not move in with their parents simply because their parents lived in China.

Rosen (1976:4), reporting on the family structure of upper-middle-class couples in Hong Kong, found that of the 11 couples (out of her sample of 20) who lived in nuclear families, 6 had done so since the inception of the marriage, but the remaining 5 had started out in the parental household. Generally, this meant that the younger or youngest of the children continued in the relatively large parental home in order to save money for an apartment into which they would move following the birth of their first child. As Rosen (1976:10-11) points out, the "volitional" nature of this co-residence contributes to a better relationship between mother-in-law and daughter-in-law since all family members are aware that the younger couple can afford to move out if the situation becomes unpleasant.

The 13 parents who are not living with any of their children remain to be considered. In only a few cases does separate residence appear to be a consequence of a weak or hostile relationship. All 4 of the couples living alone represent what is left after the children move out. All previously lived with their only or their youngest son until he moved out after marriage. Three parents live with their employers.

The remaining 6 parents, all women in their 70s or 80s, live alone. In 2 of these cases, it is likely that the child is in fact a stepchild or an adopted child with whom the informants have occasionally shared living accommodations. Despite a hostile relationship between one of these women (who has twice attempted suicide) and her daughter-in-law, the adopted son arranged several years ago for his mother to move closer to his family so that he could look after her. The other woman, sometimes lives in the rural New Territories with her son (or stepson), but usually lives in the urban area in a bedspace. On our second visit to her, we found that she had joined her son in the New Territories following her recent hospitalization. Another mother has not lived with her only son since he moved out on marriage more than twenty years ago to live in a workers' hostel.

Of the remaining 3 women (none of whom have a son) 2 cannot live with their daughters "because there is no space," but they continue to have good relations with them, and the daughters attempt to support them. The final case is of a woman who came to Hong Kong as a last resort at the suggestion of her husband's younger brother's wife in Hong Kong, and at the urgings of her neighbors in China. She has had no contact with a daughter in Hong Kong, and she is quite miserable fearing that the apartment she now tends for distant relatives in Canada will be sold and that she will be out on the street. These 3 women appear to be candidates for admission to homes for the aged, but they are not enthusiastic about this prospect. They do not want to lose touch with their friends and neighbors, and they fear mistreatment by the staff of the homes.

Other studies (i.e. Wong 1969:138, 1979:98; Hong 1970:95-98; and Mitchell 1972a:28) reveal the primacy of two generation households in Hong Kong where more than two-thirds of all households fall into this category. Mitchell (1972a:337) raised the issue of residential preferences in old age with his sample and found that the least educated and those with the lowest family income most supported patrilocal residence patterns. Hong (1970:201) also found that his data "showed that the family of the upper economic strata, which has a greater likelihood of exposure to Western culture, has a higher tendency to exhibit characteristics bearing resemblance of the Western industrial family patterns, as compared to the family in lower economic strata." These similarities were in family structure, concepts of property ownership, and in style of husband-wife interaction. Rosen (1976:11) found that couples most similar to the parental generation in income and education got along best with their elders presumably because there is less of a generation gap. Families that are most likely to be caught by the generation gap are those sending their first generation of students to secondary schools. The tragedy inherent in this situation is that these are also the families most likely to favor intergenerational co-residence and most likely to need it on economic grounds. In other words, in many cases, co-residence is not a matter of positive affect but a matter of necessity and obligation.

In summary, although nuclear families predominate in Hong Kong, the patrilocal stem family is the second most frequently occurring type. Furthermore, old people without sons can usually reside with, or at least count upon, their daughters. Wealthier and highly educated families show more features resembling Western middle-class families than do poor families. Present evidence suggests that traditional cultural values have eroded mainly in the upper socioeconomic strata. In the lower strata, regardless of value changes, the absolute need for assistance on the part of most elderly parents means a continuance of the traditional pattern of reliance on sons. Living arrangements are now more likely to include a period of separation of the generations, as children move out on marriage. Later, widowhood, illness, or poverty lead to a resumption of co-residence.

Intergenerational Relations

While most older people genuinely enjoy being with their children and grandchildren, the motivations behind co-residence are not necessarily primarily affective in nature. I once naively asked an informant whether she liked living with her son, and I was quickly set straight. "It is not a question of liking or not liking. He is my son, and I should follow him." Of those parents giving specific reasons for preferring to live with their children rather than apart, twice as many mentioned their own need for assistance as mentioned their desire for sociability. Indeed sociability is often problematic because parents and children have different values and interests but little insight into the reasons behind these differences.

Disagreements about spending habits can seriously disturb family relationships. Mrs. Yu, a recent widow in her early 60s obviously upset by financial problems with her son, acknowledged that nowadays it is a great burden for young people to take care of their parents because they have to pay rent, school fees, and raise their own children first, leaving no money for the care of the parents. She then indirectly berated her children for their spending habits, stating that in her day people were proud to save money and to wear the same clothes for a long time. One person would proudly point to a garment and say "I paid $20 for this"; and the other would add with greater pride "I paid only $15 for mine." Nowadays, however, people compete to spend more money; for example, a youngster will show you a shirt and announce that he paid $50 for it, and then the other will proudly announce that he paid $60 for his. People now think that radios and television sets are necessary to be happy.

When she finished talking, her oldest son could no longer restrain himself and exclaimed that he could not understand why old people needed so much money. If they had a large sum of money, he ventured, they wouldn't know what to do with it and would probably spend it on a trip around the world! He clearly resented the fact that his mother gambled away much of her money playing mah jong. He added that so far as he could see, old people in financial difficulties should blame themselves for their plight. "Why didn't they save money before? Why didn't they marry later? Why did they have so many children (he has seven younger siblings)?" He turned to me with an expression indicating his belief that he had convincingly indicted the older generation for poor planning.

When I volunteered that in the old days parents arranged the marriages and the individual had little say, and then, once married, the couple were almost under orders to have children right away, Mrs. Yu wholeheartedly agreed—*mouh cho* ("You said it."). Her son was unimpressed and replied that as an airline employee his own plan is to travel around the world, find the place that most suits him, settle there, and save money. Then, he added triumphantly, when he is old, he will be able to give money to people instead of having to ask them for it!

On another occasion Mrs. Yu stated that a major problem of older people is that they have no one to talk to. They can not talk with young people because their ways of thinking and their interests are so dissimilar. Young people want to go to the beach or picnics, but old people do not like to do those things. She admitted that her own children urge her to go out and walk around for the exercise, but she said she is too lazy to do so. Other parents complain about their children's taste in clothes, with reference to style, expense, or considerations of modesty. Still others fret about the health risks their children ignore during pregnancy and in the first month following childbirth.

Many parents have doubts about the way young people select their mates. Mr. Lam, 71 years old, did not himself have a "blind marriage." He had known his bride before the wedding because she was a relative on his mother's side and came from a village only four or five miles from his own. He thought that they had a realistic knowledge of one another's character before they married, and that, therefore, there were no big surprises after the wedding. Contemporary courtship patterns, however, do not provide much opportunity for understanding the partner's behavior in the marriage situation. Mr. Lam several times mentioned that whenever he takes his little grandson for walks in the parks, he sees couples everywhere. Shaking his head with disgust, he reported that some are embracing, and others sit with the head of the one in the lap of the other.

About fifteen years ago, when his jewelry and curio shop was doing little business, Mr. Lam spent his time writing to people overseas and ultimately acquired over one hundred pen pals in nearly every country imaginable—Fiji, Tahiti, New Zealand, Mexico, Taiwan, the United States, and Italy. Almost all of his correspondents were young, and, though he claimed to have both male and female pen pals, he spent most of the time talking about the young girls. He spoke quite proudly of the fact that these young people told him their innermost problems, and he always tried to comfort them with his advice. One girl had a very serious family problem and was contemplating suicide, but he wrote her out of it.

He himself never revealed his age or marital status to these friends because he feared they would immediately cease writing to him, but he said he never intended to hurt anyone. The writing, he said, was actually his way of doing anthropology, of finding out what people around the world think. It also seemed to be an effort to find out what young Chinese people think for all his correspondents were young Chinese. Was he, in fact, trying to gain greater understanding of his own children by this means? Was his pride in his ability to advise these youngsters a reflection of his possible inability to advise his own children?

Value differences between the generations do not automatically result in open conflict. Mitchell (1972a; 1972b) and Salaff (1974; 1981) suggest that the major way conflicts are avoided in the family is to delimit certain areas of decision-making in such a way that the adult child assumes increasing control over matters that are of greatest concern to him, such as job and mate selection and leisure activities. Matters that pertain to the welfare of the whole family, such as where to live, whether or not younger children should continue in school, and the purchase of costly consumer items, remain more in parental hands. The younger the child and the more conventional the structure of the family, i.e. employed father and housebound mother, the less influence the child has in family matters.

As mentioned earlier, few young people rely on parents or other relatives when seeking employment. The common saying, "When at home rely on parents; when outside rely on friends," was usually explained to me in terms of job-seeking. Mitchell (1972b:172) found only 6 percent of young men working in family enterprises. He also noted (1972a:365) that at every level of family and personal income, the self-employed are the most likely to take care of their fathers, and he interpreted this as an urban form of the traditional pattern; that is, that these sons have jobs inherited from their parents and thereby are especially obligated to provide for them in old age.

When I asked older people about the concept of filial piety and how it influences life in Hong Kong today, two themes emerged. The first was that co-residence is not the measure of filial piety; rather, the significant point is that children should be concerned about and care for their parents. Ideally, co-residence is a means to this end, but if it is not a realistic means then separate maintenance of the parents is quite acceptable. No parents agreed with the proposition that the moving out of a son at marriage is an unfilial act. Second, the expression of filial piety takes different forms depending on whether the child is a son or a daughter. Parents are the financial responsibility of their sons, though co-resident unmarried daughters also must contribute to the household's expenses. Wong (1979:110) found that about three-quarters of the parents interviewed in his research considered it a filial duty of the children to support them. This expectation was held regardless of whether the parents themselves were employed with a regular income or whether the children were married with their own families to maintain. Other parents were more flexible in their expectations saying that it would depend on their actual situation. The nature of the economic support provided by children varies tremendously. For example, a parent living with a married child might receive no actual income from him although all his basic needs are met. Alternatively, a non-co-resident child might make monthly payments of more than $100 HK or might send money intermittently and in very small amounts. Wong (1979:111) found that in actual practice, almost all children who had started working claimed to have given money to their parents. Most did so regularly once a month, whereas others did so on holidays, birthdays, or occasions of need. The amount contributed ranged widely but clustered mainly aroung $100 HK to $400 HK. Salaff (1974:8) refers to a 1970 survey of 660 young factory workers which found that 40 percent of the workers gave all of their income to their families, and 88 percent gave at least half.

According to the Social Service Needs Study (1977:49), the median amount contributed monthly by relatives and friends to the elderly was $111.40 HK or $1336.80 HK annually. However, only 41 percent of the elderly receive income from this category. Some 22.8 percent receive income from employment with a monthly median of $463.99 HK; and according to the Green Paper (1977:6) 73 percent of those aged 75 or over receive the Infirmity Allowance. The Social Service Needs Study (1977:50) concluded:

> It was very clear from the findings that the family, relatives and friends played a primary role in the support of the elderly. The fact that less than 3 percent had a pension reflected the inadequacy of the present social security system which did not cover retirement pensions. The role of personal accumulation, e.g. from investments and savings, seemed to be negligible. Should the family be unable to support them, many would have to rely on public assistance for maintenance as the other income sources were not too significant.

Reliance on daughters for financial support is still more problematic than reliance on sons. In a 1974 study of 27 unmarried working daughters, Salaff reported that the family claimed a minimum of three-quarters of the girl's income. Following marriage, however, a daughter's responsibilities shift from financial support to emotional support. A filial daughter will visit her parents regularly, help out if they are ill, and continue financial support if she is able and the parents require it.

Female employment patterns are a major factor in the lesser financial role played by daughters. According to the Census (Hong Kong 1972:74), women's participation in the labor force rose from 32 percent in 1961 to 37 percent in 1971. While female teenage employment increased during this period, male teenage employement decreased—a reflection of increasing male attendance at secondary and post-secondary educational institutions. As the daughter-in-law of one of my informants explained, "Nowadays girls are no longer considered *siht bun fo* (goods on which money is lost), because they go to work early to pay for their brothers' school fees." By 1981 49.5 percent of women 15 and older were described as economically active (Census and Statistics Dept. 1982:16-18). Female labor force participation peaks at 79.7 percent in the 20-24 age group. Shortly after marriage and the beginning of childbearing, female employment drops drastically—to 56.8 percent for those age 25-34—and never goes any higher. It is also likely that a significant proportion of married women work only part-time. By contrast, male employment rates remain above 90 percent between the ages of 20 and 54.

Women also suffer from unequal pay for equal work. As Fessler (1976:8-9) points out, it was not until April 1975, following more than 25 years of efforts, that female civil servants, including teachers, doctors, and nurses, were legally entitled to receive the same pay as their male counterparts. However, women in the private sector have been less organized and presumably continue to receive unequal wages. These basic economic facts of lower participation rates in the labor force and of unequal pay, coupled with the traditional belief that a woman's income should go to her conjugal family and not to her natal family, serve to limit the amount of financial assistance a married daughter can make to her elderly parents.

The financial assistance children provide parents, whether directly in the form of cash or indirectly through the sharing of a residence, is not simply a repayment for past favors. Most parents continue to perform many services for their adult children and cannot be considered mere passive dependents. Among my own informants, of 45 women living with relatives (usually their children), 20 claimed major responsibility for at least 2 household tasks, and a majority of these perform 3 or more such tasks, particularly marketing, cooking, and cleaning. The tending of grandchildren seems to be considered the primary responsibility of the mother or of the older siblings of the grandchild. Of 11 elderly women with no household responsibilities, 3 were employed outside the home, 6 had health problems, and only 2 were idle.

Of 31 men living with relatives (usually a spouse and children), only 7 said they perform 2 or more household tasks, whereas 20 stated that they have no household responsibilities at all. Four of these "helpful" men have working wives, one has a disabled wife, another has both a working son and a working daughter-in-law, and the last performs token work such as watching the door and answering the phone when other household members are absent. Of the 20 men with no household responsibilities, half are still in the work force: 3 full-time, 4 part-time, and 3 temporarily out of work but currently seeking employment. The remaining 10 men described themselves as retired: 3 of them are over 75 (such as Mr. Go), 3 others are in poor health, and another is very deaf. The remaining 3 are recently retired men; 2 feel the burden of free time and the other does not. One of the two (Mr. Lam) subsequently rejoined the work force as a self-employed middle man in art and curio transactions.

Fifty-five of my informants have non-co-resident children living in Hong Kong. While these children live in many different parts of Hong Kong, there is a tendency for them to cluster on the same side of the harbor as their parents. Some parents have several such children living in their own neighborhood, and these children (or one of them) not only tend to stop by daily but sometimes also take their meals with the natal family. When Mitchell (1972a:387) asked about visiting, he found that many adult children see relatively little of their parents, though these are not necessarily elderly parents. Thirty-five percent of the men and 32 percent of the women who do not live with their parents say they visit them once a week or more, but 26 percent of the men and 32 percent of the women visit their parents less than once a month or never, though Mitchell does not take into account visiting by telephone. Many of these infrequent visitors work seven days a week or have heavy family responsibilities. Mitchell also found (1972a:406) that

> married adults seem to get along quite well with their parents-in-law. . . . Fifty-eight percent of the men and 50 per-

cent of the women visit their "spouse's parents" at least once a month (among those who have these parents-in-law in Hong Kong but not living with them). In fact, they visit their in-laws about as often as they visit their own parents, and instead of these forms of involvement competing with each other, they are mutually supportive. Those who visit their own parents more often are more likely to visit their parents-in-law quite often as well.

He also found older parents-in-law (those aged 55 or over) reporting good relations with their children-in-law. Only 4 percent reported getting along "quite badly" or "very badly" with their sons-in-law though 8 percent reported bad relations with a daughter-in-law.

Family Interaction and Mobilization

There are two points in the family life cycle at which parental concerns about support are most likely to be aroused. The first occurs when the parents are in their 50s or 60s and the remaining children are contemplating marriage. The second occurs when parents can no longer provide for their daily needs because of poverty, illness, or isolation. Families resolve these crises in a variety of ways depending on the resources they have available. Daily living, moreover, calls for family strategies and mobilization of resources, and here too families come up with varied solutions, as the following cases illustrate.

The Seun household consists of 69-year-old Mr. Seun, his wife, and their two unmarried sons. In addition to the cubicle in which the two sons sleep, the family rents a double bedspace with Mrs. Seun sleeping on the upper bed and Mr. Seun on the lower. They also rent a small upper space for storage purposes. The Seuns have lived at this Sham Shui Po address for six or seven years, and for the preceding seven years lived just a few doors further down the street. Consequently they are quite familiar with their present co-tenants and their numerous neighbors. The Seuns keep both a talking bird and a very large well-fed cat.

They could easily afford to move to better private accommodations, but they had set their hearts on public housing. In the past they turned down a chance to move into public housing at Choi Hung Estate because it was too far from Mr. Seun's work place, and he feared getting dizzy riding the buses. Within the past year, they learned that they had lost their eligibility for public housing as the combined incomes of Mr. Seun's two younger sons exceeded the maximum allowable for a family of four. Ironically the government adheres to this limit only during the time of consideration of the application; once a family moves into public housing, there is no limit set on the amount of income it may have, nor is there any change made in its monthly rent.

Mr. Seun's eldest son is married and lives with his wife and four children just a few blocks away. In the winter, Mr. Seun takes the three oldest grandchildren (all primary school students) to and from school while the youngest one stays with him and his wife during the day. His daughter-in-law takes her lunch break at Mr. Seun's, joining her school-age children and the baby who stay on through dinner. At dinner they are joined by the eldest son who later returns to his own dwelling with his wife and children, though sometimes one or two grandchildren are left with the grandparents overnight. In the summer, when the children are out of school, Mr. Seun's daughter-in-law quits her job at the sewing factory to supervise the grandchildren and help out her mother-in-law. For all practical purposes, she and the grandchildren live there during the day, returning home with the eldest son only at night.

Mr. Seun's youngest son (aged 26) is known as Third Uncle to the grandchildren, and it is he rather than Mr. Seun who plays the role of taskmaster when the grandchildren are around. Mr. Seun himself is very indulgent towards his one grandson and three granddaughters, and while he occasionally supervises their homework, it is Third Uncle who is likely to scold them for sloppiness or carelessness. Second Uncle is rarely around as he works on an ocean liner and returns to Hong Kong only when his contract expires. According to his most recent letter, he is due back in about four months. Half of his salary is automatically sent by the shipping company to Mr. Seun, who retired several years ago. All of Mr. Seun's sons have followed in his footsteps occupationally; all are bakers—Mr. Seun, his eldest son, and youngest son in hotels, and the middle son on an ocean liner.

Mr. Seun also has two married daughters, the elder with three children and the younger with five. The younger one lived on the same street as her parents up until a year ago, when her family moved to public housing near Tsuen Wan. She used to visit every day, but now that is not possible. The older daughter lives with her family in government quarters for the fire service in the same district as her parents, and she visits at least once a week. Neither of the Seun daughters is living with her parents-in-law. One set of in-laws lives in Macao (where the Seuns lived for several years), and the other set is deceased. Mrs. Seun's brother also works on an ocean liner and stays with the Seuns between contracts. After a morning in the teahouse drinking and reading the paper, Mr. Seun returns to his bedspace for a nap. In the afternoon he watches television or plays mah-jong with his neighbors. He pronounces himself quite content with his present situation. His health is good (though his poor vision somewhat restricts his travels); his sons provide for him, and he is able to fill his time playing with his grandchildren, snacking, or socializing with his neighbors, co-tenants, and former workmates who occasionally drop by. The snug security of Mr. and Mrs. Seun would doubtless be a source of envy for another couple in Hong Kong, Mr. and Mrs. Tai.

When I first met the Tai family of parents and two unmarried daughters, the four of them lived in one of the older resettlement estates and were very dissatisfied with their surroundings. The room they lived in was so small that one of the daughters had to sleep on the floor at night, and their neighbors were rough and rowdy young men. The two daughters were the sole supports of the family as Mr. Tai, then aged 63, had quit work a few years earlier for health reasons. He had worked at construction sites as a dynamite blaster, but high blood pressure frequently made him dizzy; one day he had a stroke, which left him partially paralyzed. Following his hospitalization, he had acupuncture treatments, which fortunately restored his ability to move. He still required monthly checkups and, whenever he went out for exercise, had to be accompanied by his wife.

In the next year and a half, both his familial and his health circumstances underwent great changes. Both of his daughters married and moved out, not only out of the resettlement estate, but completely out of Hong Kong. One daughter married a Westerner, who worked in the firm where she was a secretary, and went to live in the southern United States; the other married a Chinese man living in San Francisco. Both daughters continue to support their parents financially and keep in touch by letter. Both called long-distance at Lunar New Year, and one has already begun proceedings to bring her parents to the States. She emphasizes, however, that her father should be in good health to be sure of the approval of their application.

Unfortunately, Mr. Tai's health has continued to decline. In the month preceding my visit to him, he had been hospitalized three times (twice with kidney/bladder obstructions and once with constipation). At the time of the interview, he was in a dazed state—as a consequence either of taking medication or of genuine mental deterioration—though he was still alert to some things. When his harried wife began to make inquiries about homes for the aged, he quickly burst out, "I don't want that! I don't want that!" Neither Mr. nor Mrs. Tai has any other close relative in Hong Kong; they came here in 1949 as refugees. Mr. Tai knows that there are some cousins in Hong Kong, but he has had no contact with them for years. For these two parents the future is very uncertain.

Like the Tais', the Leungs' household consists of a set of parents and their two unmarried daughters, both in their 20s. Mr. Leung, aged 66, retired two and a half years ago after more than forty years with a shipping company. At the time of his retirement from the position of tugboat pilot, he received a lump sum payment of $30,000 HK. Now the family is supported by the two daughters. Second Daughter teaches in a pre-primary Christian school (she is a Christian) and contributes $200—300 HK a month to the family. The Third Daughter contributes $300-400 HK a month.

The Leungs' oldest daughter married five years ago and lives with her husband and two small children in Hung Hom, not far from her parents' residence in Ho Man Tin Estate. When she decided to marry a co-worker from the factory, they agreed that they would not move in with his mother who is now living with her own daughter. She continued to work until the birth of her first child. Now that her second child is nearly two years old, she has stopped doing plastic flower work at home and has gone to work in a factory making watch bands. Mrs. Leung stays with the grandchildren in Hung Hom, though the daughter is able to return and share lunch with them. Sometimes Mr. Leung, in the course of his daily walks, joins them for lunch and even dinner. In fact, Mrs. Leung has just about taken up residence with her eldest daughter inasmuch as she returns to spend the night at Ho Man Tin only once or twice a week. In addition to providing meals to her parents, the oldest daughter also occasionally gives them money.

Mr. Leung is in reasonably good health, though a few months after his retirement, he was operated on for an ulcer. Even though he had suffered from stomach trouble for over five years, he had put off the operation. He explained that so long as he was working, he could attend the union clinic for free treatment, but that once he retired, he had to pay for private doctors himself or go to a public clinic. Ultimately he went to a public clinic and was advised to have surgery. He had delayed the operation partly because he feared that once his employers learned of it, they would force him to retire. This was their right since technically he should have retired at 60, but his boss had allowed him to work until the age of 64. Mr. Leung also admitted that he had been doubtful of the ability of the young doctors to perform the surgery successfully; in the Chinese medical tradition, surgery has been one of the least prestigious specialties. To maintain his good health, Mr. Leung has been advised to eat small quantities of food and tea many times a day and to exercise daily—thus, his long morning and afternoon walks.

The Leungs have been long established in Hong Kong. Both Mr. Leung's father and grandfather are buried in Hong Kong, and he has three younger brothers here. He and his wife are boat people who moved ashore only twelve years ago, and all of his brothers are still employed in some aspect of marine work. They were not a fishing family but a transport family and had lived in a boat moored in the typhoon shelter. Now even his son-in-law is involved in marine work, having joined a government department as an inspector checking boats for smuggled goods. The Leungs are nostalgic about their water-borne existence and like to contrast the cooperativeness of the boat people with the selfishness of the land people. When crossing from Kowloon to Hong Kong, Mr. Leung has never taken the tunnel bus, preferring instead to cross by ferry.

Mr. Leung appears to be on good terms with his brothers (he has no sisters) and with several of his former co-workers who live in the same area, but he too has his worries. For one thing, he is extremely bored and wants desperately to find a part-time job that will not require too much physical labor, but he does not know how to find one. Secondly, he is concerned about his future. The dwelling unit he now occupies is intended for occupancy by a family of four; should one member drop out, the remaining three are allowed to stay on. Should two members drop out, however, the remaining two will have to leave the housing estate because there are no units certified for the use of such a small household. Until a few years ago, Housing Department policy required all children to move out upon marriage so as to avoid overcrowding. Because this policy was detested by residents and frequently violated, the government compromised by permitting the parents to select one son or daughter to stay on after marriage, with the younger couple ultimately succeeding to the tenancy.

What will happen when his two remaining daughters marry? Mr. Leung and his wife have discussed this problem with their daughters, but no decision has been reached, and Second Daughter has kept pretty quiet, which Mr. Leung interprets as a lack of enthusiasm. He suspects that his third daughter will marry before the second. If she moves out, they will be left with the second daughter. But what if she too moves out on marriage? Mr. Leung has never directly stated this, but the parents appear to have their coolest relationship with Second Daughter. At the age of 16, she converted to Christianity on her own initiative, having been a student at a missionary school in the typhoon shelter. At first, her parents opposed her conversion, but they have since grown used to it. The rest of the family are not Christian, and they still keep shrines to the earth, sky, and kitchen gods. Second Daughter will not eat the foods prepared as offerings to these gods.

Although the Leungs have only daughters, families with sons face exactly the same problem. Whereas in private housing there is no legal limit on household size, such a limitation in public housing means that decisions must be made by the children long before the parents reach the stage of physical infirmity that usually signals the reunification of a household. Since more than 40 percent of the Hong Kong population currently live in public housing—and this proportion is steadily growing—a substantial number of families must deal with this problem. Among my primarily working class informants, tenancy rights to public (or private) housing seem to be the major benefit an elderly parent can bequeath to a child.

Just up the hill from the Leungs is Oi Man Estate, containing some of the newest blocks of public housing in Kowloon. Its giant towers sparkle in the sun and catch the occasional summer breeze. Mrs. Ip, a 75-year-old widow, her daughter, son-in-law, and five grandchildren were very pleased to move into their one family unit after years of sharing space with co-tenants in a dark and damp building near the waterfront. At long last they could sit inside their home in the daytime and not have to put the lights on. The window easily illuminates the wall opposite which is plastered with large color posters of the grandchildren's favorite pop music stars.

Against the wall at a right angle to all the posters stands a large cabinet built especially for the display of religious artifacts. On the top of the cabinet sit pictures of Kwan Gung, a righteous and loyal general from long ago, and of a bodhisattva or Buddhist "saint." The upper part of the cabinet contains a shelf divided into three chambers, one containing the ancestral shrine, the middle containing a statue of Kwun Yum, the Buddhist goddess of mercy, and the third containing a picture of the god Wong Tai Sin. Oranges for both the ancestors and Wong Tai Sin are usually on display. In the bottom right-hand corner of the cabinet is a recess for the earth god's tablet in front of which Mrs. Ip usually places three sticks of incense. In addition, a sky god is housed on the balcony, a kitchen god in the kitchen, and a door god at the front entrance to the apartment. Mrs. Ip was one of the most religiously oriented individuals I encountered. She had even purchased a copy of the Chinese Almanac so that she could interpret the results of her divination efforts at the temple of Wong Tai Sin.

Mrs. Ip's devotion to Wong Tai Sin might have been partially a result of her having so few supporters in the here and now. Her husband and six of her children had starved to death during the war. Only Mrs. Ip and her oldest girl survived those years. Several times during her life, Mrs. Ip had entered into kai relationships with young men in the hope of expanding her kinship circle, but she had mixed results. One of the young men had gone off to the United States. Another had committed suicide after being hounded by creditors to pay off his gambling debts. A third works on the docks in Hong Kong, and a fourth is a head waiter in a restaurant in Sham Shui Po. Mrs. Ip's 70th birthday celebration was held at his restaurant, and she is convinced that he was responsible for the exceptionally good dishes that were served. At one time, a Chinese visiting from the United States had wanted to marry her daughter, but Mrs. Ip had heard that life in the United States is very hard. She did not want her daughter to lead a hard life—nor did she herself want to emigrate. Her daughter ultimately married a co-worker from her factory. This young man's own parents were already dead, and he had no objections to having Mrs. Ip continue as a member of the household.

The move to Oi Man increased the demands on their family income because they had to do extensive work on the interior of their apartment before they could move into it. They had also invested in new furniture. At that time, the family had three breadwinners—Mrs. Ip's daughter, son-in-law, and the oldest grandson. Since the other grandchildren were all in their teens, they were able to perform most of the tasks about the house. Mrs. Ip herself led a relatively relaxed daily life, which she needed to do because she suffered from congestive heart disease. Over the past few years, she had been hospitalized several times and had continued to take a variety of medications for her heart condition as well as eye drops for glaucoma. But she adapted well at first to life in Oi Man and could be seen sitting on the benches or on the low walls surrounding flower gardens near the shopping plaza, chatting with other older women just about every day.

These easy days ended when her oldest grandson was hospitalized for a kidney operation. At first the family thought that the operation had been a success, but they gradually realized, despite positive signs from Wong Tai Sin, that his condition was deteriorating. Mrs. Ip's daughter quit her job so that she could look after him, staying with him at the hospital long after visiting hours were past and encouraging him to eat. Mrs. Ip became extremely depressed.

One morning about two weeks after the death of the grandson from kidney failure, Mrs. Ip failed to stir from her bed. Her daughter pulled aside the blanket which hung from the upper bunk and found Mrs. Ip barely conscious and unable to move. She was rushed to the geriatric ward at Princess Margaret Hospital suffering from total paralysis on one side of her body as the result of a stroke. There are few rehabilitative facilities in Hong Kong, and Mrs. Ip was transferred to Fanling Hospital, a general hospital in the New Territories. Her daughter was greatly distressed, but absolutely had to return to work. How could she possibly get out to the New Territories to visit her mother and be assured that her mother was receiving adequate care? Mrs. Ip, unable to speak, could only try to catch her daughter's eye to reassure her that she understood that the situation was beyond the family's control.

Mrs. Wu, an 83-year-old widow from Shanghai, lives in her own apartment in Hong Kong. Though she has two sons and two daughters, she does not at the moment live with any of them. Her two daughters are married and living in the United States; her two sons are in Hong Kong. Both she and her husband are highly educated. Mr. Wu had gone abroad to study before the Republican Revolution and returned to China as an engineer. Since he was associated with the Nationalist government, when the Communists gained power he and his family had to flee to Hong Kong, where he died in 1952. In 1963, Mrs. Wu accompanied her older son's family to the United States. The family gained admittance as political refugees, and her son continued to work for the company he had worked for in Hong Kong. However, the company felt that he was more useful to them in Hong Kong and requested him to return. He and his mother did so though his wife stayed in the U. S. long enough to acquire a "green card"* which has long since expired.

When she returned to Hong Kong, old Mrs. Wu moved in with her second son and his family, but her strong personality precluded

---

*A green card states that the owner has permanent resident status in the U.S. and does not require a visa for re-entry into the U.S. should he travel abroad.

good relationships. Her daughter-in-law did not want to change her life around, and Mrs. Wu requested her older son to purchase an apartment for her. She and a companion in her 50s moved into the apartment together. The two women had a long and close relationship. The companion had joined Mrs. Wu's family along with the first daughter-in-law, whom she accompanied as a maid. By the time she was 80 years old, Mrs. Wu was already effectively homebound. She filled her days reading newspapers and watching television—she kept three sets on simultaneously. She was also, according to one relative, "getting a little funny."

Mrs. Wu kept quiet for several months the fact that she had discovered a lump in her breast. When her relatives learned of the situation, they insisted she undergo treatment. Mrs. Wu resisted. "Look, I'm over 80 years old. What kind of treatment can they give me? Radiotherapy or surgery. Probably surgery, and I'm too old to suffer that." She was finally persuaded to undergo two months of radiotherapy. About a year later, the family again insisted she go for a course of radiotherapy as another tumor had appeared on her shoulder, only a few inches from the site of the first tumor. Mrs. Wu agreed to it only after receiving assurances that she could be treated as an outpatient and would not have to be hospitalized. Nevertheless, she was so tense and anxious that on getting up on the morning she was scheduled to renew therapy, she fell out of bed, sustained a fracture, and had to be hospitalized anyway. She entered Queen Mary Hospital as a private patient and shared a room with three other patients. Her two sons are bearing the cost of her medical treatment, are encouraging her to work with a physical therapist, and hope that she will regain her mobility and not remain confined to a wheelchair. When she is released from the hospital, they will hire a private nurse to take care of her in her own home.

Both Mrs. Ip and Mrs. Wu require long-term care. Both have supportive families. Yet one will be confined to a distant general hospital and the other will be cared for in her own home. These two different outcomes are the direct result of the shortage of subsidized community-based services. Since home care programs are extremely few, consumers desiring this type of service must turn to the private sector. To utilize the private sector requires considerable financial resources—resources which Mrs. Ip's family does not have.

In summary, the relations between elderly parents and their adult children vary greatly. Differences between the generations do not inevitably lead to intergenerational conflict because children have the option of moving out and restricting interaction, because adult children have acquired primary control over the decisions of greatest personal importance, and because children avoid situations of potential disagreement by not consulting their parents on sensitive issues. Despite the possible friction these differences can cause, most parents and children continue to be involved in extensive mutual support systems. One reason for such mutual support is that filial obligations are expected to transcend personal feelings. It is not simply a question of liking or not liking; equally, if not more, important is the fact that the two generations genuinely benefit from their interaction. Elderly parents may be housed, clothed, and fed by adult children; but elderly parents, especially women, contribute in turn a substantial proportion of labor to the households of the children. Neither Mr. Leung's eldest daughter nor Mr. Seun's daughter-in-law would be able to work without the child-care their older relatives provide.

Both the Leung and the Seun family situations illustrate the dangers of concentrating exclusively on household composition. By residence criteria, both these families are clearly nuclear families, that is, elderly married couples with their unmarried children; but by relational criteria, such as aid flows and visiting, they are clearly what Litwak (1965) describes as modified extended families. While not all non-co-resident children have relationships with their parents as intense as the eldest Leung daughter and the eldest Seun son, my own observations suggest that most parents have a close relationship with either a co-resident child or at least one of their non-co-resident children. On the other hand, the close ties of some children permit the very loose ties of their siblings. Thus, some children make no financial contributions to their parents and pay only infrequent visits on holidays or ceremonial occasions.

Extended Kin Relations

In Hong Kong, collateral kin (i.e. siblings, aunts/uncles, cousins, and nieces/nephews) do not seem to be a major source of interaction or of assistance. A major reason for this is the *absence* of such kin. Among my 99 community informants, for example, only 24 have any siblings in Hong Kong; 14 have one sibling, 4 have 2, 4 have 3, and 2 have 4 or more. Sixty-five have no siblings in Hong Kong, and another 10 either did not answer the question or do not know the whereabouts of their siblings. Some of my respondents are clearly the last survivors of their generation, whereas others left siblings behind in China (25 cases) or saw them migrate overseas (5 cases). However, those having brothers or sisters in Hong Kong do not appear to have much interaction with them. Only 5 people could remember having seen such a relative within the past two months. Those older people with brothers and sisters in China have almost as much contact with them (albeit by letter) as do those having such relatives in Hong Kong. I encountered no cases of elderly siblings living in the same household, though there were a few cases in which they lived in the same neighborhood, and there was one case in which the families of a brother and a sister occupied adjacent units in a resettlement estate.

The nature of the relationship of adult siblings who have long lived apart is problematic. It is not clear what, if any, responsibilities they have towards each other beyond ritual visits at the New Year or Ching Ming festival (the spring ancestor worshipping occasion). Smith ([1914] 1970:251) reported that

> the mere act of dividing property seems to extinguish all sense of responsibility whatever for the nearest kin. It is often replied when we ask why a Chinese does not help his son or his brother who has a large family and nothing in the house to eat, "We have divided some time ago."

Once when I was asking about relatives outside the household, an old man said he had no such relatives, whereupon his daughter burst in with "What about Uncle-So-and-So?" The old man shook his head bitterly and said, "He wouldn't help me when I needed him. I no longer consider him my brother."

Extended kin, however, do seem to have an important backup role to play; should an individual have no children of his own to depend upon, other relatives, usually nephews and nieces but sometimes cousins, will help out. Combining my data gathered from 75 people visited in homes for the aged in 1973 with that gathered from 22 residents of a hostel for the elderly in 1975, I found the following distribution of prior living arrangements, (see table 2). The sample is categorized on the basis of "closest" relative in Hong Kong; that is, though a man might have both a spouse and a brother in Hong Kong, he is categorized only as having a spouse.

Lineages, however, appear to have been characteristic of rural China rather than of urban China. After briefly reviewing the literature, Baker (1977:502-04) provided the following reasons for the comparative absence of lineages in traditional cities. First, the strength of the rural lineage rested on its control of land. Sojourners had no

TABLE 2.
Closest Kin in Hong Kong and Prior Living Arrangements
of Those Living in Homes or Hostels for the Elderly. (N = 97)

Living Arrangement	Closest Kin in Hong Kong							Total
	Spouse	Son	Daughter	Sibling	Extended Kin or In-Law	Distant Kin	No Kin	
Spouse	8							8
Son		3						3
Daughter			3					3
Sibling				3				3
Extended Kin or In-Law		1	2	2	12			17
Distant Kin						1		1
Employer				2	2	1	12	17
Friend		1	2	1	3	1	6	14
Institution	1		1	1			5	8
Alone		3	2	2	3		13	23
Total	9	8	10	11	20	3	36	97

incentive to build lineages in the city since their land rights and descendants were all in the village. Second, the greater economic opportunities in the cities required quick and flexible responses to changing investment conditions. In the face of such opportunities for individual advancement, the motivation for the kind of collective unity supporting lineage organization was weakened. Third, the greater residential mobility in cities probably militated against settled and enduring kin ties.

If these reasons account for the relative absence of urban lineages in traditional China, they seem even more credible as explanations for the relative absence of lineages in contemporary urban Hong Kong. The majority of migrants to Hong Kong came from Guangdong province and especially from the Pearl River delta. This is precisely the region in which lineages had enormous corporate holdings. According to Chen (1936:34) over one-quarter of the cultivated land in Guangdong and about half in the delta region were corporately held. Such wealthy lineages exerted great retentive powers on the loyalties of temporarily absent members. On the other hand, not all lineages were wealthy, and members of poorer lineages who resided in the city probably had weak ties to home lineages and lesser loyalties to the lineage system as a whole. As Ahern (1973:82) points out, nonresident members of lineages in Taiwan have the responsibility for managing corporate affairs when their turn comes up in the annual rotation. They also benefit by returning to the village to reap the fruits of lineage activities such as feasts which are paid for out of the profits from corporate lands. Nonresident members of lineages lacking corporate property have no incentive to remain associated with an organization devoid of economic benefits.

A second reason for the relative absence of lineages in Hong Kong is that investment opportunities are diverse and rapidly changing. Whole industries, such as wig-making, can rise and fall in just a few years. There is not the same security which owning land provides, though more cautious investors are now putting their money into apartments. Jobs are obtained primarily through friends or direct applications and less frequently through relatives. Thus, lineages have little economic significance and have failed to develop.

Third, while residential mobility within Hong Kong is quite high, it is probably less significant as a factor in the absence of lineages than Hong Kong's relative isolation from its rural hinterland. The home base of most lineages is China, where the lineage halls stand and the ancestors are buried. The present population in Hong Kong would have to start its lineages from scratch. In traditional China the lineage system and ancestor worship were mutually reinforcing, though the strength of one was not absolutely correlated with the strength of the other. Ahern's data (1973) effectively silences those who maintain that all (non-Christian) Chinese worship their ancestors. She found that the obligation to worship depended on a number of generally accepted rules: (1) if X inherits property from Y, he must worship Y; (2) if X is Y's only descendant, he must worship Y; (3) if X is the most obligated descendant, he must worship Y. Thus while descent is important, it is not a necessary, and only sometimes a sufficient, condition to worship the ancestors.

Ancestor worship is by no means universal in Hong Kong. Mr. Seun, for example, has no ancestors in Hong Kong. His wife returns to China annually to worship, but apparently hers is the last generation that will do so. Mr. Seun said that he does not expect his sons to worship him. Mr. Leung, even though he is the eldest son and has two generations of ancestors buried in Hong Kong, does not have custody of his family's tablets. Since he has only daughters, who would normally worship their husband's ancestors, a younger brother's family has custody of the ancestral tablets. Another informant, Mrs. Wun, though she is the only survivor of her husband's line, worships neither ancestors nor gods. Data from the Social Service Needs Study (1977:33) further illustrates the restricted nature of ancestor worship. Only 22 percent of their sample stated that they worshipped ancestors, while another 37 percent stated that they worshipped traditional gods. It is likely that a good proportion of those worshipping traditional gods also worship ancestors. Perhaps what is more significant is that 12 percent of the respondents were Christians, and another 22 percent indicated that they worship nothing at all.

What these findings suggest is that many people do not feel sufficiently obligated (e.g. have not received property or favors) to find worship necessary. Such sentiments do not make the development of lineage ties—which are based even more on economic considerations—a likely occurrence in Hong Kong. Indeed, if the fraternal ethic of cooperation within the joint family can be extinguished by household division, how much more likely is the lineage to crumble when there are no economic incentives to keep it together. Mitchell (1972a:419) found patrilineages nearly nonexistent in urban Hong Kong.

Only one or two of our informants claimed they belonged to a clan organization, but these organizations are not patrilineages in the traditional sense. Instead, they are "name" associations composed of people of the same surname, regardless of whether their members can establish any kinship connection with each other. And these associations provide very little if any service to their members.

My own informants confirm Mitchell's findings. Very few belong to a surname association, and most of those who do joined in order to participate in the burial insurance programs sponsored by the associations; by making monthly payments into a fund, they are guaranteed a funeral and burial at death.

Baker (1977:509-10) distinguished among lineage, clan, and surname associations in traditional Chinese cities. Whereas lineages were characteristic of the rural areas, and membership was dependent upon descent, clans were an urban phenomenon utilized primarily by the elite and deliberately formed with only the flimsiest of known or ascribed genealogical ties. Baker does not believe that common surname associations were of great importance in Chinese society and suggests that where they did exist, they were likely to be mutual aid groups for the poor in the largest cities. The emergence of such "voluntary" kin associations as clans and surname organizations in the cities has also been noted by Bruner (1970:133) in Indonesia. What seems to have happened in both urban environments is a "redistribution" of kin sentiments and of opportunities for joint action. In the absence of conventionally constituted lineages, the nuclear or stem family assumes almost complete responsibility for its own members, and the clan or surname group takes over responsibility for community-wide action. The middle ground has disappeared.

In summary, extended kin, siblings, aunts, uncles, nieces, nephews, and cousins, appear to play only a minor role in the lives of elderly Chinese. Though many of my informants have no kin from these categories living in Hong Kong, those who do have quite limited interaction with them. Collateral kin appear to be most significant for those people lacking closer kin, lacking spouses or descendants. The patrilineage which in the village was the next largest corporate group to which an individual belonged and from which he could claim assistance is almost nonexistent in urban Hong Kong. Instead "voluntary" kin groups operate in the community sphere, but their activities are more specialized and narrow than those of the rural lineage. This absence of the patrilineage has meant that increasingly exclusive responsibility for kin resides in the nuclear or stem family.

Old people in Hong Kong are highly conscious of the fact that they cannot take for granted what they assume their own parents and grandparents did. They are aware that they must continue to inculcate the value of filial piety and at the same time to determine which child is likely to be most amenable to and most capable of supporting them in old age. This situation is particularly delicate because, in the absence of the patrilineage, few outside pressures can be brought to bear on a recalcitrant child. As Bott (1971:390) points out:

> Urban families are not isolated since members maintain many relationships with individuals and groups outside the family. But they are more "individuated" than families in relatively small, closed communities. Many of the individuals and groups to which an urban family is related are not linked up with one another, so that although each external individual or group may control some aspect of familial activity, social control of the family as a whole is dispersed among several agencies. This means that each family has a relatively large measure of privacy and freedom to regulate its own affairs.

It is precisely this freedom which produces anxiety for many elderly parents. Should they lose control of their child, they have scarcely anyone else or any place else to which they can turn.

6 Community Support Systems

Informal Support

Most works dealing with traditional Chinese social relations are concerned almost exclusively with the role of the individual as a family or a lineage member. Relatively little has been written about the role of extra-kin ties. Such neglect is surprising in view of the fact that the bond between friends constituted one of the five cardinal relationships upon which the traditional Confucian social structure was based. Perhaps this concentration on kinship has been helped along by the fact that, particularly in southeast China, villages often consist of a single lineage—thus all one's neighbors and most of one's friends are simultaneously relatives. In the city, kin ties, while still important, are supplemented by more formal ties to district organizations, surname organizations, and the like. In the city, the individual becomes aware of alternative networks operating for specific rather than diffuse purposes. This awareness is more characteristic of men who go out daily to work; unemployed women remain dependent on the local neighborhood to a much greater degree, in developing social relationships beyond the family.

As discussed in the previous chapter, the position of the older person within the family has been undergoing change in Hong Kong. The distribution of power within the family, the living arrangements, and the sources of emotional gratification are quite varied. There is considerable evidence in the American literature (Johnson 1971; Hochschild 1973) that old people, while maintaining and even increasing their involvement in family affairs, also enjoy contact with their age-mates (with the exception of a minority who share the stereotypical view of the elderly and refuse to acknowledge their own membership in the category). Rosow (1967) and Blau (1973) note that while most older people retain close, affectionate ties with their children, such ties are not able to satisfy all of the emotional needs of the parent. Studies of friendship patterns indicate that homogeneity of age, marital status, sex, education, and socioeconomic status is characteristic of all age groups. Almost by definition, children are unable to meet at least the first of these qualifications. Hochschild (1973) suggests that while a parent, in a sense, relives his life through his children, he continues to live his present life with his peers. Only with a person who faces the problems common to aging can an older person truly share his fears and gain emotional support.

How true this theory is with respect to elderly Chinese is not clear. Chinese are encouraged to take the long view back to the ancestors and forward through the descendants. The present generation of old people, however, can be regarded as pioneers. They are the first generation to have grown up in a more or less traditional China and yet had to face the fact that they are aging in a modern urban context. Lopata (1973:180) points out that the urban environment itself can pose considerable obstacles for those whose backgrounds are rural, since the methods intended to bring

> another person into the "best friend" category are designed to start with already known semi-friend positions and to begin early in life. These characteristics have made the development of a new friendship extremely difficult in modern urban centers, where it must start from mere acquaintance or even some candidate-searching action through the whole life cycle. Traditionally the culture of all but the upper classes does not contain such friendship building mechanisms. In fact, their development has been hampered by a village-like distrust of all strangers and the assumption of permanency and ascribed nature of "true friends."

Clark and Anderson (1967:306) also noted the significance of time as a factor in friendship and in the apparent reluctance of older people to seek new friends. Niebanck (1965:136) found that old people living in residentially stable neighborhoods were able to maintain long-standing friendships. Furthermore, the neighbors were the major reason people gave for liking their location; these social ties were the greatest impediment to a voluntary move. A number of my own informants were living in close-knit communities of fellow countrymen, and they perceived the possible breakup of their networks through urban renewal as an unmitigated disaster.

Old people, however, just when they may need friends the most, when they are retired or widowed, often find that their circle of friends is contracting. Friends die or move away, and the physical limitations that often accompany aging may make it difficult to keep up old ties. Rosow (1967) suggests that making new friends is especially difficult for old people unless they are located in an area where the density of old people is very high, unless a majority of the households in the immediate vicinity contain at least one older person. Lowenthal and Haven (1968) make the additional point that even more significant than the quantity of friends an individual has is the quality of the ties. In their study, the presence of a confidant, whether a friend or a relative, served to protect the morale of the individual from the normal "insults" of aging (though not, interestingly enough, in the case of health problems).

That some old people have difficulty in developing a fuller social life has led, in the United States, to a proliferation of senior centers and other clubs specifically organized to facilitate interaction among the elderly. However, as Niebanck (1965:139) indicates, several studies suggest that elderly persons do not really have much interest in these clubs or their activities. Here again the lack of involvement may be an outgrowth of the time factor mentioned earlier. For a person wary of strangers and uncertain of his own social skills, a visit to a club of strangers is a dismal prospect. This is a very different experience from seeing people in, say, the neighborhood church one has attended for several decades.

Friends

The semantic range of the word friend is extensive in both American and Chinese cultures, and several qualifiers are used to distinguish the degrees of intimacy characteristic of particular relationships. Although precisely what is meant by each qualifier also varies, there does appear to be a fairly consistent use of terms with respect to relative intensity. At the least intense end of the scale is the term *jauyuhk pahngyauh* ("wine and meat friend"), with the connotation of a non-enduring relationship—"Wine and meat a thousand friends retain, but in need will one of them remain?" In Hong Kong, much social life occurs in restaurants and tea houses, and it is customary, when a group of people have been eating or drinking together, for one person to pay the bill. Diners struggle to grab the check or to push aside the hands of the other contenders proffering money to the waiter. A suggestion to split the check is usually frowned on and may be interpreted as small-mindedness on the part of the person making the suggestion, inasmuch as it can imply an unwillingness to enter into a new social relationship. At one gathering, an individual is put into the social debt of the payer of the bill, but he is expected to right this balance at a future encounter. Mr. Go's flourishing of $100 bills is in this tradition, though the practice is by no means limited to the senior generation. The inability to marshall resources sufficient to pay for several people may depress a person's social participation. True friendships, however, should not be terminated because one party can no longer keep up his share. The problem is more likely to inhibit the development of new friendships than to terminate old ones.

At a similar level of intensity is the term *poutung pahngyauh* ("common" or "ordinary friend") with the connotation of positive but not special feeling. At the next level of intensity are the terms *hou pahngyauh* ("good friend") and *louh pahngyauh* ("old friend") with connotations similar to those of the English terms. The "old" refers specifically to the enduring quality of the friendship rather than to the age of the participants. The importance of the time element in making friends is clearly expressed by the common saying, "A long road tests a horse; long-drawn out affairs test a friend." At the level of most intimate friend or confidant are the terms *jigeige pahngyauh* ("friend who knows my self") and *jisamge pahngyauh* ("friend who knows my heart"). In some cases such friendships are so intense that they culminate in *git baai hingdaih* ("sworn brothers") or *gam laahn jimui* ("golden orchid sisters," sworn sisters) relationships, the model for which is drawn from the fourteenth century historical novel *The Romance of the Three Kingdoms*. According to Doolittle ([1865] 1966 2:228-29):

> It is a very common practice for those who are intimately acquainted with each other, and who cordially love and respect each other, to adopt each other as brothers. Oftentimes women who dearly love each other adopt each other as sisters. Men who adopt each other as brothers sometimes do it by kneeling down and worshipping Heaven and Earth simultaneously, or by burning incense, with kneeling, before an image of the god of war, or of some other popular idol. Others swear, under the open heavens, to be faithful brothers to each other, imprecating awful curses in case they should become unfriendly and not fulfill the duties of brothers to each other. . . . The vows are considered binding as long as one of the original parties survive, no matter whether the

relative positions in society remain unchanged or not, whether one becomes rich and honored, and the other becomes a bankrupt or a felon.

Such sworn relationships are less frequent nowadays, but they can still be found particularly among aged domestic servants, who entered the relationship when they were young or middle-aged (Sankar:1978). In the United States old people are usually found to have fewer friends than young people for a variety of reasons such as the lessened mobility brought about by retirement, reduction of income, or ill health, which serves to make contact with former associates more difficult. A lack of social skills in urban living may make it difficult to initiate new friendships, and this difficulty is compounded by the shrinkage of the age-group from which they are most likely to draw new friends. At the same time, the need for friends remains quite high and, in the absence of kin, probably increases.

In Hong Kong, the return to China of some old friends and the relative absence of extended kin probably leave many old people isolated from their peers. Most of the friendship characteristics associated with elderly Americans apply equally to elderly Chinese. A majority of informants stated that they now have fewer friends than they had when they were 50 years old, and they attributed this fact primarily to having lost natural opportunities to interact with them. Retirement for many men meant no more mealtime association with co-workers, and moving to a new location often meant the loss of co-tenant or neighborhood-based friendships for women. Those few informants who made new friends encountered them in the course of walking around or sitting in public areas near their homes, or through other friends. They did not tend to meet them in clubs or other formal organizations. Two-thirds, however, said that they have made no new friends at all in recent years. These responses were to questions regarding friends in general; but when asked specifically about "good friends," nearly 50 percent of the informants said that they have no good friends. Most striking was the basic difference between the sexes; women were much more likely to say that they had no good friends. The present living arrangement of the older person, whether with family members or alone, does not seem to affect the number of good friends a person has.

When asked whether they had any intimate friend with whom they felt comfortable talking over personal matters, a majority of both men and women said that they have no intimate friend, but men were more likely than women—37 percent to 21 percent—to state that they do. This apparent lack of close friends on the part of women does not mean that they have no intimates in whom they can confide. There is a Chinese saying to the effect that men have friends and women have relatives, which suggests that women are more likely to obtain emotional sustenance from this latter source. At another interview session, I simply asked informants whether there was any person (as opposed to a particular friend) with whom they shared their personal problems. The responses to this question were almost identical for men and women; 47 percent of the men and 43 percent of the women identified such a person.

Literature dealing with the traditional structure of the Chinese family (e.g. Lang 1946) tends to emphasize the father-son and mother-son ties. Whereas father-son ties are the authority focus of the family, mother-son ties are usually perceived as the affective focus of the family. Among my own informants, only 10 parents singled out a child as a confidant. Seven women cited a daughter (of these 7 women, 5 have no sons), but *no* woman cited a son. Sixty-five informants have sons in Hong Kong and 65 have daughters yet only 2 fathers picked sons as confidants, and 1 father who has no sons picked his daughter. (Ten informants responded that their families (in general) shared their personal problems.) Spouses did not rate highly as confidants. Out of 32 married informants, only 3 specifically said they share their personal thoughts and problems with a spouse.

Traditionally couples were not expected to be especially close. Overt signs of affection in public even between a married couple were discouraged and ridiculed. Family or sex-segregated peer groups were the major social settings. Couples did not socialize as couples. Among the Western educated, this separation was, of course, less marked, but even among young people in contemporary Hong Kong, sex segregation remains high. Dating is usually group dating first, and when a young man and a young woman pair off on a regular basis, they are assumed to be heading for matrimony. Changing partners after a month or two of dating or dating several individuals simultaneously, even if very casually, raises the eyebrows of peers and parents alike.

Older people themselves seldom think of remarrying, least of all remarrying someone of the same age for companionship. An older man might remarry a younger woman "to take care of him," but a marriage between two old people for companionship seems incredible and continues to be a matter engendering ridicule. Several old women laughed loudly on learning that such marriages do occur in the United States. One elderly couple, a widow and a widower, met as residents at a congregate housing facility (known locally as a "hostel"). The director of the hostel considered them an exemplary couple and in conversations in front of other hostel residents pointedly emphasized the tenderness with which they treated each other in times of illness. At least some hostel residents were unimpressed and complained that sellers in the market gossiped about the couple. According to the *Hong Kong Standard* (15 Sept. 1976) of the 36,479 marriages registered in the 1975-76 year, there were only three cases in which both the husband and the wife were 70 or more years old.

The congregate housing facility mentioned above offers one possible solution to individuals seeking additional friends. Rosow (1967) found that older people in the United States prefer to select their friends from among age-peers, and that the availability of such peers conditions the formation of friendships. However, an examination of friendship patterns at Wah Hong Hostel suggests that cultural and personality factors continue to inhibit many older people from converting acquaintances into "true friends." Wah Fu Estate contains the first housing built by the government specifically for the elderly. Two floors of one block were set aside for the hostel, which opened in 1969. The block is located on a promontory and provides a magnificent view of the water and nearby islands. According to a handout sheet introducing the hostel, nine voluntary agencies and three Government Departments co-operated

> to provide attractive accommodation for 120 ambulatory independent elderly persons in a Public Housing Estate. It is the first project in the community designed to provide non-institutional housing for the aged, and it plays a useful and necessary role for them. It is clear that for many elderly people life in an institution is not the right answer - what they want is a home in which they can enjoy a full, active and normal life. This is what the Hostel aims to provide.

Unlike residents in a traditional home for the aged who often live many to a room, take their meals in common, and share communal washing facilities, the hostel residents retain a large measure of the freedom they had in the community. Four residents live in each of the 30 units, which contain a large living and sleeping area, a small kitchen, balcony, and toilet off the balcony. They are free to watch television in the common room provided on each floor, to engage in handicraft activities in their rooms, to do their own cooking and cleaning, and to come and go as they wish. There are buzzers by each bed so that a staff member (who is on call 24 hours a day) can be summoned in a medical emergency. The residents may spend up to seven nights a month outside of the hostel and may accumulate such time to take longer trips to Macao or China. The hostel provides ten regular social activities every year, including two picnics, four birthday parties (one for each season), feasts on Mid-Autumn Festival, Dragon Boat Festival, and the "Winter Day," as well as get-togethers with the residents of the other hostels since opened in Hong Kong. In addition to these hostel-sponsored activities, other activities are carried out by church and private agencies, which, for example, sponsor *tai chi* exercise classes or bring in youth groups to sing at Christmas time.

Priority in admission to the hostel goes to old people who are poor and have no relatives. While the expenses of most residents are met through public assistance, there are a few who pay their own fees. Residents do not have total freedom of action however. The choice of roommates is up to the hostel staff; people apply as individuals (except in the cases of a few couples) and vacancies (which now occur only through deaths) are filled from the waiting list. People are not allowed to change their room except under very special circumstances; for example, the two residents who met and married in the hostel were allowed to transfer to a room with another married couple. Similarly, gambling, as in cardplaying or mah-jong, is not allowed, nor may residents keep large appliances such as refrigerators or televisions in their rooms. Nevertheless, residents consider themselves much better off than those living in traditional homes for the aged, and the government departments and voluntary agencies have considered the hostel such a success that by 1982 15 were in operation, including some which provided meals.

Though the possibilities for social interaction are greatly increased in a setting such as the hostel, this does not appear to have been a major factor, or at least not a primary factor, motivating people to apply for entry. Most residents came to the hostel out of financial necessity, though perhaps others, in the newer hostels, may now perceive advantages of a social as well as a financial nature. The locating of the hostels in blocks of public housing estates means that, unlike in many of the secluded homes for the aged, the residents can still participate in ordinary everyday activities such as going to the market and the tea house.

Before conducting my own research, my expectations, based on

Rosow's (1967) findings, were that hostel members would (1) have more good friends than community dwellers, (2) have a smaller change in the number of friends between age 50 and now, (3) be more likely to have made a new friend recently, and (4) be more likely to have a confidant. Only the second assumption was borne out. Responses reveal scarcely any differences between community dwellers and hostel residents with respect to the number of good friends. Just as in the community sample, hostel women were less likely than hostel men to say they have any good friends (37.5 percent to 50 percent). Forty-two percent of hostel residents compared to 26 percent of the community residents stated that they have as many friends now as they did at the age of 50. Surprisingly, however, only 2 of 22 respondents said that they made new friends in recent years. When asked whether they had any intimate friends, only 2 hostel residents responded positively, and of these 2 confidants, 1 is a cousin living outside the hostel and the other is a room-mate. The relative absence of confidants again points out the significance of the time element in providing intimacy in a relationship. Few of the hostel residents knew other residents prior to entry and are unlikely to feel they have known their co-residents long enough to become very close.

The fact that many hostel residents are embarrassed about the circumstances which led them to apply for admission also inhibits the development of close ties. Language differences in the hostel are a problem for residents and staff alike. "Northerners" tend to be located near each other, but the only Hoklo speaker in the hostel proved very disruptive until another Hoklo speaker was admitted. In the opening of a hostel, the language problems of the applicants are taken into consideration, but this is much more difficult to do when admissions are one at a time from the waiting list.

In summary then, old people in Hong Kong have, in the absence of extended kin or other close relationships, become increasingly and in some cases exclusively dependent upon their immediate families for social gratification. They frequently find their social circles narrowing as mortality and reduced mobility lessen the opportunities for interaction with friends. Women are the primary victims of these reduced opportunities for two reasons: (1) they tend to be more dependent on long-term association such as that provided by kinship or a stable neighborhood, and (2) they frequently lack the social skills to convert casual friends into closer friends. The influence of these two factors seems quite strong in Hong King.

Neighbors

Hong Kong residents are frequently said to lack a sense of identity, and this can, as we have seen, probably be attributed to three factors: (2) most older residents were not born in Hong Kong and still think of China as their homeland; (2) the anticipated expiration of the British lease in 1997 creates insecurity and causes many residents to view Hong Kong as a temporary residence only; and (3) Hong Kong is a British Colony which means minimal political power to the residents and reinforces their basic lack of interest in its affairs. All of these, combined with language differences, neighborhood instability, and long working hours, serve to limit both the inclination and the opportunities for interaction among neighbors. There are almost no occasions when neighbors *as neighbors* mobilize other than to protest or to resist the destruction of their housing by government bulldozers. Ironically, but not surprisingly, squatters and occupants of the housing estates with the fewest amenities appear to have the strongest neighborhood ties (Kan 1974). Squatters organize fire-fighting and rescue teams to protect their lives from fire, flood, and mudslides. Everyone must cooperate to be assured access to public facilities such as water and toilets. Families living in self-contained units in permanent structures tended by hired staff have fewer reasons to cooperate for joint action. Historically, such housing has been the province of the well-to-do who are less locally based anyway.

There are two major types of neighborhood-based formal organizations in urban Hong Kong: the *gaaifong* ("neighbors") associations and the Mutual Aid Committees (MACs). Both of these organizations owe their origins to government (and private) concepts about the nature of welfare and mutual aid in the Chinese village. The first gaaifong was established in 1949 with official encouragement. According to Wong (1972:50) the gaaifongs serve essentially three functions:

1. To act as social welfare organizations which give charity and relief, provide a limited scheme of social security, and work to strengthen the integration of the Chinese community.

2. To serve as channels of communication between the authorities and the Chinese people representing Chinese community interests on the one hand and publicizing Government community policies on the other.

3. To provide a source of prestige and social status to the leaders.

Wong found the leaders to be traditional in their orientation and interested in encouraging the retention or restoration of such values as filial piety and respect for the aged by holding annual banquets or entertainment programs for the elderly. By the mid-1970s, however, these functions were increasingly being turned over to the Government. For example, in February 1976 the Social Welfare Department's Community and Youth Office in Sham Shui Po coordinated the programs for Senior Citizen Week. The gaaifongs' greatest impact on the elderly comes in the form of burial societies or "death gratuity schemes." In 1977, the Green Paper (p.51) reported that nearly 18 percent of the older population were members of burial societies (not all of which were run by gaaifongs) and that the median monthly payment of the members was $10.13 HK. My own informants were more likely to belong to a burial society than to any other form of organization. Participation consists simply of making the monthly payment. In both the recreational and the burial society activities of the gaaifongs, old people are merely the passive recipients of services. They are rarely involved as active planners or implementers of programs.

The MACs are somewhat different; they are based on smaller residential units than the gaaifongs, such as a single multi-story building, and though membership is entirely voluntary, members are expected to be more actively involved (Scott 1980). Mr. Leung, for example, takes a turn as a night watchman once a month for his MAC. For these reasons, the MACs, which were first organized during the Government's Fight Violent Crime Campaign of 1973, may be more successful in stimulating neighborly interaction. The number of MACs in the urban area continued to grow—reaching 4,245 by the end of 1980. Compared to the residents' committees characteristic of cities in the People's Republic of China, however, the MACs and their activities are scarcely visible. A former Shanghai resident noted in the mid-1970s:

> I left China feeling that we try too hard to control people's lives and we keep too tight a rein on what they do after work in their homes. Here in Hong Kong, however, neighborhood life is so impersonal that I wonder if my Shanghai experience couldn't somehow be applied here. Maybe we should try to organize some kind of Hong Kong residents' committee—

not to snoop on people or to mobilize them politically, but just to help them keep the place clean, to take pride in their surroundings, or simply to get them to know one another. What's missing in Hong Kong is people in the neighborhood feeling part of some group. In Hong Kong almost everyone is a stranger. As a result there is dirt and chaos, and people don't care about each other. In China there's too much control and in Hong Kong there's not enough (Frolic 1980:241).

In a stable village, there are many opportunities to develop relationships with neighbors over a long period of time. In a village, community organizations consist of people already known and flow naturally out of ordinary interaction. In the city, however, where there is considerable residential mobility, it is difficult to depend solely upon the passage of time for the development of friendships. Furthermore, one's neighbors may be involved in unfamiliar lines of work and speak unfamiliar dialects, which hamper interaction. Since most community organizations in Hong Kong are artificially stimulated by outsiders, either by the government or by volunteers, they do not flow naturally from everyday life and consequently are unable to attract many members. All of these factors contribute to a lack of community spirit. Nevertheless, social life does exist beyond the bounds of the family. Despite their minimal involvement in formal neighborhood organizations, some of Hong Kong's elderly are able to participate in informal local friendship groups and helping networks. Others maintain or try to maintain the friendships they made at the workplace. Urban living offers a variety of opportunities for social life outside the family, but the taking of these opportunities requires some individual initiative.

Among my own informants co-workers, or rather former co-workers, are significant sources of interaction, but because co-workers frequently do not live in the same neighborhoods, the level of interaction with them tends to fall off much more rapidly than the level of locally-based interaction. Mr. Leung, the recently retired boat pilot who lives with his wife and two daughters, is a good example of a man closely bound to his former colleagues, several of whom retired at the same time he did. When I first met him in 1974, a few months after his retirement, he continued to have weekly tea with these men. He was at that time quite restless and liked to take walks during which he occasionally dropped in on former co-workers, though he remarked, "I always call on others, but others seldom call on me." He was looking forward to a move to a public housing estate because several of his former associates lived in that general area.

When I next visited him in 1976, he had succeeded in moving to the housing estate and still met his former colleagues for tea. He had made no new friends, but seemed to retain close ties with his old ones; he stated that he was quite comfortable talking over confidential matters with them. On the other hand, he was still restless and wondering how to go about finding some part-time work. He has joined the MAC in his building, but he is not involved in any other organized activities. Mr. Leung is also active within his kinship network having three brothers in Hong Kong, at least one of whom he sees on a weekly basis. He is also increasingly involved with his two young grandchildren, and he will probably turn more and more to his family for social gratification, as he does not seem to know how to go about making new friends.

Unlike Mr. Leung, 73-year-old Mr. Wu has spent most of his life in association with co-workers and fellow countrymen, the two categories frequently overlapping. He never married, he said, because he never had enough money, but he does have an older brother and his family living in Hong Kong. Mr. Wu's first attempt to find a job in Hong Kong was with a printing company, but he became ill early in his apprenticeship and was forced to return to China. When he recovered sufficiently to return to Hong Kong, the company would not take him back, so through the introduction of friends he began the same work he had left behind in China, serving as a shop assistant. He usually lived in the shop that hired him, but as he got older, approaching 60, he had difficulty finding a shop to keep him for any long period of time. He then became a casual day-laborer, going every morning to a certain street where people came to hire workers for the day or for specific short-term tasks. Such jobs did not provide lodging, but he was able to stay in the rear of a shop of a co-villager with several other co-villagers. He did not have to pay any rent, but he helped out picking things up when the shop was closing for the night.

When he was in his mid-60s, his co-villagers alerted him to the possibility of living in the new hostel for the aged. At first, he was not interested, thinking instead that he would save the option for a later date when he would be in greater need of such a facility. However, as his friends pointed out, it would probably be easiest to join the hostel when it was opening up because subsequent vacancies would become available only upon the death of a resident. Once in the hostel, Mr. Wu ceased to have much interaction with his co-villagers and fellow countrymen. They have not come to see him nor has he gone to see them. On the other hand, he and his older brother exchange two or three visits a year—one or the other taking the hour long minibus trip to the opposite end of Hong Kong Island. In the meantime, Mr. Wu seems to be on good terms with the hostel residents. He has assumed responsibility for the care of the plants in the sitting room, and he takes great pride in his calligraphy, having prepared several New Year sayings for the hostel. He attributes his good writing to the days when he wrote the prices for goods in shops. While he has no intimates, Mr. Wu seems to be well-adjusted and competent in managing his social affairs. His years of experience in group living have provided him with the social skills necessary to win acceptance and still maintain his own interests.

Eighty-year-old Mrs. Wun, on the other hand, is an extreme example of the person whose social interaction is locally based. Removal to a hostel would probably terminate her present relationships without replacing them. Since she first came to Hong Kong about 50 years ago, she has worked and lived exclusively in or around Western District on Hong Kong Island. She now has not a single relative in either Hong Kong or China. Her two young daughters and her husband all died when she was in her mid-20s. At that time, her father-in-law ran a fruit stall in Hong Kong, so Mrs. Wun left China to replace her deceased husband as his assistant. By the time he died, her natal family of parents and younger brother had migrated to Hong Kong and moved in with her. Her brother disappeared after being taken into custody by the Japanese, and Mrs. Wun tried to support the family by selling fruit, first as an illegal peddler and subsequently as a licensed one, though she had no fixed stall from which to operate.

For more than twenty years, Mrs. Wun lived a few blocks away from her present residence and was on good terms with her numerous co-tenants. Eventually, their decrepit residence was declared a dangerous building, and the residents were forced to scatter. An old woman from the same district in Guangdong told her of her present residence, and she has been living here in a bedspace in the rear corridor of a small metalworks shop for the past ten years. Since the corridor containing their two bedspaces is small and dark, Mrs. Wun and her co-tenant actually spend most of their time sitting outside the rear of the metal shop in an alleyway that contains four more bedspaces—all occupied by old women from the same Guangdong district as Mrs. Wun and her co-tenant, though Mrs. Wun did not know them until she moved here.

The alley is sloped so that water drains away; it is reminiscent of the village alleys of the New Territories with chickens and rats keeping watchful eyes out for food. The old women have no refrigerator and so are forced to keep only minimal quantities of food around, and these are suspended in plastic bags or baskets from a wooden and canvas structure built from scavenged goods, which serves as a roof over the sitting area. Mrs. Wun and her co-tenant do not have to pay any rent, but as they use the water supply of the metal shop, they are assessed $5 HK a month as a water fee. They cook on wood burners in the alley using for fuel scraps of wood given them by a nearby carpenter or scavenged from construction sites or shops using wooden boxes. Most of their clothes have been given to them, and when they need help in repairing their "roof", they can usually get assistance from the nearby male workers.

Mrs. Wun spends most of her time sitting quietly or playing a card game characteristic of her native district with the other old women. Whenever we visited her, these women were also present, sometimes playing cards and sometimes cutting the tails from the stems of beansprouts. The beansprout seller in the nearby market gives them this task whenever she does not have the time to do it herself and pays them a small amount. Fortunately, Mrs. Wun lives very close to the market and, as a former seller herself, knows many of the stall owners. In any case, she is occasionally given gifts of food by local people. Whenever she is too sick to buy her own food, she can count on her neighbors, the other old women, to buy it for her. They also help out in times of illness by offering advice or by accompanying her to a clinic or a doctor, though these are indeed rare events, as Mrs. Wun prefers not to seek formal medical services.

Mrs. Wun survives on public assistance, the Infirmity Allowance, and the charity of her neighbors. Her social life does not extend beyond the five women living in the corridor or the alley. She has neither the inclination nor the money to participate in social activities of a more formal nature. She gives the impression that she is quite tired of her life and has several times remarked that she never really expected to live this long. Although her material standard of living is very low, she is at least able to share the company of other old people with similar experiences and values ("We can talk about everything," she once said), and she can count on their assistance in time of need.

Not more than a ten minute walk from Mrs. Wun lives Mrs. Lau. Like Mrs. Wun, Mrs. Lau is a widow from Dongguan, a district of Guangdong, but unlike Mrs. Wun, she has lived in Hong Kong for only thirteen years. Mrs. Lau has a son and a daughter in China as well as a son and a daughter in Hong Kong. Many years ago Mrs.

Lau's older son in Hong Kong asked her to come and help his wife with the grandchildren, but her younger son in China did not want her to leave until he was married. When she finally did come to Hong Kong, she first lived with her older son's family in Western District, but when the building was declared dangerous, they moved to Central District. This move proved to be a very good one for Mrs. Lau, as two co-villagers including her father's brother's wife were their co-tenants. Unfortunately, this building too was declared dangerous, and the Laus had to move again. This time, however, the family split up. Mrs. Lau's son actually has two wives and two sets of children in Hong Kong. Mrs. Lau had been instrumental in the arranging of the first marriage and found it uncomfortable living with her son's secondary wife. Mrs. Lau's son rents a flat in Western District, the front part of which he uses as a workshop for making silver jewelry (very simple earrings, chains, and bracelets) and the back part of which (where Mrs. Lau lives) he sublets to others. His father-in-law also lives there, and his brother-in-law works with him in the shop. At night, both the brother-in-law and Mr. Lau return to their wives and children living elsewhere.

Mrs. Lau cooks the meals for her son and occasionally pinches rings together to help him out and to earn some money for herself. In fact, she sends all the money that she doesn't spend on cigarettes—her only indulgence—to her children in China. She used to return to China annually, but for the past two years her rheumatism has made it difficult to go. She would like to return to China to spend her last days, but her older son will not allow her to go, saying that she will not be able to get adequate food. Even were he to send money to her, he explains, she would still have to use ration books, so her diet would be much more restricted than in Hong Kong.

Mrs. Lau is very dissatisfied with her social situation in Hong Kong. Her present residence is very difficult to reach, being located on the 3rd floor of a building perched high on the slope behind Western District's commercial area. The fellow countrymen who used to visit her in Central District cannot climb the many stone steps necessary to reach her, and even her young grandchildren complain of the climb. Because she has moved several times since coming to Hong Kong, she has not been able to make new friends. She says that people in Hong Kong do not want to make friends with her as they consider themselves refined and her a country bumpkin. Mrs. Lau reciprocates by describing Hong Kong residents as overly concerned with their appearance and interested only in spending money. She cannot tolerate extravagant trips to a teahouse because she knows how her descendants in China are suffering from lack of food. She loves to tell old Chinese folk tales, but few people in Hong Kong seem prepared to listen to them.

Because of her rheumatism, she is not really able to get around. If she had someone to go with, she would try to participate in some outside activities, but she doesn't know anyone. She does not regard her (secondary) daughter-in-law's father, a co-tenant, as a suitable companion. She once remarked that if there were somebody who would live with her and talk with her, she would be very happy— "even if the person is not from the same village." Unfortunately, her location makes it difficult for her to meet new people easily, and her own co-tenants are mostly unsuitable younger people.

As these four cases suggest, a wide variety of factors work together to influence the level of social activity of older people in Hong Kong. The mere fact of being old seems a less significant predictor of social activity than other variables such as length of time spent in Hong Kong, the nature and availability of co-tenants and neighbors, and the health of the individual concerned. Perhaps the next generation of old people in Hong Kong—those maturing in an urban environment—will have a different view of the role of formal organizations and will utilize them as a means of expanding their social networks. Alternatively, should population growth slow down and residential stability increase, perhaps there will be no need for such organizations. In the meantime, many older people are frustrated by the lack of opportunities for increasing interaction with their peers.

Formal Support

Prior to 1948, social welfare activities in Hong Kong were the province of private, charitable organizations. Some of these organizations were run by Chinese such as the Tung Wah Group of Hospitals while others were run by foreign missionaries such as Caritas. Except with respect to homes for the aged, the elderly were not viewed as a group with needs different from those of the general community. The sick, the disabled, the victims of natural disasters were provided temporary care without regard to age.

Official government involvement in social welfare activities began in 1948 with the establishment of a Social Welfare Office within the Secretariat for Chinese Affairs. In its early years, its responsibilities included protecting women and girls and handling suicide and repatriation cases. In 1958, the Social Welfare Office became an independent department which gradually expanded its services until, twenty years later, it operated through six divisions: the Group and Community Work Division; the Family Services Division; the Rehabilitation Division, which served the disabled; the Probation and Corrections Division, which provided services for the courts and operated correctional institutions for young offenders; the Social Security Division, which was responsible for public assistance and other social security schemes; and the Elderly Division, set up in August 1978 to develop services and facilities for the elderly. In 1979, this divisional structure gave way to a new regional management structure to coordinate the by then overlapping and fragmented programs.

Historically, the private (voluntary) sector relied on local and foreign donations to carry out its work. However, in the 1960s, as demand for services began to increase and as donations from abroad declined, the private sector came to rely heavily on government subventions. By 1980, subventions accounted for over 90 percent of the budgets of many of the private agencies, with most of the remaining funding coming from the Community Chest. Such heavy dependence on government grants has hampered the expansion of small innovative programs such as home help and community nursing. Until the agencies are convinced that their programs will be funded by the government, they are reluctant to broaden them beyond the limits of their other budgetary resources. Community nursing programs struggled for government recognition for five years before receiving a 100 percent subsidy (Little 1979:3).

By the early 1970s, the elderly had gained recognition as a specially vulnerable group. Attention had been drawn to their needs by the spectacular expansion in the 1960s of homes for the aged. Prior to 1955 there had been only three such homes in all of Hong Kong. By 1973 there were 21 such homes, and both the public and private sectors were taking steps to determine what direction policy planners should take. The government itself had organized a special Interdepartmental Working Party on the Future Needs of the Elderly. The Hong Kong Council of Social Service, the coordinating body for most of the voluntary agencies in Hong Kong, had created a committee to look at both community and institutional services for the elderly with an eye to developing standards for these services. The basic conclusion of these committees was to emphasize services which would allow the elderly to remain in the community rather than to enter institutions, but given the substantial waiting lists for homes for the aged, they recommended expansion or construction of several additional homes in the meantime. Similar recommendations were made by the writers of the Green Paper four years later. The development and utilization of these various residential, economic, social and medical services intended specifically for the elderly or having a large elderly clientele are described separately below.

Homes for the Aged

Residents of homes for the aged actually constitute a very tiny proportion of the elderly population. Of the approximately 507,000 people over the age of 60 in Hong Kong, fewer than one percent live in such institutions. Homes for the aged are not nursing homes. They provide residential facilities and minimal services, such as communal meals, to individuals who are reasonably healthy, mobile, and relatively independent in daily living activities. Nearly all of the homes are run by religious organizations, Christian, Buddhist, or Taoist. In 1973, I visited 19 of the 21 then existing homes and subsequently returned to 6 of the homes to interview residents (See Ikels 1975). Hostels for the elderly are frequently included in government listings of homes for the aged, though they differed originally in having no central cooking facility and in being located in public housing estates. Most of the Buddhist and Taoist homes are located in rural areas, making contact with nonresidents difficult.

The rapid expansion of homes for the aged in the 1960s caused many Hong Kong residents to wonder about the nature of the Chinese family. How was it possible that old people could be living in ever increasing numbers in this non-family context? To answer this question, I interviewed 98 residents (including those subsequently interviewed in the hostel) and found that the majority of people in homes for the aged simply do not have any children in Hong Kong, and indeed, frequently have no relatives at all in Hong Kong. Some never married, others lost all their children in infancy or during the war, and still others left them all behind in China. Fewer than one-quarter of the informants, 21 out of 98, had children in Hong Kong prior to entry into a home, and the reasons for not now living with them vary greatly. Twelve people had only one surviving daughter. In most cases, the daughter had long been living with her husband, often with his parents as well. If the parent had been living with the daughter, usually an economic hardship drove them to separate. In only 2 cases were bad relations between mother and daughter apparent.

In no case had a man alone lived with his daughter prior to entering a home though 2 couples had so done. There continues to be a fairly strong resistance to the idea of living with daughters, even among men who really have no other alternatives. One of my community informants who was in semiretirement, though still living with and being supported by his employer, sighed that maybe it was alright for a woman to live with her daughters, but it would be "embarrassing" for a man. At that time, he had three married daughters in Hong Kong and was considering going to a home for the aged. When his daughters and employer heard of this plan, however, they raised such protests that he decided to remain with his employer.

The situations of the nine people having a son or sons in Hong Kong were somewhat different. Nearly everyone who had at least one locatable son in Hong Kong had lived with him prior to entering the home, and the reasons for their separation varied.

1. One man suffered from high blood pressure, and his doctor had advised him to move to a more quiet environment while his wife stayed on with the children. The whole family lives in the same housing estate as the informant (a hostel resident), and they visit frequently.

2. In another hostel case, the son died and the daughter-in-law had to go out to work. The informant's wife stayed on to look after the grandchildren while he came to the hostel to ease the burden.

3. One woman's only son had only recently been discharged from a home for the handicapped. His mother had previously worked at the home, but at about the time her son was released, she was too old to continue work. He could not support her so she came to a home for the aged.

4. One man had retired to China to live with his younger son, but on finding that he was not wanted, came back to Hong Kong to seek his older son, an unmarried seaman. When he was unable to locate him, he moved in for several months with the family of his elder brother's son in the same housing estate where he now lives in a hostel.

5. Another man also failed to locate his older son, so he lived with his younger son. However, their relationship was not good, and he applied to move into the neighboring hostel. He has not seen his son for several months and takes a dim view of intergenerational living, saying "Quarrels are inevitable."

6. One man with several children living in Hong Kong had lived with one of his sons in a carpenter shop, but for obscure reasons

moved into a home. This man showed some signs of mental incompetency, and this may have been a factor in his removal from his son's residence.

7. A woman was removed from her elder son's residence (and was not picked up by any of her other children) because of her very poor eyesight.

8. Another woman served as a domestic servant in her adopted elder son's home until she broke her leg. Thereafter, she lived with them for several years until another relative, the daughter of her husband's elder sister, suggested she enter a home.

9. One woman came to Hong Kong from China in the 1960s to find that her stepson did not want her to move in with him. She then lived alone and attempted to support herself until she was hospitalized. She came to the home from the hospital.

As these cases suggest, people come to the homes for a wide variety of reasons, but usually there is some precipitating incident that makes it difficult to maintain the status quo. The death or moving away of a key household member is a frequent reason, but the most common reasons seem to be illness (acute or chronic) or loss of dwelling, usually because it is torn down but sometimes because the owner reclaims it. A significant proportion of people come into the homes as the result of a gradual loss of health, inability to continue employment, overcrowding, exhaustion of savings, or a combination of these factors.

The majority of the residents were previously employed in traditional sectors of the economy, such as unskilled labor or domestic work, and as such did not have any fixed age of retirement. Most worked until they simply could work no longer. If they had been long-term employees, they often continued to be looked after by the employer and to perform nominal tasks. In the case of domestic servants, it was often the employer who arranged for placement when he was no longer able to support her or planned to emigrate.

Those women employed as short-term domestics usually looked out for their own interests and maintained a bedspace or other accommodation, such as a *jaai-tong* (Topley and Hayes 1968:136; Sankar 1978), to which they could go between jobs or to which they retired to live with other retired domestic servants. *Jaai-tongs* or *chai-tongs* ("vegetarian halls") are operated by religious bodies and individuals and are not usually considered homes for the aged by the government. Some of the secular jaai-tongs represent the last gasp of the anti-marriage movement that occurred in the silk producing districts of Guangdong in the early part of this century. Membership is acquired by payment of a lump sum, which ranges from a few thousand to more than ten thousand Hong Kong dollars. For older and retired persons, the jaai-tongs offer some security by providing shelter, board, and help and care from co-members in times of illness and infirmity. The Green Paper (1977:21) estimates that several thousand older women live in jaai-tongs, but there has been no systematic study of them nor of their living conditions.

Income Maintenance Programs

Prior to 1971, individuals in need received grants of foodstuffs from the government and private agencies. In 1971, however, the government set up a Public Assistance Scheme to provide cash assistance to families and individuals whose incomes fell below a prescribed minimum. The target population included the disabled, dependent children (defined as those under 15), and the elderly (originally defined as those over 54). Able-bodied persons over 15 and under 55 without family commitment were not within the original scope of the scheme. By 1978 two changes had occurred. Applicants now have to be 60 years of age before applying as elderly, and able-bodied unemployed applicants between the ages of 15 and 59 with one year's residence in Hong Kong are now eligible provided they are registered for employment with the Local Employment Service of the Labour Department. Over 60 percent of the recipients of public assistance are elderly. The Green Paper (1977:5) estimated that about one-half of all elderly living alone were recipients of public assistance.

The income maintenance program reaching the greatest number of the elderly is the Special Needs Allowance Scheme which includes a cash allowance to the severely disabled and the elderly infirm. This scheme was first introduced on 1 April 1973 as the Disability and Infirmity Allowance Scheme. Regardless of income, anyone certified as severely disabled by the Director of Medical and Health Services was eligible for the Disability Allowance, which is identical to the amount a single individual receives through the Public Assistance Scheme. Anyone reaching the age of 75, regardless of income, was automatically assumed to be "infirm" and received a monthly payment of one-half the Disability Allowance. Neither the Disability Allowance nor the Infirmity Allowance was considered income for the purpose of calculating eligibility for public assistance. Originally, residents of homes for the aged were not eligible for the Infirmity Allowance but received instead a monthly "pocket money" grant. In 1978 as a result of recommendations made in the Green Paper, the Infirmity Allowance was renamed the Old Age Allowance and administered along with the Disability Allowance as part of the Special Needs Allowance Scheme. It was further extended to individuals in homes for the aged and to include those who had reached the age of 70 though limited to those who had been residents of Hong Kong for the five preceding years. The number of people drawing disability and old age allowances at the end of 1981 was 202,692 compared with 183,366 at the end of the previous year. Expenditure on these payments in the 1980-81 fiscal year totalled $306.3 million HK, an increase of $69.4 million over 1979-80. The Old Age Allowance provides $225 HK monthly to each recipient.

Social Services

Home help and home-delivered meals reach a very tiny proportion of the individuals in need of them, according to the Green Paper (1977:13). Home help is delivered through 18 centers and is not restricted to the elderly. According to Little (1979:3), there were two distinct models of home help and difficulty in determining which model to emphasize hampered the government's willingness to provide funds to other agencies interested in starting home help programs of their own. St. James Settlement, which aims primarily to serve the elderly, utilized mainly volunteers, who were supervised by a social worker, and a home helper. Meals were delivered and laundry taken to the Settlement to be washed. The Family Welfare Society which has a family focus utilized mainly part-time helpers, who made longer visits and themselves did the cooking and washing on the premises.

Social clubs and community centers reach a larger proportion of the elderly. In 1972 there were only 10 social clubs and 6 community or social centers for the elderly which together reached not more than 1,500 people. By 1978, 60 social centers and clubs reaching 6,000 older people were in operation. Nevertheless, the impact of this increase in the total number of clubs and centers does not seem very great. For example, the Social Service Needs Study (1977:45-46) found that 77 percent of their sample had never heard of such clubs, and fewer than three percent of the sample knew that they were places for recreation. Community or multi-service centers, of course, do not limit themselves to providing recreational opportunities. They also offer social work and preventive health services such as blood pressure readings. Very few of my own informants mentioned attending centers or social clubs for the elderly.

In 1972, 3 of these organizations were selected for a study by the

Research and Evaluation Unit of the Social Welfare Department. Ninety percent of the sample were female, 82 percent (2 men and 111 women) were widowed, and 44 percent were living alone. These are higher figures of widowhood and single living than for the aged population as a whole and reflect the fact that the clubs for the aged were intentionally located in areas with a population having these characteristics. The preponderance of females in the clubs serves to discourage male participation. I once asked Mr. Lam, the man who had so many youthful pen pals, why he didn't seek the companionship of other old people by visiting a club for the aged. He shook his head in distaste and exclaimed that he had nothing in common with the members. "All they talk about is family business! Mothers-in-law complain about daughters-in-law, and daughters-in-law complain about mothers-in-law."

The basic reason for noninvolvement, however, appears to be that most older people do not look to formal organizations for purely social gratification. When asked by a 1971 survey of elderly residents of Wong Tai Sin resettlement estate (Leung 1971) what functions organizations catering to the special needs of the elderly should perform, only 11 respondents mentioned the provision of recreational activities—far fewer than mentioned financial assistance (142), help with residential problems (57), medical care (45), or help in obtaining employment (29). Only 6 respondents suggested that the organizations help old people to make friends.

Medical Services

The leading causes of death in Hong Kong are cancer, heart disease, cerebrovascular disease, and pneumonia (accounting for 27, 15, 13 and 8 percent respectively of all deaths in 1981). Among the elderly, there are striking differences between the sexes in the occurrence of respiratory ailments and in perceived state of health. For example, of the 8,192 cases of tuberculosis discovered in 1975, elderly men accounted for 1,137, but elderly women for only 348. With respect to perceived state of health, however, women claimed to be suffering from more health problems than men.

In order to obtain a rough indicator of the health and disability status of my informants, I rated them on the basis of such criteria as occurrence of most recent illness, length of disruption of daily routine by illness, presence of chronic conditions, hearing or visual deficits, and other potentially handicapping conditions. All the information was obtained by asking the informants directly, and no confirmatory physical examinations were carried out. The ratings ranged from a low of zero to a high of eight. Mr. Go, for example, merited a one on the basis of his poor vision. Mrs. Wong received a three due to her frequent bouts of rheumatism, occasional "head troubles," and some vision difficulty.

The mean scores by sex differed substantially: 2.1 for males and 3.9 for females. In every age-controlled comparison, the mean score for men was exceeded by that for women. The *highest* mean score by age for men occurred in the 85 and over age group (3.5). This was the *lowest* mean score for women occurring in both the 60-64 and 75-79 age ranges. When I visited 74 of these people the following year and reinvestigated their health status, I found that while the mean scores had increased—possibly due to more careful follow-up questioning—the sex differences remained the same. The mean score for men was 3.0 and for women 4.8, and in every age-controlled comparison, the mean score for men was exceeded by the mean score for women. Palmore (1975:32) found similar differences in perceived health status among Japanese and stated that this phenomenon seems to be "a universal tendency at all age levels in all modern societies studied." The extent to which these scores reflect real differences in morbidity or cultural differences requiring one sex to deny illness and the other to proclaim it is not clear.

Whichever the situation, the elderly utilize a wide range of techniques and services to maintain their health. Although I describe the medical services generally available, it is important to keep in mind that traditionally the Chinese have placed great emphasis on individual responsibility for both health preservation and its restoration. Thus, most elderly have already attempted various forms of self-treatment before they arrive at an outpatient clinic. Furthermore, their concepts of the origins of their illness frequently differ from Western scientific concepts and affect the likelihood of their compliance with a doctor's orders.

Two points must be kept in mind when discussing the availability of medical services in Hong Kong: (1) medicine operates in a bicultural context, there being Western medicine and Chinese medicine; (2) there is public (i.e. government-subsidized) medicine, and there is private medicine. Furthermore, Western medicine is subsidized while Chinese medicine is not, and this fact is one explanation for the greater utilization of Western medical services. Osgood (1975:1059) found that in his island community,

among the poor and the illiterate who comprise most of the

population of Lung Chau, modern medicine wins out as much because it is free, or cheaper, as for any other reason. There is also the prevalent notion that if one system is better, there is no harm in a little of the other.

According to the *Annual Departmental Report* of the Director of Medical and Health Services (Hong Kong 1976:4), at the end of 1975 there was a total of 18,561 hospital beds available to the public in Hong Kong. Of these, 8,533 were in government institutions, 7,849 were in the 21 government-assisted institutions, and 2,179 were in private institutions. In all, there were 4.3 beds per 1,000 people, but this figure does not tell the whole story. For example, of the 1,898 beds in Queen Elizabeth Hospital, the largest general hospital in Kowloon, 302 were temporary, and in Castle Peak Hospital, the only psychiatric hospital in Hong Kong, 679 of the 1,921 beds were temporary (Hong Kong 1976:Table 41). This means that many patients were on cots in corridors or in other available space, making for incredible crowding and creating pressure for rapid turnover. Despite efforts to improve the situation by the construction of extensions to already existing facilities and of a new psychiatric hospital, the number of beds per 1,000 dropped to 4.2 by the end of 1981.

In 1975, about 9 percent of those aged 65 and over received inpatient treatment in medical wards, and 10 percent received treatment in other specialties. The average length of stay was 6.1 days in medical wards and 10.1 days in other specialties (The Green Paper 1977:11). Overall, 473,628 inpatients were treated in the various hospitals and maternity centers of Hong Kong in 1975. Of these 252,942 were cared for in government institutions, 147,240 in government-assisted institutions, and 73,446 in private institutions. Government-assisted hospitals were generally established as charity hospitals and as such charge no fees or only small fees. Originally, and still partially, dependent on donations from private sources for their operating costs, these hospitals have gradually reached the point of nearly total dependence upon the government. According to one officer of the Tung Wah Group of Hospitals, government "deficiency grants" account for more than 95 percent of Tung Wah's budget for medical services. Tung Wah operates three general and two convalescent hospitals which provided care to 49 percent of the inpatients treated in government-assisted institutions. Outpatient services are also free at the Tung Wah Hospitals, and these are the only institutions that also have traditional herbalists and *tit da* doctors ("bone setters") working in a hospital setting; however, their services are not covered by the government "deficiency grants" because the government supports only Western medical services.

The quality of the care provided in some of the charity hospitals has been questioned by many observers. One high-ranking government doctor told me that charity patients have complained of not seeing a doctor for weeks at a time. There are also private hospitals that, though often run by missionary organizations, still charge fees and have been known to suddenly dump patients on public hospitals when the patients were no longer able to pay the bills. Given the overcrowding in some of the hospitals and the pressure for beds from patients suffering from acute conditions, the plight of the chronically ill elderly person is most unenviable. The director of one of the hostels for the elderly related that sometimes when hostel residents become ill and require hospitalization, doctors refuse admittance on the grounds of a lack of beds. Doctors have even said, in essence, "Look, we have just a few beds, and you are asking us to choose between someone in his 20s who can be up and about and back to work in a couple of weeks and someone in his 70s who might not leave the bed for more than a year."

None of my informants mentioned having hospital or medical insurance, and superficially none would appear to require it since the costs of treatment are extremely modest. Patients in the general wards of government hospitals are charged $5 HK a day which covers a bed, diet, X-ray examinations, laboratory tests, drugs, surgery, and any other forms of special treatment required. These charges may be waived for some patients. There are a limited number of private and semi-private rooms at some government hospitals; the charges for maintenance in these rooms are much higher, and all treatment procedures are separately billed. There is (or was) also, however, an additional informal hospital charge known locally as "tea money." This fee is paid to the nonprofessional staff who bring food, remove soiled sheets, and otherwise attend to the patient's comfort. A letter to the *South China Morning Post* of 17 July 1974 from an "observer" indicates just how significant this unofficial payment can be.

> Over a period of months we have observed some elderly patients in a hospital near Wong Tai Sin. . . .
> The small matter of finger and toe nails becomes a big matter to patients unable to trim their own. They may be in a hospital for months on end without having them clipped.

Ragged, long nails are most uncomfortable, but apparently the duty of checking finger nails is not assigned to anyone. In these hot days, many of the patients complain of itching backs. Lying on a wet sheet, over a hot rubber sheet with plenty of wrinkles, and crumbs of food and peeling skin, with an itching back that cannot be reached for scratching. . .

A cool bath, or a back rub might solve their itching. But baths are only for those who pay. The going price is $5-$6, and I have seen money change hands on many occasions. Moreover someone must stand by to see that the bath is actually given.

And as for patients who have no relatives and no money. . . ?

One informant said that each *amah* (maid) is responsible for several rooms, and that whenever she went to visit her mother at Queen Mary Hospital, she paid $2 to $5 HK. But Mrs. Ip's daughter, whose son was in Queen Elizabeth Hospital at the same time, said that the hospital workers (at least in government hospitals) no longer dared to accept tea money. Both of these women were describing the tea money situation during the summer of 1976 when the government had instituted an anti-corruption campaign with the abolition of tea money as one of its objectives. The long-term results of this campaign remain to be seen.

People aged 65 and over constitute about 9 percent of all general outpatient attendance and 18.2 percent of all attendance at specialist outpatient clinics. The charge at government operated clinics of $3 HK includes the consultation as well as medicine, X-rays, and laboratory tests, but the charges at government-assisted and private hospitals vary greatly. As far as the elderly are concerned, there are at least four serious shortcomings with the medical services provided by the government: (1) there is no government-subsidized dental care for the general public except for emergencies, (2) there is only a minimal appointments service for the out-patient clinics, (3) there are scarcely any long-term care facilities, and (4) there is no subsidization of traditional modes of treatment.

One of my informants, a 79-year-old man, suffered a stroke while visiting his relatives in China during the 1976 Lunar New Year. At first, he experienced nearly total paralysis of his right side, but after receiving medication, injections, and acupuncture in China, he showed some improvement though he remained quite feeble. Once back in Hong Kong, he continued to require treatment, but as he could not endure the anticipated long wait in line, he wondered whether I could arrange an appointment for him at a government clinic. I received a quick brush-off from a spokesman for the Medical and Health Services Department, and when I attempted to persuade the Social Welfare Department (from which my informant was receiving the Infirmity Allowance) to intercede on his behalf, I was told they could not "interfere" in the policies of another department.

Services for those requiring long-term care are in extremely short supply. In 1977, so-called "care and attention" homes provided only 316 beds, with an estimated demand of over 1,500 beds (Green Paper 1977:Exhibit 15). By 1980 the supply had increased only to 324. These residential facilities provide general personal care and limited nursing care—but not medical care—for old people who require assistance in activities of daily living and who, for physical and social reasons, are incapable of continuing to live in the community. Infirmaries are intended for patients with chronic physical or mental conditions who require constant nursing care and some medical supervision. In 1981 there were 953 infirmary beds in Hong Kong. By early 1983 the private sector was moving to meet the demand for nursing homes. Some 20 or so "profit-making" homes were reported in operation; their fees ranged from $2,400 to $4,500 HK a month (*South China Morning Post* 25 April 1983). Clearly, the vast majority of those in need must remain in a community setting under private care, as clients of community nurses, or dependent on their families and friends.

The community nursing service was instituted on a very small scale in 1967; by 1973, 5 centers (all in the voluntary sector) were providing these services through a total of 11 nurses. It was on the basis of the work being done by these 5 centers that the Working Party recommended the expansion of the community nursing program in 1973. However, by 1976, though the service had expanded to include 26 1/2 nursing equivalents and 3 more centers, and had 2,676 active cases, the funding of the program was still the responsibility of the agencies involved. Generally, the fees charged by the nursing service covered only 10 to 18 percent of their expenses (Carter 1976:39). The elderly make up about one-fifth of the community nursing patients, and their six major medical problems in order of frequency are those involving paralysis, post-surgical care, some element of chronicity requiring dressings and general nursing care, chronic heart problems, diabetes and its complications, and finally chronic conditions with urinary or bowel involvement. Thus the elderly are concentrated in the long-term care conditions, whereas most of the other age groups require only short-term care, such as maternity cases. By 1979, the government was sufficiently convinced of the value of the nursing service that it took over its expenses. In 1980, 6,859 patients were treated.

Approximately 30 percent of the 3,029 registered physicians in Hong Kong are employed by the government, but in addition to these recognized doctors, the police estimated there to be more than 1,000 people illegally practicing Western medicine in the mid-1970s. Not only do these people freely dispense controlled medicines and poisonous drugs and perform surgical procedures in their homes, but they freely advertise in the Chinese press. Some are refugees trained in well-known hospitals in China, but others are totally untrained. Such marginal practitioners tend to concentrate in the poorer or outlying areas of Hong Kong. Osgood (1975:804-5) found that of the 8 physicians with some type of Western training practicing in Lung Shing, all were unlicensed refugees from China. There were also 4 doctors practicing Chinese medicine in Lung Shing, not including "druggists of the Chinese medicine shops who actually diagnose and prescribe."

Osgood's reluctance to include these "druggists" among physicians is symptomatic of the difficulty in determining just what constitutes a Chinese physician or Chinese medicine. While there are professional associations of traditional practitioners in Hong Kong, they do not have the right to prohibit or prescribe what Chinese practitioners may do. In fact, any Chinese who has paid the business registration fee may set himself up as an herbalist, acupuncturist, or "bone-setter" (tit da doctor). The government has intervened minimally, and primarily in situations involving the use of modern medical treatments by traditional practitioners (e.g. they may not possess antibiotics, make use of X-ray equipment, or give injections). According to Lee (1975:224), in 1969 there were 4,506 Chinese practitioners of various kinds, and though this was nearly double the number of Western-trained practitioners at that time, they did not carry double the case load.

Considerations of expense and convenience affect preferences for treatment. When I went to a traditional herbalist on the recommendation of my landlady, I paid $20 HK for a diagnosis and a prescription for a sore throat. My landlady did not think this was out of line, and indeed, though it was certainly more expensive than going to a public clinic, it was not much more than a private Western doctor would have charged. The herbalist was also readily accessible, whereas longer waits would have been anticipated in a private Western doctor's office, and a much longer wait in a public clinic. On the other hand, the latter two places prescribe medicine which can be quickly injected or ingested, in contrast to an herbalist's prescription, which requires several hours of boiling prior to ingestion.

The Treatment of Illness

Assumptions about the causation of illness obviously affect the selection of treatment methods. Most of my informants attributed their ills either to the six elemental causes of wind, cold, heat, damp, dryness, and fire or to dietary imbalance. All foods are classified as to "hot" or "cold" (though their natural condition can be altered by the cooking process) and, therefore, have to be carefully balanced to ensure health. Most people, however, do not seem to be concerned about possible dietary imbalance until they have already begun to manifest symptoms. While few old people referred to the germ theory of disease, this theory is not irreconcilable with traditional beliefs—if one had paid more attention to one's diet, the germs would not have been able to gain a foothold.

Because of these concepts of causation, most elderly people—and many younger ones—manipulate their diets or try traditional herbal or prepared medications before seeking, or in combination with, Western treatment. The common opinion of Hong Kong residents (Lee 1975:229), which most elderly persons seem to share, is that while Western medicine can be very effective in removing the symptoms of a disease or in curing infectious or acute diseases, it is less reliable than Chinese medicine for dealing with the underlying causes. Chinese also frequently complain that Western medicine has many dangerous side effects that do not occur with Chinese medicine.

The terms Western medicine and Chinese medicine are taken from the Chinese language. A *sai yisang* (Western doctor) is a doctor trained in Western medicine; a *jung yisang* (Chinese doctor) is a practitioner of traditional herbal medicine—a doctor who takes the pulse as the primary diagnostic procedure. Most *sai yi* in Hong Kong are Chinese in ancestry as are all the *jung yi*. My own informants resorted to a Western practitioner more often than to traditional practitioners, though certain ailments such as fractures and dislocations were nearly always taken to the traditional *tit da* ("fall-hit") doctor, known in English as a bone-setter. These doctors are usually associated with the martial arts schools—where people are hit and fall down—and are a separate category of practitioner from the herbalists. In his study, Lee (1975:229) found that when asked to compare the effectiveness of Western and Chinese medical practices, informants overwhelmingly endorsed the traditional tit da practitioner (86.5 percent to 8.2 percent) when it came to sprains and fractures. The only other ailment Lee's informants considered more amenable to Chinese treatment was rheumatism, by a two to one ratio. Rheumatism, however, is most likely to be treated at home by the application of oils rather than by visits to a doctor.

Acupuncture, the Chinese medical technique best known to the West, is also practiced by a specialist, but my informants rarely resorted to it (see also Topley 1975:265), and two people volunteered that they knew people who had become worse after treatment.

Among my own informants prevention of disease by proper diet and treatment by herbal remedies and the skills of the tit da doctor are much more important than other traditional practices such as acupuncture, respiratory techniques, and massage.

Several informants pointed out that in the old days in the villages the scarcity of doctors meant that the ordinary villager had to be familiar with the medicinal herbs which could be gathered in the nearby hills. The utilization of such knowledge in urban Hong Kong is an impossibility, and young people cannot identify the herbs known to their elders. They must go to the herbalist for all the ingredients. The average Chinese in Hong Kong is as dependent on the herbalist for traditional medication as he is on the Western-trained doctor for Western medication. The traditional lore is being lost. This is not the case in the People's Republic of China where the government is making a vigorous effort to gather and test as much of the traditional lore as possible. Families are urged to submit their secret prescriptions to institutes for standard scientific testing.

The present generation of old people are caught between two medical systems. Many of their assumptions about the causes of illness are dismissed by the experts. In the home, their opinions may be respected for a while, but the grandchildren soon learn that these home remedies have little currency in school or with the government. When a health problem is not responsive to self-medication, the older person may find that his preferred mode of treatment is too expensive for the family (or himself) to tolerate. A simple fracture, for example, requiring two months of daily visits to the tit da doctor may run in excess of $500 HK. The necessity of relying on Western (subsidized) medicine, particularly when surgery is a likely course of action, can cause long delays in seeking treatment. Thus, for many old people the physical suffering and distress which accompany serious illness are augmented by worries about expense and the appropriateness of the treatment.

The greatest problem, however, lies in the lack of facilities for those requiring long-term care, such as victims of stroke or patients with fractures that must be kept immobilized for long periods. Some families attempt to provide this care themselves, but, sometimes, at considerable personal cost. One of my elderly informants had tended a daughter who had been rendered paralyzed, mute, and blind by a fever in childhood nearly forty years ago. In the meantime, the other children had grown up and moved out. They refused to take in their old mother later because she could not abandon her helpless daughter, and they did not want this pathetic creature in their own homes. No institution would admit the daughter because she was already receiving care from her aged mother. When I first met this old woman, her greatest worry was the care her daughter would receive when she herself was no longer able to provide it. In the end, the daughter died very suddenly, but the mother had become so alienated from her other children (who supported but did not visit her while their sister was alive) that she insisted she would go to a home for the aged rather than to her children when she could no longer make it on her own.

This is admittedly an extreme case, but it illustrates well the kinds of strain that long-term care can place on the family. In the absence of extended kin or neighborly ties, the family gets little respite from the constant attendance such a person may require. Not surprisingly many old people live in dread of becoming such burdens.

PART III
Aging in Greater Boston

7 Greater Boston—The Context of Immigration

The Impact of the Historical Background

As we have seen, Hong Kong has long been a destination for Chinese emigrants, but by no means has it been the only destination. In the eighteenth and nineteenth centuries, despite laws against emigration, tens of thousands of men left their ancestral villages in the coastal provinces of Guangdong and Fujian to work in Southeast Asia and eventually in North America. Many of those who went to Southeast Asia (Indochina, Thailand, Malaysia, Indonesia, and the Philippines) eventually brought their families along or intermarried with the local population. Those who went to the United States or Canada faced a very different situation. The distance, the climate, and the mobile nature of the work (primarily mining and railroad construction) were not conducive to the relocation of Chinese families. Public opinion and, in some instances, law prohibited intermarriage. By the time the Chinese labor force had been driven into other occupations, primarily in the service sector, discriminatory legislation made it nearly impossible for Chinese laborers and Chinese women to immigrate.

In 1882 Congress passed the Chinese Exclusion Act, the first but not the last piece of legislation to restrict immigration and naturalization on the basis of race. For the next 60 years, Chinese laborers were denied entry into the United States, and the term "laborer" was sometimes interpreted to include also white collar workers and professionals. Women were assigned the status of their husbands and were similarly denied entrance even when their husbands were already in the United States. In 1924 the Asian Exclusion Act banned all Chinese women (except the daughters of United States citizens) from entering the United States as permanent residents, a ban which was applied even to the wives of American-born Chinese.

137

There were ways around this legislation of course. Smuggling, including the smuggling of Chinese women for prostitution (see McCunn 1981), was one route; jumping ship was another. As recently as 1978, 305 Chinese seamen failed to return to their ships by the time they were due to leave American ports (U.S. Department of Justice 1978:19). In 1906, what for many San Franciscans was a disaster turned out to be a blessing for many of the Chinese. The building that housed the birth and immigration records was destroyed by the fire that followed the great earthquake. As a result, many Chinese were able to claim American birth or citizenship. In addition, many claimed to have fathered children in China on trips home. As alleged children of United States citizens, these sons (and in a very few cases daughters) were permitted to enter the country. A huge market for false birth certificates developed. Suspected "paper sons" were detained on Angel Island in California (and at the New England Detention Center in East Boston) for months while Immigration and Naturalization officials attempted to determine the authenticity of their documents.

The vast majority of the men who came to the mainland United States during these years originated from one region of Guangdong province known as Sze Yap. This region was comprised of the four counties of Taishan (Toisan), Kaiping (Hoiping), Enping (Yanping), and Xinwui (Sunwui). They spoke a dialect of Cantonese referred to in Hong Kong as Sze Yap but in the United States as Toisanese. The speakers of standard Cantonese cannot ordinarily understand it, and Sze Yap speakers are considered a linguistic minority in Hong Kong.

By the beginning of this century Sze Yap families had adapted to the long-term absence of their menfolk. By the time he reached his late teens, a young man would leave the village to join his father or other male relative in the United States. He either helped them in a family enterprise or was sent by them to work for someone else. If he could return to the United States legally (as the child of a citizen rather than as an immigrant), he would usually risk a trip back to China where his parents, usually his mother, had selected a bride for him, a daughter-in-law for herself. He would remain long enough to assure a descendant and then return to the United States leaving his wife and child with his mother. When his father reached his early 50s, he would retire to the village expecting to live off the fruits of his invested income as well as the money sent back by his son, still resident in the United States. At this stage of life, the older couple hoped to be able to relax and to turn over execution of household responsibilities to their daughter-in-law.

There were, however, sons who were not as filial as they should have been—sons who became indebted through gambling or who took up with other women. Some sons, though able to maintain a flow of cash back to the village, were unable to return themselves. These were men who had been smuggled in or feared exposure of their "paper son" status. (The flavor of the lives of these quasi-bachelors is well-captured in the writings of Siu 1952, 1953; Nee 1972; Kingston 1977, 1981; and Chu [1961] 1979). In this context, filial piety or responsibility to parents included: (1) marriage to a person of one's parents' choice, (2) acceptance of a job under the direction of one's father or male relatives, (3) economic support of the parental household, and (4) the freeing of parents from responsibility in old age.

This family pattern began to change in the late 1940s and early 1950s. First, restrictions on the immigration of Chinese women were gradually lifted. With the abolition of the Exclusion Laws during the Second World War and the passing of the War Brides Act, the wives of servicemen were allowed to enter the United States. According to Nee (1972:410) approximately 6000 Chinese women entered the United States under the latter. Then, Displaced Person and Refugee legislation meant that those who had fled to Hong Kong or been stranded in the United States as a result of the change of government in China in 1949 had the opportunity to come to or remain in the United States. Further, the restructuring of immigration legislation in the 1960s led to a tremendous increase in the Chinese and Chinese-American population in the country in the 1970s. The population soared from 435,062 in 1970 to 806,027 in 1980. Finally, the incentive to return to China for a relaxed old age had been removed. The government of the People's Republic of China alternately harassed the families of the so-called Overseas Chinese or attempted to persuade them to redirect their investments away from their relatives and to the village as a whole. As men found themselves increasingly unlikely to retire to China, they came under pressure to bring their parents and spouses to the United States or at least to Hong Kong.

Currently eligibility for immigration to the United States rests largely on the possession of kinship ties or special skills. Spouses, parents, and dependent children of United States *citizens* are not subject to any numerical limitations. Other immigrants, however, fall under a national-origins quota system. There is a ceiling of 170,000 immigrants per year from the Eastern Hemisphere, and no single country can fill more than 20,000 slots in a year. Individuals born in Hong Kong fall under the United Kingdom's quota. As a British "dependency" Hong Kong is entitled to no more than 600 slots a year. In 1982 the United States government announced that for purposes of immigration it would henceforth treat the People's Republic of China and the Republic of China (Taiwan) as separate entities, thereby, in effect, doubling the number of slots available to Chinese.

Immigration quotas are determined by a preference system which has as its objective the reunification of families. A summary of the preference categories is listed below.

First Preference: Unmarried adult sons and daughters of U.S. citizens;

Second Preference: Spouses and unmarried sons and daughters of aliens lawfully admitted as permanent residents, i.e. aliens who are "green card" holders;

Third Preference: Members of certain professions and persons of exceptional ability in the sciences or arts;

Fourth Preference: Married sons and daughters of U.S. citizens;

Fifth Preference: Brothers and sisters of U.S. citizens;

Sixth Preference: Skilled or unskilled aliens whose services are needed in occupations for which workers in the U.S. are in short supply;

Seventh Preference: Certain refugees.

Having a close kinsman who is a United States citizen is clearly the most effective means of obtaining an immigration visa to the United States. In the spring of 1980, the United States opened a consulate in Guangzhou and was promptly swamped with visa applicants. A consular official processing these applications expressed his belief that Taishan (a county in Guangdong province) would soon be depopulated! In 1982 the United States government was considering eliminating the Fifth Preference. No more than 24 percent of the annual per-country immigration quota of 20,000 is set aside for Fifth Preference visas, though unfilled quota allotments from higher preferences may be added to lower ones. While some countries do not use up their Fifth Preference quota, many Asian countries face a large backlog. As reported in *Sampan* (January/February 1982), a bilingual monthly newspaper, Fifth Preference visa applications filed in July 1977 for China were being considered in early 1982; and in Hong Kong, brothers and sisters of U.S. citizens currently have a nine and a half year wait (*Sampan* April 1982).

Sometimes these regulations set up unintended hardships. For example, in 1979 a 65-year-old woman emigrated from Guangzhou via Hong Kong to join her husband in the United States. She had previously lived with their only child, a married son, and his family and fully expected them to follow her. However, shortly after her arrival in Boston, her husband died while their son's visa application was still under review. As a result, her son did not receive a visa. The mother, a noncitizen, was distraught when she realized that she would have to become a citizen before she would be able to sponsor her married son.

People from Sze Yap, mostly retired laundrymen and their recently brought over kin, probably constitute the bulk of the older Chinese population in the United States. The men, having been in this country as far back as the 1920s and 1930s, usually have some competence in English ranging from survival English to genuine bilingualism. The women, however, are largely illiterate, non-English speaking, and the older they are at the time of immigration, the more dependent on other family members.

Another very different source of older Chinese are those who originally came to this country in the 1940s for training in science and engineering. In their 20s and 30s then, they are in their 60s and 70s now. Most of these people, estimated by Lee (1958) to number between 4,000 and 5,000, had come to the United States with the intent of acquiring skills useful in the war effort against Japan or in the rebuilding of their country after the war. When the Chinese Civil War broke out, and their sponsoring agencies and companies hastily relocated to Taiwan, they were stranded. Some elected to return to their home areas; others went to Taiwan. Those who hesitated too long found themselves unable to return to the Mainland, when during the Korean War, the United States government forbade their return on the grounds of national interest.

The family backgrounds of these people are strikingly different from those of most of the families mentioned earlier. They are most likely to be from regions other than Guangdong province, to have had parents who were Christian and well-educated, to have been sent to teacher-training institutes and colleges run by missionaries in Beijing and Shanghai, and to have selected their own spouses in a love-match. While their siblings remained behind with their parents, they were allowed to go abroad to develop the skills which would help build a strong China. Many lost touch with their families in the aftermath of the Chinese Civil War. Others learned that their families' status had undergone a complete reversal and had to devise ways of assisting them that would not politically handicap them further. These former students settled in suburban locations near the universities and research facilities in which they ultimately found employment. They had little contact with the Toisanese-speaking immigrants in China-town or in the laundries in the suburbs. There were, of course, some individuals from well-educated, Cantonese-speaking families in Guangdong who came to the United States to study, but they were not typical of the majority of the Guangdong immigrants. The high visibility of these scholars and professionals has led to some misconceptions among the American public at large. Many Americans view Asian Americans in general and Chinese Americans in particular as successful minorities. Both Hsu (1971:6) and the United States Civil Rights Commission (1980) have pointed out that the apparent prominence of Chinese Americans with a high level of education compared to the United States population as a whole is misleading and does not in most cases reflect bootstrap upward mobility. Furthermore, while the percentage of college graduates is high, the proportion of adults with fewer than five years of schooling is also high when compared to Americans generally. This is especially true among the older women.

The next category of older people is perhaps the most diverse. These are parents whose children came to the United States in the past two or three decades, perhaps as students or as spouses of American citizens. When the parents reached retirement or widowhood in Hong Kong or Taiwan, the children acted as their sponsors to enter the United States. These parents may be monolingual or bilingual, of modest means or well-to-do, traditional in outlook or highly "westernized".

There are also older American-born Chinese. According to the Pacific Asian Elderly Research Project (1978:11), in 1970 two-thirds of the Chinese elderly were foreign-born, the highest percentage located in the Northeast region and the lowest percentage in the West. Because of the immigration patterns in recent years, the proportion of older people who are foreign-born has actually been increasing. Of the 114 people over the age of 60 for whom we have information, 82 percent are foreign-born and 18 percent are American-born. (For a broader discussion of the Chinese in America see Lee 1960; Kung 1962; Sung 1967; Miller 1969; Lyman 1974; and Chen 1981.)

Boston Chinatown

The arrival of Chinese in the Boston area is believed to date back to the eighteenth century. According to the Boston 200 Corporation

(1976) New England merchant ships, carrying on an extensive trade with China, sometimes took on Chinese crewmen, but these men did not settle permanently in Boston. The first records of permanent Chinese settlement go back to 1875 and the nearly simultaneous arrival of two groups of Chinese laborers. The first were contract laborers who came from the West Coast to construct the Pearl Street Telephone Exchange near South Station, the terminus of railroads coming in from the south. The second were factory workers in the shoe industry. According to McCunn (1979:54), at the close of the American Civil War

> the boot and shoe industry was just starting in California. The firm Buckingham and Hecht refused to pay American workers the wages they demanded, so the workers went out on strike. The Chinese learned the work quickly, and other boot and shoe factories started hiring them.

Within a few years the Chinese constituted more than half the footwear work force in California. The recession of 1875 dealt a devastating blow to the footwear industry, and at about the same time, workers in a shoe factory in North Adams, Massachusetts went out on strike, and Chinese were imported from California to replace them. These men eventually drifted to Boston. Thereafter, a small but steady stream of Chinese immigrants moved to Boston, concentrating in the South Cove area. Of the 250 Chinese in Boston in 1890, 200 lived in the area around Oxford Street. By 1935 the Chinese inhabited the entire area of present-day Chinatown north of Kneeland Street and then gradually moved into the more desirable housing to the south as other immigrant groups moved out (Sullivan and Hatch 1970:1).

Because of the restrictive immigration legislation, family life was nearly impossible, and Boston Chinatown did not have a significant American-born population until the 1950s. Between 1890 and 1950, the Chinatown population increased from 200 to only about 1,600. This population was almost entirely Sze Yap in origin, and the norms of village life continued to operate sometimes to the puzzlement of the young, American-born residents. One young woman related that she found it distasteful the way people "took for granted their right to tell you how to behave." People did not hesitate to tell her how a proper Chinese girl would act.

> They would tell you to wear skirts not pants. Not to smoke. They would want to know where you came from. I would

be in a store just to buy something, and the salesperson would ask where I was from, what was my name, what was my genealogy. I didn't see how any of this was relevant to a sales transaction.

Proper behavior in children was stressed, and just as in the village, parents did not want to be accused of being soft on their children. Thus discipline, especially public discipline, served two purposes— correcting a child and demonstrating to the community that one was an effective parent. A middle-aged man who grew up in Chinatown during the 1940s and 1950s related that when he was a youngster, people did not hesitate to correct you or report you to your parents. "Then the parent would probably take your pants down and strap you right there on the street. It wasn't the strap I feared so much as being hit like that in front of everyone else. It was embarrassing. I made a point of not getting caught outside." A public scolding, how- ever, could not be safely extended beyond the immediate community. In the early 1960s, for example, one 82-year-old man stepped out of a Chinese restaurant to discover a (non-Chinese) youth from another part of the metropolitan area relieving himself in a doorway. When he attempted to rebuke the youth, he was thrown to the ground by the offender and died of his injuries shortly thereafter.

By 1970, Chinatown had expanded over four census tracts that included the core South Cove area as well as parts of the nearby South End. The population had increased to 3,306 Chinese by 1970 (and to 5,633 by 1980) and included so many people of unknown origins that old-timers began to feel displaced. Parents also came to fear a loss of control over their children, and most observers had come to view Chinatown as a problem-ridden community.

Prior to the 1970s, the two dominant organizations within China- town were the Chinese Consolidated Benevolent Association (CCBA) and the Chinese Merchants Association. The latter regulated business matters whereas the CCBA was viewed as an umbrella organization which articulated the political concerns of the Chinese community to the outside. These two organizations and their constituents have his- torically been viewed by both insiders and outsiders as the Establish- ment. Opponents of these organizations have also accused them of "protecting" gambling establishments and of intimidating employees by threatening them with exposure of their illegal status.

As elsewhere in the United States (e.g. Nee 1972), Chinatown organizations were originally organized by and for men living in a bachelor society. These various associations served the interests of their membership only and did not as a rule provide services to non-members. Twelve family associations composed of individuals sharing the same surname or several surnames linked by a historical or mythical event, and with branches in other cities in the United States, were able to keep men in touch with their home villages and to provide a basis by which capital might be loaned to start a business (e.g. Siu 1953; Light 1972). Such associations owned or rented clubhouses and, sometimes, rooms that provided living accommodations for destitute older members. The family associations elected representatives to the CCBA.

In 1982 in addition to the family associations, the CCBA had representatives from the following organizations: the American Legion Chinatown Post #328, the Chinese-American Civic Association (CACA), the Chinese Economic Development Council (CEDC), the Chinese Evangelical Church, the Chinese Freemason's Association, the Chinese Merchants Association, the Chinese Women's Club of New England, the Hip Sing Association (a merchants association), the Hoy Kew Association (a social club), the Kew Sing Music Club, the Kuo Min Tang (Chinese Nationalist Party), the Ni Lun Association (a seamen's association), and the South Cove (Chinatown) YMCA.

Some of these organizations, such as the CACA and CEDC, were latecomers to the CCBA having come into existence only in the late 1960s and early 1970s. Unlike the traditional organizations, which are largely composed of Toisan speakers from Guangdong, the CACA and the CEDC are composed of bilingual, suburban-dwelling Chinese with concerns of a broader nature than the traditional CCBA. Many are business and professional people who focus their interests on Chinatown and worry about community-wide needs such as health and housing, economic development, bilingual education, and information dissemination. The CACA, for example, publishes the bilingual monthly newspaper, *Sampan*. The *Sampan's* editor-in-chief is also the producer of Boston's only TV program, "Asian Focus," that weekly highlights issues of special interest to the Greater Boston Asian community.

The increasing size and diversity of the Chinatown population have also made some groups aware of the tourist potential of the community. In 1969 the first annual August Moon Festival was held in Chinatown. This is basically a harvest celebration, which occurs in the eighth month of the lunar calendar. In 1981, this festival was scheduled to coincide with the thirty-seventh annual Chinese American Invitational Volleyball Tournament. Under the auspices of the CCBA the Chinese community of Boston served as the hosts for forty volleyball teams from all over the United States and Canada. This annual event was first organized by GIs of Chinese heritage to provide a framework for the continuation of close friendships formed during their years of active duty during World War II. Since 1944, the tournaments have been held in rotation among the various Chinatowns of the United States and Canada.

In 1979, as part of the City of Boston's Summerthing program, the Chinese community organized the first Dragonboat Festival. Still extremely popular in Guangdong and Hong Kong, this festival commemorates the drowning of a virtuous official who tried unsuccessfully to warn the emperor of treachery. Teams of rowers compete on the Charles River, and with the demise of the Summerthing program, the Chinese community itself has continued to sponsor the Dragonboat races. The majority of these sponsors represent new rather than traditional concerns of the Chinese population. The Asian American Resource Workshop, Asian Women, Chinatown People's Progressive Association, the CACA, the CEDC, Quincy Community School, Greater Boston Chinese Cultural Association, and the Chinatown Little City Hall, but no family associations, and not even the CCBA were recorded as sponsors of the 1981 festival.

Many of these new organizations arose to meet community and individual needs that were either not the domain of the more traditional organizations or too massive to be tackled by them. Some of these needs were the direct result of the changing nature of the Chinatown population; there were a large number of aging men, the first generation of Chinese immigrants to spend their final years in the United States; there was an influx of women into this predominantly male world; a growing number of Chinese Americans were questioning their past and seeking a satisfactory identity; and young and aggressive urban immigrants were arriving from Hong Kong. Other needs were manifestations on the local level of national concerns. The Civil Rights Movement and the War on Poverty stimulated community activists to seek wider involvement of the residents in resolving local problems. The thaw in United States relations with the People's Republic of China allowed the expression of the political or cultural sympathies for the homeland that had for the past thirty years been confined to expressions of support for Taiwan. There were also, however, major threats to Chinatown's integrity that were the direct result of its particular location, and many of the new organizations arose to tackle these threats.

According to Sullivan and Hatch (1970), the situation of Boston Chinatown at the end of the 1960s was dismal, and this assessment was generally shared by its residents. It was a problem-ridden community whose only advantage over other larger Chinatowns such as in San Francisco and New York was that it could see what was happening in those cities and try to take action before those same problems became unmanageable in Boston. Housing, health, social services, employment, education, and community services were all perceived as problem areas.

Housing: Chinatown faced a series of devastating land losses in the late 1950s and 1960s. Highway construction of the Southeast Expressway and the Massachusetts Turnpike Extension not only took away housing but also greatly increased the traffic flow through Chinatown's narrow streets and added to air pollution. The Tufts–New England Medical Center (T-NEMC), located in the middle of Chinatown, was in the process of expanding and continues to do so to this very day. The Chinatown Housing and Land Task Force was established primarily to monitor T-NEMC expansion which competes for space for new housing as well as with commercial and industrial development. Hundreds of Chinese women are employed as stitchers in garment factories located in buildings leased from Tufts and are threatened with loss of their jobs unless these factories can relocate nearby (*Sampan* March 1982). While garment factories are often viewed as sweatshops, they nevertheless offer flexible employment to women with childcare responsibilities and with limited English skills close to their homes. The displacement of these factories is considered calamitous by community spokesmen, and major efforts to assist them in relocating nearby are underway.

Health: Despite the presence of a large medical institution in its midst, Chinatown was not adequately served by the medical establishment. Cultural misunderstandings and language difficulties discouraged residents from going to T-NEMC for treatment. The provision of Mandarin-speaking staff could not help Cantonese and Toisanese-speaking patients. Accordingly, the first community need addressed by the CACA was for a community clinic with Cantonese-speaking personnel and a bicultural understanding of medical problems (Gaw 1975).

Social Services: There were few social services available in China-

town, and the language barrier further depressed resident participation. When community needs were few and primarily those of men,
they were met within the community by the old-time organizations
or simply went unmet. A lack of demand for social services reflected
more a lack of knowledge than a lack of need. When individuals
knowledgeable about public and private programs available elsewhere
turned their attention to Chinatown, they became very concerned
about the issue of access.

Employment: Much of Chinatown's working population, both
then and now, has been handicapped by a lack of English training.
Even if highly skilled technically, these workers found that a lack of
English proficiency condemned them to low level jobs until they could
master enough English to pass exams for licensing. In the meantime
many worked in restaurants.

Education: This problem was closely related to employment, but
there were other adult language needs as well. For example, immigrants hoping to reunite their families had to acquire enough English
to pass the naturalization test.

Community Services: Sullivan and Hatch (1970) reported a tremendous need for improvements in municipal services. These included
better police protection, traffic management, and sanitation. Historically, one of the major reasons for the low city priority placed on
Chinatown has been its miniscule voting population. For many years,
Chinese as resident aliens could not vote, and a lack of knowledge of
English or of issues outside of the community did not stimulate great
public concern for participation in the electoral process. Even more
recent immigrants from Hong Kong, where only a minority of the
population were allowed to vote, are not highly motivated politically.
During the 1970s, voter registration drives were held. Now, however,
just as awareness and eligibility are on the increase, the Chinatown
population risks being overwhelmed by a political reform originally
intended to increase the representation of minorities in city government. Previous city-wide elections for seats on the City Council were
subject to criticism: simple majority vote allowed for greater representation of the dominant ethnic groups at the expense of minority
groups. A return to a district basis for City Council seats was expected
to allow residentially concentrated minorities to elect representatives
more familiar with their points of view. When the district lines were
drawn up on the basis of the 1980 Census, Chinatown leaders found
that Chinatown had been lumped with South Boston, an almost exclusively white community, and with the South End, an extremely

heterogeneous community, and they feared that their population would remain unrepresented.

Despite this litany of problems, Sullivan and Hatch (1970:88) concluded on an optimistic note: "While the magnitude of these problems cannot be minimized, the relatively small size of Boston's Chinese community is a factor in its favor, as is the unity of its leadership." This perception of unity was not entirely accurate. In fact, as in any community, there were differences of opinion about how to deal most effectively with the problems faced by Chinatown's residents. During the late 1960s and 1970s, for example, young professionals, often American born and living in the suburbs, were more confident of their own abilities than of the establishment's to negotiate with state and federal bureaucracies to secure funds for local projects. They believed that the often non-English-speaking members of the CCBA were not willing to recognize their limitations in this regard. On the other hand, the CCBA had long represented the community to outsiders, and without its cooperation or at least its nominal support, new organizations were seriously weakened in their assertions that they understood and could articulate the needs of the community. Indigenous community activists—those who had grown up in Chinatown—were caught between their own beliefs that the CCBA moved too slowly, that leadership was awarded primarily to those who had proven themselves in commercial activities, and their realization that seniority was still an important basis for respect in the community.

International political issues also served to divide the community. The Chinese in America have long been forced to be sensitive to the implications of American foreign policy and to be on the alert for outbreaks of racism directed explicitly against them as Chinese. In defense, many adopted a low profile. According to Nagasawa (1980), the dispersed nature of the Chinese population in Phoenix, Arizona resulted from a deliberate decision by community leaders. They believed that a scattered population would reduce blatant racial conflict and strongly opposed the establishment of enclaves such as those in San Francisco or New York. The internment of the West Coast Japanese and Japanese-American population during the second World War served as a warning to the Chinese and Chinese-American population, when shortly after that war, Sino-American relations deteriorated. The American embargo on Chinese goods forced Chinatown suppliers to shift from China to Hong Kong or Taiwan-based wholesalers. The Kuomintang (Nationalist Party), which had been actively supported since the turn of the century by Overseas Chinese, continued to rely on its American allies when it relocated in Taiwan. Thus, the China-town leadership became wedded politically and economically to Tai-wan, even though their families, for the most part, remained in their home provinces on the Mainland. Persecution of their families during land reform and subsequent political campaigns hardened their re-sistance to accommodation with the People's Republic of China. When the United States began to change its policies towards the People's Republic of China in the 1970s, Chinese sympathetic to the goals if not the means of the Communist Revolution began to organize into "friendship associations." Most Chinatown residents would prefer that the two factions suppress their differences rather than air them publicly.

The Vietnam War provided another example of how United States foreign policy and racism affected the adaptation of the Chinese in America. Although the allies and the enemies of the American forces were of the same race, derogatory terms describing the Vietnamese in general sensitized Americans of other Asian ancestry to the hostility that lurked just below the surface. One man described his experience as a student trainee in a Veterans' Administration hospital:

> I had never been exposed to mental patients before, and I had assumed that they would be tied down or doped up. I didn't realize they would be walking around, and there I was—an Asian surrounded by Vietnam War schizophrenics who went berserk when they imagined themselves sur-rounded by Asians. When people from here (Chinatown) heard that was where I was going, they couldn't believe it. They imagined that guys would beat me up and lock me in some small room out of sight somewhere. Actually nothing happened until my last day there. I told my supervisor af-terwards about my feelings about being placed there, and there was real surprise. It had never occurred to them about the Vietnam War and my being Asian.

Psychological issues, such as self-image and identity, and policy issues, such as alliances with other minority groups, also split the Chinese community. Many younger Chinese-Americans were dis-appointed by the relatively passive stance taken by their elders. They argued for greater self-affirmation. They wanted Asian-Americans to challenge stereotypes and to stop worrying about projecting an image acceptable to white America. They wanted to examine their historical experience as an ethnic group and to publicize the resourcefulness which they had developed to survive in a hostile environment. In Boston, students organized the Asian-American Resource Center to provide a meeting place for those seeking to promote the expression of the Asian-American experience through art, culture, and historical education.

Advocates for self-respect and racial pride followed the Civil Rights and Black Pride Movements with great interest. They could identify themselves with the deprivations experienced by blacks and could appreciate the goals which blacks laid out for their full participation in American society. This interest did not, however, lead to a Third World Movement in the Boston area. Many of the long-term Chinese immigrants had learned that identification with blacks led to being treated as blacks. Prior to the recent past, the best way to avoid being treated as black and thus suffering educational, economic, and political deprivation as they did was to maintain as much separation as possible. Loewen (1971) described the process whereby the Chinese in Mississippi caught "between Black and White" managed to move from a status just above blacks to just below whites over the course of several decades.

In addition to the historical racial dilemma, contemporary aspects of urban living, particularly displacement, have contributed to the rise of resentment by many older Chinese against Blacks and Hispanics. Several retired laundry operators lamented having been forced by crime, and in one case a firebombing, to abandon their marginal laundries in neighborhoods that became predominantly black. While many laundry operators were forced out of predominantly white neighborhoods, the immediate causes were more likely to be perceived as a result of technological advances—home washing machines and permanent press clothing. Furthermore, many of these long-term immigrants had come to the United States with expectations of long lives of hard work. Many of the social programs which now exist to assist poor families were totally unavailable in their day. Accordingly, they relied upon themselves, although now in old age, they are willing to accept housing subsidies, foodstamps, Medicaid, and Supplemental Security Income (SSI). When they compare their recollections of those deprived youthful and middle years with the relative bounty received by younger poor minority people today, they are indignant. Thus there are serious generational differences in willingness to unite across racial lines.

The arrival of more Westernized—in the sense of having had greater exposure to Western media—immigrants from Hong Kong in recent years does little to improve the situation. It was a very sobering experience in Hong Kong to realize that the vast majority of the population have knowledge of black Americans from two contexts only—from servicemen on leave in the entertainment districts and from motion pictures. American and European films which attract crowds in Hong Kong tend to be action-oriented and to deal in stereotypes. Blacks were seldom depicted in roles that Chinese were likely to admire. Such one-sided exposure to black Americans does not pave the way for cooperation or identification. A small proportion of Chinese and Chinese-American youth who have refused to accept either Chinese or middle class values express some admiration for the tough stance taken by some black (and white) youth, but when this admiration translates into behavior seen as rebellious or irresponsible by parents, these youngsters are in serious trouble with their families.

At a conference in May 1981 of Boston and national Chinese-American leaders, speakers decried the lack of unity and of a political force within the Chinese community in Boston. Because of the many competing groups, there has been little coordination of services; instead, there has been a duplication of services with agencies competing for the same funds (*Boston Globe* 10 May 1981). A slumping economy and a federal government with a more restrictive allocation of funds to social services were beginning to take their toll by the early 1980s. Perhaps the major success story was the opening of the South Cove Community Health Center (SCCHC) in Chinatown, with services provided by personnel speaking Toisanese, Cantonese, Mandarin, and Vietnamese. In addition to medical care, the Center also provides intepreter and escort services as well as assistance with social service applications. Adjacent to the Center is a congregate housing facility occupied primarily by elderly Chinese. This latter building also houses an Adult Day Care Center on its second floor and a senior center (The Chinese Golden Age Center) on its first floor. The senior center provides low-cost Chinese-style meals five days a week as well as some social activities, such as outings, crafts, and language classes for citizenship aspirants. The major casualty in terms of services for the elderly has been a nursing home. Despite a long-recognized need for such an institution and the existence as early as 1978 of two groups attempting to meet that need, none had been built as of 1982.

Beyond Chinatown

Between 1970 and 1980 the number of people of Chinese ancestry in the United States grew from 435,062 to 806,027. The growth over the same period in Massachusetts was from 14,012 to 25,015. (Actually, the population of Chinese ancestry is considerably greater than these figures suggest since a substantial number of Indochinese refugees, although nationals of Vietnam, Cambodia, or Laos, are of Chinese ancestry. In 1982 estimates of the Indo-Chinese population in the Boston area were around 5,000 (*Sampan* January/February 1982). Over half of the Chinese population (13,559) was concentrated in four areas in and around Boston. The greatest concentration occurred in Chinatown and its hinterland of the South End which together were home to 6,279 people of Chinese ancestry. The vast majority of the elderly and the poor live here. The Brighton-Allston district of Boston lies at the extreme west end of the city and is connected to the rest of it by a narrow strip of land parallel to the Charles River. Immediately south of this strip of land is the town of Brookline. Brighton-Allston and the western part of Brookline hold the next largest concentration of Chinese in the state—4,721. Directly across the Charles River from Brighton-Allston lies Cambridge with its population of 1,571 Chinese. Newton, which borders Brighton-Allston on the west, has 988 Chinese. These three latter districts hold the bulk of students and professionals. The three counties in which these cities and towns are located together contain over 80 percent (21,627) of the Chinese in Massachusetts. (All of the above figures were extracted by the author from Summary Tape File 1A of the 1980 Census.)

Unfortunately the proportion of elderly Chinese in the population is not yet available, and data from the 1970 Census is extremely out-of-date. Nevertheless, for illustrative purposes I include some national figures on elderly Chinese as reported by the Pacific/Asian Elderly Research Project (1978: 11-12). Chinese elderly 65 years and over constituted 6.2 percent of the total Chinese population in 1970. In 1960 the sex ratio of elderly Chinese males to elderly Chinese females was 301 to 100. By 1970 it had dropped to 131. This change reflects the new immigration trends—men are bringing over their elderly wives. While over half (54.8 percent) of the males 75 years and over immigrated before 1925, only 35.9 percent of the females did. For elderly Chinese males the median school years completed was only 6.7 compared to 8.6 for the total population. For Chinese females it was only 4.4 years. Most of this education was in village schools in China, which are not comparable to American schools of the same period. These contrasts between men and women in immigration timing and in schooling serve to reinforce cultural proscriptions against socializing of the sexes. Even in the case of elderly couples who have been married for more than fifty years, there is often a tremendous gap in shared experience which makes reunions in the United States a very mixed blessing for some.

Large numbers of Toisanese and Cantonese-speaking Chinese first expanded beyond Chinatown into the South End when they were displaced by highway construction projects in the late 1950s and 1960s. Others moved a little further into Brookline, which was considered especially attractive because of its educational environment. A heavy proportion of Brookline's population is of Jewish ancestry, and many Chinese see similarities between themselves and the Jews with respect to attitudes towards schooling and achievement as well as towards close family ties. Furthermore, following the steps taken in Boston beginning in 1974 to desegregate the schools, many parents became concerned about bussing of their children. In Chinatown, the one way to assure that one's elementary-school-aged child attended the neighborhood (Quincy) school was to enroll him or her in the bilingual education program which was held there. In Brookline, however, children automatically attended their neighborhood schools. By 1978 there were so many Chinese children in the Brookline classrooms that the system inaugurated a Chinese bilingual program. The Brookline Chinese Parents Committee which started out as a small group in 1974 had about 100 members by 1982 (*Boston Globe* 11 May 1982). In 1977 they organized a Chinese school to teach their children Cantonese and other aspects of Chinese culture.

Brookline and Brighton–Allston have a mixed population of immigrant parents who are interested in familiarizing their children with American culture as rapidly as possible and American-born parents who are fearful that their children are losing an appreciation of their Chinese heritage. Many of the earlier suburban Chinese, those who came originally for advanced degrees in the 1940s, faced this acculturation issue over two decades ago. These primarily Mandarin and English-speaking Chinese had few contacts with the Chinatown Chinese. Their work-mates were largely non-Chinese. Their children attended public schools in primarily white communities. In an effort to stimulate a sense of Chinese community in their children, they founded organizations with social and cultural objectives. In 1956 they founded the Greater Boston Chinese Cultural Association (GBCCA), which by 1982 had a membership of more than 350 families. According to the *Sampan* (April 1982) its goals are primarily "sponsoring and developing the understanding, study, education, promotion and appreciation of the Chinese arts, literature, history and language for members and the general public." Three years after its founding, the GBCCA established the Newton Chinese Language School and in 1972 the Lexington Chinese Language School. These two schools teach Mandarin whereas the Quong Kow Chinese School in Chinatown teaches Cantonese (in its earliest years it taught Toisanese). Just as the Chinatown community in Boston maintains contacts with other Chinatowns through the surname associations and the annual volleyball tournaments, the suburban Chinese maintain (and establish) ties with other suburban Chinese through "Chinese family camps" organized in vacation spots during the summers.

Chinese language churches also serve both the Chinatown and the suburban Chinese Christian populations. The Chinese Evangelical Church, located in the extreme southeast corner of Chinatown, offers bilingual (Cantonese and English) services and has a diverse membership of long-term and recent immigrants plus students from Hong Kong. Just across the Massachusetts Turnpike Extension in the South End stands Holy Trinity Church whose Catholic congregation is nearly one-half Chinese. The Chinese Christian Church of New England in Brookline and the Chinese Bible Church of Greater Boston in Woburn offer services in Mandarin and English and have congregations of northern Chinese or Taiwan origins.

Most of the members of these churches were already Christians when they came to the United States, though some converted only after arrival. The satisfactions of belonging to a small church mean a great deal to many of the older people. While some were clearly committed to doctrine and the Bible, others admitted to feeling comfortable around old people like themselves. In some cases the churches are valued primary groups which offer assistance in transport, housing, and visitations when ill. They are also important as referral agents. In addition, as Palinkas (1980) points out, the churches provide a means of coping with the anxieties of acculturation. Sermons stress the continuity between the Christian and the Chinese traditions, and faith provides a means of seeing difficulties through.

As the historical sketch and current profile above indicate, discussing the Chinese in America (or Greater Boston) in general does not get one very far. While nearly all Chinese are aware of their shared status as a minority group, they are also aware of the tremendous internal differentiation of this group. Individuals from one subpopulation are often amazed by the beliefs and practices of those from another. Because of their particular immigration experiences, even members of the same group frequently have difficulty communicating with each other, especially across generational lines. Examples of this diversity are provided in the subsequent chapters.

8 Greater Boston—The Variation

The Moys—Long-Time Boston Residents

Mr. and Mrs. Moy are both in their early 70s and grew up in Hoi Ping, a county adjacent to Toisan. Mr. Moy's father had come to the United States through the purchase of a birth certificate that stated he was a U.S. citizen. He later returned to China for a stay of several years, where he produced more sons on paper than in fact and and sold his surplus birth certificates to other families in his village. He later brought over both his sons to work in a large laundry in Roxbury, a section of Boston.

Mr. and Mrs. Moy had a traditionally arranged marriage and are living proof that this kind of marriage can work. Throughout my contact with them, they were mutually supportive and generally tolerant when expressing disagreement. Like many of the older generation, Mr. Moy believes that the advantages of a "blind marriage" outweigh the disadvantages.

> You can trust your mother to pick the girl. She will check back three generations to determine the health of the family and its background. She will investigate the character of the girl to see whether she is industrious. Her relatives will have had the opportunity to observe the girl growing up. It is better to find a girl through your own relatives rather than through a matchmaker. Your relatives raised you and can be trusted.

The Moy's older son, even though American born, subscribed to a modified version of this procedure. He had reached his 30s without finding the kind of girl he considered suitable for a spouse. His relatives pitched in to help him find the right girl. The Hong Kong-based

157

mother-in-law of one of his sisters sent the family a set of pictures of prospective candidates. Then Mrs. Moy and her son went on a several months trip to Hong Kong where they checked out these and other girls. They had been favorably impressed with one girl from the beginning, and she eventually became the Moys' first daughter-in-law.

In 1926 right after his marriage, Mr. Moy came to the United States where he joined his father and older brother. In 1928, his older brother returned to China to supervise the construction of a house in which the brothers and the father would all live together with their wives following their retirements from the laundry business. In 1929, Mr. Moy himself went back for a two year stay during which time his wife gave birth to a daughter. Shortly thereafter, the two brothers returned to Boston and persuaded their father to retire as he was already about 50 years old. While his older brother operated the main laundry (which he continued to operate until it burned down only a few years ago), Mr. Moy opened various branch laundries, finally settling on a laundry in Brighton-Allston.

In the meantime, he had devised a way to get his wife admitted into the United States. She came in as the unmarried daughter of one of his friends who claimed successfully to be a U.S. citizen. A week after her arrival in 1938, the Moys, having already been married for twelve years, were officially married in Boston. They continued to operate their laundry well into the 1960s, but by 1969 Mr. Moy found that the work was beginning to exceed his capacity. He was getting old, and the wet clothing was too heavy for him to carry. Leaving his wife in charge of the laundry, he began working full-time in a friend's Chinese restaurant with the objective of earning enough quarters to qualify for Social Security. About three years ago, he shifted to part-time work. The laundry did not prosper. When Mrs. Moy and her son closed the laundry for the duration of their Hong Kong match-making trip, he handed the keys over to the owner of the property and asked him to dispose of the equipment.

Mr. Moy's father died in China in 1948. His mother was the only family member residing in the village when it underwent land reform. Because she owned land, which she had purchased through the remittances sent to her by her husband and sons, she was classified as a landlord and ordered to turn over any money and jewelry in her possession. She refused. She was then imprisoned and forced to send Mr. Moy a letter requesting money for her release. He declined to do so as he believed that the Communists were not sincere but only interested in blackmail. If he gave them money once, he reasoned, they would hold her forever and just keep requesting money. Although his mother was nearly 70 years old at that time, she was made to walk on her knees over broken glass and to ford a stream in which she risked drowning. The Moys did not learn this directly from her but from other relatives. Like many people who underwent severe hardship in China at that time—or earlier as during the Sino-Japanese War—she seemed to prefer to forget her suffering.

Eventually the Moys were able to bring her to the United States. She had somehow managed to reach Hong Kong but at one point became ill and was hospitalized. From that time on she did not function properly mentally. In 1974 one of the Moy daughters went to Hong Kong to accompany her grandmother to Boston. She moved in with Mr. and Mrs. Moy who watched over her carefully. Her behavior was sometimes incomprehensible to them. For example, old Mrs. Moy would not use the toilet. Instead she brought containers into the bathroom and used them for elimination. Whether she viewed the containers as chamber pots or as a means of preserving the excrement for fertilizer was never clear. Sometimes she would gather together a pile of clothes and stuff them behind the radiators in the belief that she was somehow burning offerings for the ancestors. She also had a terrible memory. She frequently stood in the door to the bedroom staring at Mr. Moy and wondering out loud who this "big man" was.

In 1978 old Mrs. Moy died at the age of 96. She had been in failing health for some time, but Mr. Moy did not want to send her to a hospital. He felt that she could get better care at home, and he himself fed her in her last days. At the very end, he had to use a straw to put drops of water into her mouth. From the tone of their conversation whenever they touched on this topic, it was clear that the Moys derived great personal satisfaction from having done all they could for this lady in her final hours. Perhaps they felt a bit guilty for what she had had to experience during land reform—or perhaps they saw their behavior as a model for their own two sons.

The Moys are fortunate in having all four of their children living within a short distance of the parental home. Their two sons, in fact, live with their own families in the same three-family house in which they grew up. The Moys own this house and occupy the middle floor. Their two daughters and their families live in the next town. Once every week, all the children and their families assemble for dinner at the Moy residence. The Moys do not receive any money from their children except in the form of rent or gifts such as major birthday celebrations. The two sons pay their heating costs and just enough rent to cover the property taxes.

The Moys do not expect money. They had managed to save during their years at the laundry, though they never made very much. In the 1950s they cleared only about $150 a month, and in the 1960s about $200 a month. From this they had had to send money back to China to support old Mrs. Moy as well as their oldest child who had been born before Mrs. Moy came to the United States. Nevertheless, they had managed to save enough to buy three houses. In the 1970s they had had to sell one of the houses, but they still own the one they live in as well as the one a daughter's family inhabits. Mrs. Moy still makes her own clothes. She enjoys window shopping, but instead of entering major downtown department stores, she turns off into a side street to purchase remnants from a garment factory.

Producing filial children and investing in land were the keys to a materially adequate old age. Many Chinese in this country attempted to continue in this tradition, but some now have ambivalent feelings about having voluntarily scrimped and saved for their old age. Mr. Moy remarked:

> I had a cousin who came to the United States about the same time that I did. This cousin did not work hard and save like I did. He had a wife in China, but he preferred to be independent. At times I saw American women going in and out of his apartment. I warned him that he would be sorry, that he would be poor in his old age, that nobody would take care of him. To everyone's surprise, the government gives money to those who are poor including those who did not work hard in their youth! Many Chinese receive Social Security. If they don't have enough money, they can apply for SSI. If they still do not have enough, they can apply for foodstamps. I wish I could be one of the elderly in Chinatown. They have Social Security and welfare. They also have an expensive room in which to live, but they only have to pay about $70 a month in rent. Who says these benefits are not desirable? If I had not worked hard in the past, I would be eligible for welfare and a room in Chinatown.

Mrs. Moy for her part has also decided to make up for lost time. She does not want to have to worry about money any longer.

> I should enjoy myself as much as possible because I do not

have that much time on earth. I do not care to have a great deal of money because I cannot eat more than my body can take in. I like to enjoy myself and do what I want. If I want to gamble, I will go to my friends' houses and play mahjong. I do not like to look after my grandchildren because I had enough hard work in my early years. Raising four children gave me plenty of headaches. With grandchildren I cannot enjoy myself. I do not need my children's money because we (self and spouse) have already bought boxes (coffins) for ourselves. I was stupid when I was younger because I worked so hard and did not have any fun. I don't want to be stupid anymore.

Mrs. Moy is very comforted by the fact that her youngest child, Tom, encourages her to gamble. He himself is a gambler, though his parents were quick to point out that he gambles only his own earnings and never those of his wife, and has told her that she should not worry about the money. Even if she were to lose everything, she could always come and live with him. This is precisely the kind of talk Mrs. Moy wants to hear. She is not interested in the children's money, she has said, but in their hearts.

While the Moys now have a comfortable and warm relationship with their youngest child, this was not always the case. As one man put it, Tom typified the case of a family in which the "fathers may have moved to Brookline or Brighton-Allston, but the sons remained (psychologically) in Chinatown." In short Tom was irresistibly attracted to some of the less desirable aspects of young male culture in Chinatown (see Kendis and Kendis 1976). Tom's older brother had graduated from high school and attended college. His American-born sister had become very active in community affairs, but Tom himself had difficulty sorting out his life goals. He began to skip classes in high school. When the school authorities informed Mr. Moy, he beat his son and ordered him to return to school. As it rapidly became clear that Tom was not academically motivated, Mr. Moy decided not to force him to continue. The boy worked in a restaurant for a year before deciding to try his luck at school again. Although he had not yet graduated from high school, he was still able to gain admittance to a junior college. Mr. Moy was very gratified and provided school fees and a car. After only six months, Tom decided to return to restaurant work and began hanging out in Chinatown. The Moys are convinced that had this behavior occurred nowadays, he would have become a gangster. As it is, he is the only one in his crowd, as far as they know, to have eventually made something of himself.

At the age of 18 Tom joined his friends in renting an apartment in Chinatown near his place of work. None of the others bothered to get a job. They would go to the restaurant where Tom worked and tell the manager to charge their meals to Tom. They did not bother to pay the rent for several months on their apartment. Tom became very worried about all this and finally confessed his troubles to his parents. Mr. Moy paid the rent so that his son could retrieve his bedding and other belongings. Tom never went back to the apartment again, and he has no interest now in moving out of his parents' house. A few years ago, he and his older brother joined three others in a restaurant partnership. They have been doing very well, and the brothers have begun to buy investment property out of state. Mr. and Mrs. Moy consider him to be a financial success, and they are also happy with the young woman (from Chinatown) whom he picked out for himself.

Mr. Moy is no longer as active as he used to be. When he and the children were younger, they went on many excursions to nearby places of interest. He has seen them all many times and is no longer interested in going to the same old places. He says he would rather sit and read. In fact, he gets out of the house nearly everyday. He takes Mrs. Moy shopping or drops her off at a friend's house. Sometimes she goes to Quincy Tower (elderly housing in Chinatown) to play mah-jong while he goes to sit on the Boston Common. On very hot days they might drive to an air-conditioned shopping mall to pass the afternoon. For a half day on Friday and all day on Saturday, Mr. Moy works in a friend's fast food restaurant; this helps him to kill the time. He and his wife are not active in community organizations though they do belong to the Moy family association. Mr. Moy can readily recount the genealogy of the Moy clan and was quick to bring out a yearbook. He spoke at such length that Mrs. Moy twice reminded him that his coffee was getting cold. Women are members of these organizations by virtue of their marriage to the male members. They do not hold offices or decide any of the organization policies. Their participation is usually limited to the two annual banquets such family associations hold, one at the New Year and one in September. The food and entertainment attract the women and the young folk. The men welcome the opportunity to participate in the ritual aspects and to stand before the microphone giving speeches—though the speeches cannot be easily heard over the conversations of the others.

Mr. Moy considers himself in good health, though he does have to follow some dietary restrictions. One day when he felt so weak that he thought he would faint, he went to a Chinese doctor (a traditional herbalist who was a relative of his wife but who has since ceased his practice and moved out of state) who prescribed a traditional remedy. This helped temporarily, but one day while working at the restaurant, he had a fainting spell. His family members sent him to the hospital by ambulance, and he learned that he had an ulcer. Fortunately, he did not require surgery, but he does take medicine for his ulcer every day. Normally, he sees a Western-trained physician for serious medical problems as does Mrs Moy. She used to prepare various medicinal teas, but now that she is taking medication for high blood pressure, she is wary lest there be a drug interaction effect.

Between them the Moys have over 90 years of experience living in Boston. As a result, they are aware of the need for the older generation to compromise when it comes to dealing with the younger generation. Mrs. Moy has learned not to push. When one of her granddaughters complained about being tired when asked to help out with household chores and the girl's mother backed her up, Mrs. Moy felt that she had to hold her tongue. When a daughter-in-law declined Mrs. Moy's offer to make clothes for the grandchildren, she quietly withdrew, realizing that the daughter-in-law wanted somewhat more stylish clothing than Mrs. Moy was accustomed to making. As Mrs. Moy puts it, she "does not interfere in the children's business."

Both parents recognize the need to define a limited role in their children's lives and view this as a necessary adjustment to American life. However, according to Mrs. Moy, some of the more recent arrivals to the United States do not have the wisdom to appreciate this point of view.

> They think they are still in China and want their sons and daughters-in-law to listen to them. I know many cases where mothers-in-law are kicked out of their children's houses. The mother-in-law thinks that her son is still hers whether he is married or not. Little do they know that women have more authority here than in China. Men listen to their wives more.

She has tried to advise such people to look at the situation differently. They should not put all the blame on their children, but should be prepared to take some responsibility for bad relations themselves.

The Moys are typical of long-time residents in several ways. First, like most Chinese immigrants of the period, they came directly to

America from Sze Yap—from a village or a market town to a big city with no transitional period in Hong Kong. Second, they came, especially Mr. Moy, for straightforward economic reasons, joining fathers and older brothers in earning enough money to support the family members left behind. Third, they came in less than a totally legal manner. Their documents had been accepted by the United States Immigration and Naturalization Service when they arrived, and the costs of their dubious legitimacy were only financial. For others who came in by jumping ship or in the back of someone's truck or on someone else's reused documents, there were considerably greater costs. Unscrupulous members of the community could hold the threat of exposure over them. Fourth, they were employed in the laundry business until the very last years of their working lives. The Moys lived in the same neighborhood as their laundry. In this they differed from some of the single laundry workers who lived in the backs of their shops or commuted daily from a room in Chinatown. Fifth, even though they lived well outside of the boundaries of Boston Chinatown, they remained oriented to it. They bought their groceries there once a week, and two of their children became heavily involved in Chinatown activities. Sixth, their children were educated in the Boston school system and, except for the oldest child, exposed to American culture from birth. These parents have the experience to recognize the value differences that exist between themselves and their children. Recent immigrants find it much more difficult to accommodate.

The Huas—Suburban Professionals

The Huas (he is 66, and she is 56) had actually met each other as children when their families shared the same courtyard in China. She had even played *go* with her future father-in-law. When she approached college age, she was "introduced" to Mr. Hua who had already been studying in the United States. In 1946, already engaged to Mr. Hua, she came to the West Coast to finish her last two years of college. Mr. Hua at that time had taken a job on the East Coast. Mrs. Hua considers her college days in America as the most pleasant of her life. She had no responsibilities beyond her studies as she was the youngest of several cousins attending the same college. They all watched out for her and even did her laundry. Her abrupt relocation to the Boston area and her marriage to a man very intent on his work required major adjustments.

When I was in school, I was writing and thinking, but I couldn't find a job because English—even though I majored in it—didn't give me very good skills. So I would stay home with nothing to do. But my husband was very busy. This was a big change. I left the West Coast to come East to get married, but even at the wedding, I didn't know anyone except my bridesmaid. There were no other friends. I sort of felt dislocated, displaced—with no identity. I didn't know the other people, and I didn't care too much about them. Of course another part of it was that we knew we were going to get married since we were in China, but there was a lag of about two years. If you fall in love and get married immediately, then it's O.K. But in two years each person grows and the environment changes and the psychology also grows, but you are still hanging on to the image of two years ago.

Mrs. Hua never did find employment outside of the home, but once her children began to arrive, she found plenty to occupy her time. Despite her unfamiliarity with childcare, Mrs. Hua managed, being treated by a "natural" pediatrician, reading Dr. Spock, and following her own instincts. She also had to learn about homemaking because in China these tasks had been performed in her family by servants.

One of her few concerns was that her husband did not play a greater role in family life. He was so devoted to his work as both an academic and a businessman that he spent scarcely any time at home. His youngest daughter, on discovering him at home one Sunday, exclaimed in surprise "What are you doing here?" Mr. Hua was not responding to his paternal role much differently from fathers in China who occupied similar high status positions outside of the family. Such fathers were expected to have little to do with the children (or their wives for that matter). In addition to their economic role, their most important familial role was in moral instruction. Several China-reared informants have stated that they had been terrified of their own fathers. Dinner time had been a stern and formal affair at which their fathers had given training in ethics and values.

Mr. Hua was certainly not a father in this mould. His youngest daughter was not afraid to talk with him and share her innermost thoughts; her only problems had been in being able to catch him and in being certain that he was actually paying attention to what she was saying. While she shared her problems with both her parents, she found that their ways of responding differed. Her mother usually based her advice or analysis on her own personal experience, whereas her father was more likely to draw on axioms or philosophical statements. As the children grew older, Mr. Hua came to be a more visible presence in their lives. Some of this greater involvement was at Mrs. Hua's instigation. When the children had questions about colleges or majors, she urged Mr. Hua to guide them as he had greater academic experience than she did. When the Huas' older son complained to his mother that he really didn't have any idea about what his father was like, Mrs. Hua had encouraged Mr. Hua to join a swimming class so that the pair could spend some time together in a joint activity. While this helped somewhat, the older son continues to resent the fact that if he wants paternal notice, he has to actively solicit it. He believes that a father should be more spontaneous and concerned about a son's mental and emotional state.

The Huas were both from families closely tied to the Nationalist Party. After the Korean War, during the apparent thaw in ideological rigidity that occurred in 1956 (the "Hundred Flowers" period in which dissenters were asked to voice their opinions), some of their friends and relatives went back to China, only to find themselves embarking on two decades of persecution. (See Bernstein 1982:243-51 for the contrasting treatment meted out to two Chinese physicists trained in the United States, one of whom returned shortly after the Communist takeover and the other not until the 1980s.)

The Huas were not isolated in the United States. Both came from large families, and many of their siblings had also been educated in the United States. Mr. Hua's younger brother has been with them since their wedding. When he too married, the two couples continued to share a two-family house. In 1956 when their families were already enlarged by children and by the arrival of their widowed mother, the brothers built houses on adjoining pieces of property. The brothers had invited their parents to come to the United States from Taiwan, but old Mr. Hua died just before they were to leave. For several years, old Mrs. Hua rotated among four of her children in the United States, her two sons in Massachusetts and two married daughters living in other states. While living with one of her daughters, she broke a hip and required hospitalization. The Huas went to the hospital, where they took turns serving as translators for her. Mr. Hua's sister who was employed had great difficulty working out satisfactory post-hospital care for the old lady, and she herself expressed a preference for returning to her oldest son's house.

None of the Huas recall her as a family burden. Her grandchildren recall her fondly as not bothering anyone, and staying much of the time in her own bedroom where the children would go to chat with her. They were impressed by her bound feet and her ability to open Pepsi bottles with her bare hands. One of the Hua daughters thinks that her grandmother had the best of all possible living arrangements in old age, but she is not sure what her own parents prefer. The Huas themselves are certain that as long as they are both alive, they will prefer to stay in their own home. Only widowhood or a serious illness would cause them to think about involving the children in their search for an alternative living arrangement.

The Huas are well-to-do and have no financial worries about retirement. They continue to contribute money to their children and have paid for their undergraduate and much of their graduate education. They have also helped out with car purchases and during periods of unemployment. The Hua children range in age from 30 to 23, and all of them have left the family home. The oldest daughter, the only married child, recently returned to the Boston area and settled with her husband in a suburb about a half hour's drive from her parents. The three younger children live in three different states and are not yet settled.

The oldest Hua child has married a non-Chinese. This fact causes no problems for the Huas, who knew that intermarriage was a very likely outcome of their suburban living situation. The children, after all, have had very few opportunities to meet other Chinese. For several years, their younger daughter also went with a non-Chinese boy, and even though that relationship has been broken off, they still remember the boy warmly. However, not everyone is as tolerant of intermarriage as the Huas. The Mas have already seen two of their children marry non-Chinese, and according to Mrs. Hua,

Mrs. Ma dislikes it a lot! The oldest daughter's husband is very nice in fact. Mr. and Mrs. Ma visited them (in another state). The husband is very good, but Mrs. Ma can't stand a Chinese girl that has a relationship with a white man. She said she couldn't bear to watch them touch. There is something unnatural about having a white person touch a Chinese girl. I was shocked at my friend. I told her that I couldn't believe that she had those feelings. She is racially prejudiced. I don't know why, but she just is this way.

Mrs. Hua believes that similarity of temperament and not race is probably the single most important criterion to employ when thinking about marriage. She herself has been much involved in matchmaking, and many of her own relatives owe the introduction of their children-in-law to Mrs. Hua's sharp eyes. Mr. Hua has also been instrumental in the mating game. His younger brother's wife died leaving behind three children, only one of whom was still at home. Mrs. Hua had had to assume many of the daily tasks of the deceased wife and mother. The younger Mr. Hua and his daughter ate with the Huas every day, and Mrs. Hua drove her niece to her various engagements.

The general view of the local Chinese community was that the widower should remarry. People would come to the older brother's house and ask whether it was time to find someone for the younger. At first Mr. Hua said no, but about two years after his sister-in-law's death, he announced that it had been long enough since her death and that while his brother would certainly remember her, it was time for him to find a wife for companionship and help around the house. Mr. Hua contacted many friends and the names began to come in. Within the small national Chinese community of professionals, it was nearly always possible to learn about the availability and background of qualified candidates. Unfortunately, this had not been the case for the deceased sister-in-law; no one had realized that her family had a history of "weak nerves" that in all probability contributed to her early death. Mr. Hua's younger brother checked out several candidates before settling on a woman who had already been married and had two children.

Like Mrs. Moy, Mrs. Hua has found herself serving as an interpreter of American culture to immigrants more recently arrived than herself. One of Mrs. Hua's sisters and her husband, the Ais, came to the United States permanently only in the 1970s, though all four of their children had already spent many years here. Their oldest daughter had married a man from Taiwan whom she had met in the United States. When her parents came to the United States, she invited them to live with her, but her husband accepted this only grudgingly. He had been displeased when, earlier, his wife's brother had stayed with them for a long period. Their marriage ended in divorce, and the Ais were very anxious for their daughter to remarry. Mrs. Hua knew of an appropriate candidate describing him as "very Chinese" by which she meant that he had a smooth temperament, was quiet, and valued family ties. The Ais' daughter and this young man decided to live together prior to marriage—a decision which greatly agitated the Ais (who were no longer coresident with their daughter). Mrs. Hua spent many hours on the phone trying to reassure them that the decision was based on good intentions, that it was an attempt to determine whether or not they really shared the same values, particularly where family relationships were concerned.

When the Ais' youngest child, a boy, became seriously involved with a non-Chinese girl, they decided to take prompt action. Mr. Ai insisted that his son accompany him back to Taiwan, where he had arranged for a series of formal meetings with eligible young women. Almost all of these women were daughters of Mr. Ai's friends. Mrs. Hua related:

> At first my nephew was heart-broken, but afterwards he was O.K. Some of the friends' daughters were still in the United States and had to go back to Taiwan just to meet my nephew— he's a good catch. It would be a way to come permanently to the United States, and he would have a steady income, and it would be a good family. The girls were brought into the room one at a time. They would talk for a while and then leave. When the eighth girl came in, he fell in love at first sight. He didn't want to see any more girls, but his father said that since all of them had gotten lined up, he must see all of them. They had come so far. . . . My nephew will probably live with his bride in his parents' house. She will like it that way. She will like it better because it is her first time in the United States. The adjustment will be easier; it will be more like Taiwan. My nephew doesn't have any money now, since he is in school, so he doesn't mind living with his parents. My brother-in-law is 100 percent Chinese. He pushed the match-making more than his wife.

Watson (1975:174-77) has described a similar kind of whirlwind courtship for emigrants from rural Hong Kong. In the prospective bridegroom's village community, however, his peers rather than his parents are more likely to put together a list of girls, and the initiative for following up on the list remains with the young man. Watson attributes the greater influence of these emigrant sons who work in London restaurants to their financial independence—the parents are dependent on them for support.

The Huas were concerned with the lack of exposure of their children to Chinese culture. The children can now speak Chinese to varying degrees, but they seldom use it. As youngsters they attended one of the Chinese language schools organized by the Greater Boston

Chinese Cultural Association, but they did not like it. One of the Hua daughters has since read a book on the history of the Chinese characters and believes that if an "interesting" rather than a rote approach had been utilized in the language school, she and her siblings might have stayed longer.

The changing American relationship with the People's Republic of China has enabled the Huas to help out other family members. Now that educational and exchange programs are operational, the Huas have arranged for Mrs. Hua's oldest brother, a professor in Shanghai, to come to the United States on a lecture tour. He has been invited to lecture at the University of California, where one of his former students is now a professor. The university will pay part of his expenses and Mrs. Hua's younger brother, also living in California, will pay part. Two of Mrs. Hua's nephews (cousins to each other) are now studying at a university in the Boston area. Almost all of Mrs. Hua's American-based siblings are contributing to the education of these young men. Mrs. Hua has four siblings in China and six in the United States, though none are geographically closer than New York. In 1978, one of the younger members of this dispersed family organized a gigantic family reunion on the West Coast that lasted for two or three days. On the last day of the reunion the younger members played a game; each child had to identify all the others and tell who his or her parents were. Another gathering three years later was scheduled on the East Coast to allow those unable to travel far on the first occasion to participate.

Not every educated family from the Mainland has such a large number of relatives in the United States. Many found themselves reduced to a minimal nuclear family. Such families have frequently developed surrogate relationships with other Chinese. They formed associations based on common school ties or common professional interests. The Huas did this when they were a younger family, but no longer find such organizations so necessary. Other couples when faced with an "empty nest" have developed quasi-parental ties with Chinese students in the area. Often these ties developed out of invitations to spend a Chinese holiday with a host family. As strangers themselves at one time, the generation of the Huas understands the need of students in a foreign land for contacts with people from the homeland.

The Huas are typical of the families most frequently contrasted with those from Chinatown. They personally have very few contacts in Chinatown, and both came from well-to-do families. They do not speak Cantonese and are not members of family associations. When they first came to Boston, the Huas lived in Brighton-Allston, but they quickly moved to Watertown where they purchased a two-family house. Later they moved to their present home in a suburb out along Route 128—the highway which skirts the metropolitan area from north to south, and along which many of the high-tech industries set up in the 1960s. Many families such as the Huas were Christian and had sent their children to schools run by Western missionaries. As a result, many were already exposed to both Westerners and English before they ever came to the United States. While some encountered initial difficulties in finding places to rent, they tended to shrug this problem off, attributing it to being misidentified as Chinatown Chinese. Many of these couples espoused romantic ideals as the bases of their marriages, but did not know how to translate these youthful ideals into concrete roles in their marriages. A more traditional Mrs. Hua would not have been disappointed by her husband's limited involvement in family life, and a conventionally reared son would not have expected his father to take a spontaneous interest in his feelings. Mr. Hua and his friends are employed in professional and technical fields; most of their co-workers are non-Chinese as are their neighbors, and they are realistic about acculturation issues and understand about the likelihood of intermarriage. At the same time, they have an acute need for interaction with people who share their experience as people stranded in a foreign country.

Mrs. Chin—A Recent Immigrant

Mrs. Chin's family had fled from Guangdong in 1951. Her father-in-law who worked in the South Pacific sent back the cash which his son (Mrs. Chin's husband) invested in real estate and business ventures in Hong Kong. While Mr. Chin did all of the start up work in their prosperous laundry business, such as the site selection and the purchase of equipment, once the business was underway, she took control. She paid the wages and kept track of the clothes. One of their laundries had about fifteen employees, most of whom were from the same village, had the same surname, or had been introduced by someone known personally. They had taken their meals together and developed close ties. Now when members of the Chin family go traveling to places like New York or Toronto, they sometimes look up these former employees.

Mrs. Chin's oldest son also helped with the laundries. Her second son had originally gone to New Zealand as a student but stayed on after earning a professional degree. The oldest daughter married a man from the United States; the next daughter married a man from New Zealand. In the early 1960s, Mr. Chin became ill and realized that he was not going to live. He summoned his son in New Zealand to Hong Kong, and the family tried to work out the best strategy for the future. They had already been forced to leave China, and no one could be sure what would happen to Hong Kong. The consensus was that Mrs. Chin and the two youngest children should emigrate. The immigration restrictions of New Zealand were more severe than those of the United States, and the son from New Zealand thought that his brother would receive a better education in the United States than in New Zealand. Consequently, the family contacted the oldest daughter and asked her to arrange for their immigration as refugees.

They sold two of the laundries and an apartment to finance their trip to the United States. Any surplus cash was divided among the adult children. The oldest son remained in Hong Kong for several years with the other two laundries before coming to Boston with his own family. When they first came to Boston, Mrs. Chin and the two youngest children moved into the attic of the oldest daughter's home. The two children worked in their older sister's laundry even though her own children did not have to do so. Mrs. Chin went to work in a garment factory as a thread cutter, a job requiring the least skill. She did this partly to qualify for Social Security, and she quit when she was about 65 to look after her youngest daughter's new baby.

In 1972, Mrs. Chin's youngest son and last child to remain single decided to marry a girl of his own choosing. He had met her through a church they both attended and had known her for several years. She had been brought up in Taiwan of Cantonese speaking parents, but had lived in Boston for several years. Since the marriage of her final child marked a significant rite of passage, Mrs. Chin was entitled to make a major event of this wedding. First, an engagement party was held, which relatives of both parties attended; at this time, negotiations regarding bride-price were carried on. About a month before the wedding, Mrs. Chin arranged for the transfer of a large sum of money, chickens, ducks, roast pig, coconuts, and many small cakes to the bride's family.

Like many immigrant families, the Chins and the bride's family faced the often confusing problems of how to carry out a wedding in a foreign land. How many of the traditional elements could they reasonably expect to carry out? How much would a Christian church wedding restrict these elements? The Chins were able to blend the two traditions successfully. As Mrs. Chin's daughter-in-law explained:

> It (the wedding) was held at an Episcopal church, and we had two pastors. One was the resident pastor, and the other was from the Chinese church, so he could translate. We wanted our relatives to understand what was happening. It was just like a Western wedding except you know how Chinese like to talk—the church was a little noisy.

The bride wore white at the wedding, but changed into a Chinese-style red dress for the banquet, which was held at the China Pearl, the largest restaurant in Chinatown.

In China, since a girl normally marries out of her natal village, the wedding usually involves two banquets: one in the husband's village attended by his relatives and one in the bride's village attended by hers. Since members of the bride's and groom's families were both in the Boston area, a joint banquet was held. There were fifty-three tables at the banquet. In the negotiations, Mrs. Chin promised to pay for fifteen tables for guests of the bride's family. The bride's family volunteered to pay for an additional eleven tables' worth of their own guests. The bride's mother explained that had her daughter chosen to have a conventional Western wedding reception, it would have been the financial responsibility of the bride's family, but since she did not, they would make a contribution towards the banquet, which is normally the groom's family's responsibility. Mrs. Chin paid for the rest of the tables.

Guests at Chinese weddings normally present *huhng baau* ("red packets," red envelopes containing cash gifts) to whomever invited them to the wedding. The young couple themselves did not collect any of these gifts, which went instead to the senior generation to help defray the costs of the banquet. Their own friends of the same age presented them with non-cash gifts, which they retained. The young couple then went to spend one night in a hotel in Boston before departing on their honeymoon. When they arrived, they found fifty people in the room waiting for them. These were mostly peers who stayed around for more than an hour teasing them and asking them riddles. The following morning, the newlyweds went to Mrs. Chin's residence (which she shared with the young couple, having never been separated from her youngest son), where the bride presented her with a cup of tea symbolizing her recognition of her duty to serve her mother-in-law.

Actually, Mrs. Chin spent the nights with her youngest son and daughter-in-law, but she spent most of the days at her oldest son's apartment where she did some of the housekeeping. Her oldest son and her youngest daughter lived in the same two-family house. In the mid-1970s, several events conspired to force the various households to relocate. Dorchester, where they had lived since first moving in with the oldest daughter, was becoming a less desirable neighborhood. Her youngest son, whose family was expanding, was interested in buying a home in a better area. The youngest daughter was planning to sell the two-family house, which meant that both she and her oldest brother would have to move. Furthermore, a family investment venture had gone sour, and two of Mrs. Chin's children had become involved in a lawsuit with each other.

Mrs. Chin's youngest son found a two-family house in Brighton-Allston. Her youngest daughter-in-law had lived in that neighborhood before marriage, and her natal family still lived there. Mrs. Chin's son asked her to move along with them, and she did. In fact, she contributed several thousand dollars to the young couple's down payment. They at first refused to accept it, but she explained that when the laundries in Hong Kong had been sold, the profits had been divided among the adult children. At that time the youngest boy was only in junior middle school and had not received a share. She interpreted the down payment as his share.

Mrs. Chin currently receives Social Security as well as a monthly allowance from her youngest son, which she just puts in the bank. Her son also provides her room and board. In fact, Mrs. Chin could have a whole small apartment of her own within her son's house—a so-called mother-in-law apartment. The apartment contains a separate bedroom, bathroom, and kitchen. The kitchen appliances are not actually connected, and the room is used primarily as a study by her son and daughter-in-law. Books are everywhere including on the top of the stove. Mrs. Chin likes her bedroom location on the second floor because she likes plants, and her room has the best exposure to the sun.

When the family first moved to the house, Mrs. Chin had shared a room with her oldest grandson while the young parents shared a room with their second son. Now everyone is separated by generational status; three boys are in one room, the parents in another, and Mrs. Chin in the third. Her daughter-in-law manages the household and does all the housework, though when there are visitors or when her daughter-in-law has important business outside of the home, Mrs. Chin will babysit.

When they first moved in together, Mrs. Chin had tried to help her daughter-in-law in cleaning up after meals, but learned quickly that her cleaning standards were not the same as those of the younger woman, so she had retreated. While she believed in intergenerational living, Mrs. Chin was also aware that it could present delicate problems in human relations. For example, she knew that she and her daughter-in-law had different opinions about child-rearing, particularly on issues of discipline, and Mrs. Chin hesitated to express her opinions or to act on them. In her Toisan village, it had been customary to yell at children, to call them names such as *sei jai* ("dead boy"— the implication is one of wishing the child dead) or *neih mouh yuhngge* ("you good-for-nothing"), to threaten them, to isolate them (locking them in a storage closet or out of the house), and to strike them with little regard to possible negative consequences. These punishments were seldom graded by the nature of the child's offense, but tended more to reflect: the state of mind of the parent, how quickly he or she wanted to make the point that the offending behavior was unacceptable; the accessibility of the child, whether within reach of hand or voice; and the presence or absence of witnesses from outside the family, witnesses being a stimulus to parental action. Mrs. Chin did not dare to strike her grandchildren. She would yell at them and threaten them with punishment from her daughter-in-law, but her daughter-in-law does not strike them. She believes in talking with them or punishing them by restrictions on their freedom of movement.

Despite nearly fifteen years in the United States, Mrs. Chin does not speak English, so she is restricted in her mobility and in her choice of friends. She accompanies her son's family to a Chinese Christian church even though she herself is not a Christian. She enjoys the recognition of others that she is her son's mother. She is primarily involved in family life, crocheting blankets for all the children and attending family gatherings. Her youngest daughter and her oldest son's wife used to be stitchers in Chinatown, but the oldest daughter arranged for them to work as assemblers in a large factory on the outskirts of Chinatown, where the employees are largely non-Chinese. Mrs. Chin views this job change as part of the process of upward mobility and attends the annual picnic of the company with great enthusiasm. She really has no friends who are not also relatives. Perhaps the one person with whom she can relax most conveniently is her youngest daughter-in-law's mother, who lives in the same block, who attends the same church, and who years ago demonstrated her reasonableness in the wedding negotiations.

Mrs. Chin has considered moving into elderly housing. She twice presented her son with an application form for such housing, but he turned it aside declaring simply that she would remain with them. In fact, he was very puzzled by the request because he was unaware of any special problems with the current living arrangement. He concluded that perhaps she had just been testing him.

Mrs. Chin is in several ways typical of the older immigrants who have been coming to the United States since the mid-1960s. First, though originally from Toisan County, she spent more than ten years living in Hong Kong. Thus, she had some exposure to urban living before she came to the United States. Second, the time spent in Hong Kong provided her an opportunity to understand standard Cantonese, though she does not speak it. Third, she was brought over by a child rather than by a spouse and settled outside of the immediate area of Chinatown. Fourth, she experienced a considerable drop in occupational status as a result of her move to the United States. Though previously a successful entrepreneur, she became a thread cutter—the lowest status job within the garment industry, a position lower than those taken by many of her former laundry employees when they came to the United States. Fifth, she has no independent network of her own outside of the family. She is not a member of any organizations, and she does not have a circle of friends with whom she can chat or play mah-jong. Of all the immigrants described so far, she is the one most dependent on the family.

Being an Immigrant: Commonalities and Contrasts

Immigrating to the United States is very different from immigrating to Hong Kong. Older people who were born and raised in China and who subsequently moved to Hong Kong seldom express regrets about their moves. They often regret the unfortunate experiences of their relatives left behind, but by and large feel that economically speaking they are lucky to be in Hong Kong. When given a choice of remaining in Hong Kong or coming to the United States, older people face a difficult decision.

In 1946, Mrs. Wing, then a young wife living with her mother-in-law, left Toisan when her husband returned from the United States to escort them to Hong Kong. He wanted to bring the entire family to the United States, but Mrs. Wing had serious reservations. She asked him what life would be like for women who spoke no English and whether or not she would be able to purchase Chinese vegetables. In order to obtain reliable reports of what life in America was like she wrote to several friends who had already immigrated and begged them to tell her the true story—after all, everyone had already heard the stories that America was full of gold. Her friends wrote back that under no circumstances should she consider coming to the United States. Her husband bought a house in Yau Ma Tei in Kowloon where she raised her children. She did not come to the United States until 1965, when the social order in Hong Kong was beginning to deteriorate. Other immigrants stayed in Hong Kong until their elderly parents-in-law died because they believed that the older people would never be able to make the adjustment. Nearly every immigrant knew of older people who had come to the United States for a trial visit of several months and who had subsequently decided to return to Hong Kong. Only the direst of circumstances persuaded such people to spend their final years in the United States.

Most of the immigrants to the United States also had to deal with the restrictions placed on them with regard to contacting their relatives in the People's Republic of China. People in Hong Kong had much more direct access to information about what was happening in their home communities and could respond to pleas from relatives for assistance in ways that people living in the United States could not. Any letter from the United States indicated that the recipient had ties with the archenemy of the Chinese people and could cause them further political difficulties.

Mrs. Liu, a Christian who had received her college education in the United States, returned to China for several years before deciding to come to the United States again for graduate work in the mid-1940s. Her only sibling an older sister remained in China, and she and her husband stayed with the mother. As far as Mrs. Liu knew, her family was managing. Then in 1953, she received a letter that they had nothing to eat. She began to send them flour, tinned meats, and other items she knew to be in short supply. She wrote monthly, but her sister constantly warned her to be discreet: "You don't know the situation here. Don't send too much." In 1972, Mrs. Liu went back to China and observed her family's circumstances for the first time.

When I was there, I was careful about what I said. We were taken on tours of various factories and offices and told what they did there. Afterwards we would have to get up and tell about our reactions. I told them I admired Chairman Mao and what they have done for the people but that I myself could not be a good Communist, that I was too used to having my freedom. Of course I never said things like "I'm glad Chairman Mao took away my house and caused my family to suffer." But I didn't actually experience any of the suffering myself. I said that I did admire the fact that China was now better able to provide for all the people. Before there were a lot of poor people. There was so much suffering, but we didn't have to suffer. This is just my way of thinking. I saw how bad it was after the war in 1945. People just starved to death and were left on the street. The rich people, especially those with power, just ignored the poor. I didn't like that either. The present (1980) situation is generally better. But what they went through to get there! . . . My family's living standard shows a lot of improvement (since 1972). Before they were very disadvantaged. First they were the privileged class, and then the *un*privileged. Now they are back on their feet. Before the educated became the undesired. Before you were *guilty* of being educated and all that.

Chinese immigrants in the United States had to deal constantly with the fact that they were living in a country hostile to their homeland. Their loyalty was suspect, and they could not have direct contact with the Mainland until the 1970s. The more highly educated immigrants were also more aware of and upset by American ignorance of Chinese culture and Chinese life, and by the American tendency to fail to discriminate between Chinese and Japanese customs.

Also, immigrants to the United States faced much greater isolation than did those to Hong Kong. For those who did not speak English, settling in an area with other Chinese was the only possible way to retain a sense of control over their lives. Other Chinese were the people who could provide information about American life, access to jobs, and directions to the grocery stores. When elderly immigrants arrive in the Boston area and find their children living too far away for easy access to Chinatown, they find themselves revising their views on intergenerational living. Even those Chinese who are English speaking but who find their neighborhoods and workplaces occupied by non-Chinese prefer to socialize primarily with other Chinese. One woman sighed, "It is such a strain to always have to use English! It is a relief to be able to use Chinese."

One advantage of the United States over Hong Kong is its political stability. Sending children to the United States and following after them is an increasingly popular option for many two-step immigrants who left China for Hong Kong or Taiwan in the late 1940s and early 1950s. Another advantage over Hong Kong is that in the United States the elderly can be financially independent of their children. They are frequently appalled when they come to the United States and discover how expensive housing and educational costs can be. This was especially true in the 1960s and is still true in the case of immigrants arriving in the United States directly from China. Housing, medicine, and education are relatively cheap in the People's Republic of China though also relatively scarce. On learning that they are eligible for SSI, Medicaid, and subsidized housing, many are relieved to remove any financial burdens from their children that their presence might add.

Perhaps the greatest disadvantage of America compared to Hong Kong lies in the potential for intergenerational misunderstandings. We have already seen that there is a generation gap even in Hong Kong, but in the United States it can be much greater. Newcomers are also sometimes very surprised to discover that there are no servants in their children's houses and that they may have to perform household tasks that they did not have to perform in the old country. Just when they thought they could relax and be attended to, they may find that they are saddled with child-care and that no other adults are in the house during the day—no servants, no paid companions, no dutiful daughters-in-law.

There is no neat analytical system for predicting which individual will adapt well, will function without serious psychological disturbance, in American society. Generation status terms such as "first generation American (immigrant)" or "third generation American" are not very meaningful. People of even a second or third generation, if reared in an ethnic enclave, may be less "Westernized" than highly educated immigrants who have settled in the suburbs. Most of the people with whom I spoke were convinced that adapting to American culture (which they did not equate with losing their Chinese-ness) was a function of level of education, time spent in the United States, and the nature of the community in which one lived.

9 The Family

Issues in Intergenerational Relations

Older people, particularly those in rapidly changing societies, often have values and attitudes about family and personal goals that differ substantially from those of younger people. To a large extent such differences can be explained as cohort differences. Each cohort matures at a different point in historical time and is inevitably affected by the wider historical context. For example, persons coming of age in the 1930s faced the Great Depression. They had to search desperately for employment and to defer marriage and childbearing. Consequently, they placed great importance on securing permanent jobs and viewed staying out of debt or paying off a mortgage as major achievements. Their children, who came of age in the 1960s, faced a totally different economic environment, one of seemingly endless expansion. They often took for granted the possession of material things, and many reacted against what they perceived as their parents' timid and constricted lifestyles by embarking on lives of risk-taking, readily changing jobs, residences, and even spouses in the confident expectation that they could easily acquire others. Such contrasting approaches to life can understandably lead to parental anxiety.

Immigrant parents, however, face not only cohort but also cultural differences when attempting to communicate with their children. For example, Chinese families traditionally emphasized the male line. In the United States, however, despite symbolic acts such as assigning a child its father's surname, equality is more emphasized. A child in the United States is normally assumed to be as much the child of its mother (and her relatives) as of its father (and his relatives). Similarly, a parent in the United States can regard a daughter as a permanent family member in a way that a Chinese parent could not. In short, a family in which one generation is foreign-born and another is native-born or in which the generations have acculturated at different paces or in different ways frequently operates with conflicting assumptions about family goals. Members of such a family must pay particular attention to the nuances in each other's behavior and constantly strive to prevent differences from erupting into conflicts that threaten the integrity of the unit.

The major sources of intergenerational tension in Chinese families in the United States lie in child-rearing practices, role definitions, and goals of marriage. Secondarily, folk beliefs surrounding these arenas can lead to misunderstanding and annoyance on the part of both generations.

Child-rearing Practices

For young people eager to be accepted by their peers in American society, being different is often a source of embarrassment. They strive to be as much like their peers as possible, while at the same time trying to avoid antagonizing their parents. This is a delicate balancing act even when parents and children share the same definitions of what constitutes sensible or appropriate behavior. It is even more delicate when children feel themselves stigmatized because of "weird" parental or grandparental behavior particularly when their elders do not offer any explanations for such behavior. One young woman was severely chastised while discussing funeral arrangements with an older woman. The elder was upset that the younger had neglected to record the names and amounts of money contributed by several individuals towards the purchase of a wreath for the family of the deceased. When the younger accepted the criticism and replied that "the next time" she would be sure to record all the information correctly, the older broke out angrily into a string of unfamiliar Chinese phrases (presumably word charms against bad luck). A third party intervened to explain that it was very bad luck to say "the next time" in that context, as the phrase invited another funeral. Another woman recalled how her grandmother had started when she walked into the house wearing a white headband. White was the traditional color of mourning. A descendant walking in first thing in the morning wearing white was in a sense a harbinger of death.

In Hong Kong, I had a similar experience that, unexplained, made no sense. One of the youngsters in the family that I lived with had received a small plastic gun as a gift. He spent much of the evening excitedly walking around and shooting the various members of the household with no objections from any of the adults. The next morning as I sat at the table eating breakfast, he rushed up to me and shot me with his toy. To my and his surprise, his mother reacted instantly and furiously to his act. She ripped the gun out of his hand and struck him harshly several times. He ran screaming to the other side of the room. Noticing the look of total incomprehension on my face, she returned to the table and asked whether I understood why she had beaten the child. I confessed that I did not. "Because he shot you!" she explained. "But he shot me several times last night," I responded. "Nobody said anything then. . . . " To which she replied, in apparent disbelief of my ignorance, "But you just got up!" In short, timing is everything. To shoot someone first thing in the morning is to set the tone of that person's day. Someone whose day begins with a play gunshot may end the day with a real gunshot. One must behave very carefully first thing in the morning and in the first days of the New Year. My landlady was not unusual in applying physical force swiftly to make the point that certain behavior was unacceptable without at the same time providing the child an explanation as to *why* it was unacceptable. Verbal threats sometimes precede actual blows. My landlady admonished her youngest son by telling him that *I* would throw him out the window (we lived on the seventh floor) if he didn't keep quiet. Our next door neighbor threatened to flush him down the toilet.

Most adults who had been the objects of physical punishment in their childhoods did not seem resentful of this fact. They generally accepted it as a strategy that worked. Adults were more concerned about the possible psychological damage that could result from name-calling. Mrs. Chin's daughter-in-law, for example, was genuinely afraid that children might take seriously labels such as "dead boy" or "good-for-nothing." Even more adults objected to a common parental practice of setting up one of the children as a model for the others. The American-born daughter of Hoiping parents explained:

> They always tried to hold my oldest brother up as a model, but we wouldn't let them do this. Every time that he made a mistake we would jump in and say "See—that's what you want us to be like." We teased him so much that he said he was going to abdicate. We just didn't appreciate having to follow after him. He was favored as the older.

She added that the modeling issue had created a rift between her two brothers as the younger did not want to simply follow in his footsteps.

Other people have pointed out cases with which they were familiar in which there were similar outcomes—insecure younger siblings struggling to follow a successful older one or uncertainly wavering between attempting to follow and carving out their own paths. Children whose parents had high aspirations for them sometimes felt that they were not very bright and unable to live up to parental expectations even though they graduated from prestigious universities and earned advanced degrees. (See Kessen 1975 and Munro 1977 for a fuller discussion of the significance of modeling in Chinese culture).

Some children refuse to play the game at all. Instead of acceptance by parents they seek acceptance by peers. One man described his younger sister's rebellion:

> She was the only Chinese kid at her school until they started the bilingual program out there a few years ago. But she made it clear that she wasn't interested in hanging around with Chinese kids - they were too namby-pamby. She also didn't hang around with the White kids, but with Blacks and Puerto Ricans.

A psychiatrist serving as a consultant to a public school system with a substantial minority of immigrant students believes that the boys face a more difficult situation than the girls in adolescence. The girls even if they immigrated at the same age tend to be more skilled verbally than the boys. They prefer to date American-born Chinese boys or Caucasian boys rather than inarticulate immigrant boys. The boys also know that the stereotype of the passive Chinese causes other ethnic groups to disparage them, and in compensation they attempt to cultivate a macho style which does not contribute to their academic development. Some of these boys turn to the streets and become involved in gang activities.

Role Definitions

Parental (and grandparental) definitions of responsible parenthood are buttressed by the belief that their experience provides them with the necessary perspective to help children through life and in decision-making. One man who had been born in Boston but reared in China following the death of his parents sighed as he recounted the conflict his parents-in-law were having with their son's children.

> But, you know, it's hard for the grandparents and the grandchildren. The old people want to give instruction, but young

people don't want to take it. (What kind of instruction?) Things like when they should be back in the house. "Don't stay out after ten o'clock." "Why do you go there?" "Don't go there." "Why don't you study?" "Don't eat that. Eat this. This is good for you." They want the kids to drink herbal soups, and the kids don't want it. I'm always having to be the middleman and explain things to the grandparents. (Why you? Why not the son who lives over there?) Oh, they don't have a good relationship. And mixed marriage! That raised hell all over the place! A grandson married a Caucasian.

In arguing with a young woman about the virtues of an arranged marriage, 75-year-old Mrs. Ng stated flatly: "The parent knows more than the kid. Don't you think your parents know more than you do?" To her it was unthinkable that someone would disagree with this proposition. Similarly a (non-Chinese) scholar of Chinese philosophy shared his tactic for persuading his students that age and wisdom are linked. On the first day of class he asks them whether they feel smarter or dumber than they felt a few years ago. No college student will believe that he was smarter in high school.

Some parents who are too intent on guiding their children wind up alienating them. Other parents recognize their limitations and allow children the right to make wrong decisions. Mrs. Choi, a middle-aged immigrant from Hong Kong, brought five children through adolescence in the Boston area. She described her dilemma:

Being a parent is very difficult. There are so many ways you can go wrong. My husband says I am too softhearted, but it is difficult to change when the alternative is to be hard-hearted. You see things that your children want and know you can give to them. It is only natural for parents to want to give things to their children. I remember that when I was growing up, there were many things that I couldn't have, and I remember how I felt then. So now I want to give them things that I couldn't have. But then they come to expect these things, and they don't appreciate what you do for them. It is give, give, give, and they are very disappointed if they can't have the things. But then you wind up spoiling them.

Despite working all day when this mother goes home to her husband and four children, she finds that she must do all the housework as well. "My sons—they are typical males. They do not even consider it appropriate to wash a dish. As for my daughter—I remember how hard it was being a girl, and I know that when my daughter marries, it will all fall on her shoulders. I guess I want to spare her this as long as I can." When Mrs. Choi's own mother came on a visit from Hong Kong, she was shocked to find her grandchildren playing no role in carrying out household chores. She advised her daughter to simply *tell* the children what to do. Mrs. Choi, however, firmly believes that "you cannot tell this generation to do things," that any pressure simply intensifies their opposition. She will explain why she thinks something is bad and then hopes that the children will come to share her opinion.

> I knew when they were in high school that the two older boys were trying drugs. They knew I disapproved, but they had to try it for themselves and finally decided that that wasn't for them. Another time one of the boys wanted to take a job as a bouncer at a place in Kenmore Square. He even had to get a gun to do this. I told him it was a bad idea, but that if he had to, he could try it out. He did it for just one night and decided it wasn't for him. I have always told them that no matter what my door is always open to them.

To a certain extent Mrs. Choi's "softheartedness" serves to balance her husband's more authoritarian approach. He flatly vetoed his oldest son's choice of job in the hope of persuading him (unsuccessfully) to follow him into the restaurant business. All of his children have attended college or are college-bound and counter his efforts to dictate their employment by saying that they went to college to avoid restaurant work.

Men who grew up in China conveyed vivid images of controlling fathers. Mr. Au, a 48-year-old man whose father had become a military officer under the Nationalists, related that he and his sister were terrified of their "typical" father. They sometimes ran out of the room when they saw him coming. Their father had almost no casual interaction with them. The only time they were together was at dinner, a very formal and serious affair during which their father engaged in "spiritual training." "The Chinese have two kinds of education: school education and home or family education. The family education which emphasizes correct moral training is the most important. My father would give talks at this time." Mr. Chen, a 67-year-old man whose father had been a banker, was quite intimidated by him and explained that he had preferred to talk over his problems with his older brother rather than with his father because he was never sure how much the decisions and advice his father recommended were in his own or in his father's interests. He felt his brother would be less self-centered. There were no displays of paternal affection in his home. "The father might love you, but he does not show it. Even if you do something right, he would never praise you to your face. He might tell his friends 'This is a good boy,' but he would never tell you. It was below his dignity to say it." Both Mr. Au and Mr. Chen hoped for warmth in their relationships with their own children, but they did not aspire to the "pal" relationship that some Americans have with their children. They felt that the role of father carried with it special qualities that they did not want to abandon.

I asked Mr. Au what he thought about the American practice of using the first name in many different kinds of social contexts including the parent-child context. He disapproved:

> The use of the given name is something appropriate for friends because it implies equal status, but I would not want my children to address me by my given name. Anyone can use a given name, but very few can legitimately use the kinship term. I want to be my son's friend, but I want more to be his father. This is more special and precious and should be acknowledged.

Mr. Chen prides himself on the warm relationship he has with his children despite the fact that he has been the primary disciplinarian in the family. He described his children as "jumping up and down" when they saw him coming home "even if I had no candy to give them."

All of the Chen children are currently living out of state, and none are expected to return permanently to the Boston area. Accordingly, with encouragement from their children, the Chens have made the somewhat reluctant decision to move to California, where the children all live. As the children began to move out of the parental home, Mr. Chen attempted to modify his paternal role. He views himself as the cement of the family and once a month sends a "Bulletin" to all the children. He types up information he has garnered from each child's letters and makes certain that everyone is kept informed of everyone else's activities. He keeps a carbon for himself and now has a stack of Bulletins set aside.

Mr. Dow, a 64-year-old Hawaii-born Chinese American, also circulates a lengthy newsletter to his children. He first began this practice, through letters, when the children went off to college, to keep them in touch with what was happening in Hawaii. Later he expanded the letters into a newsletter which he sends not only to the children, but to more distant relatives, friends, and acquaintances. In 1980, he hoped to send out monthly newsletters, but he fell behind. His eight-page, single-spaced December edition was the seventh in the 1980 series. The first page of the newsletter was given over to salutations to the many recipients, such as nephews Phil and Tim in San Antonio, and Cousin Daniel, Ph.D. at GE. Probably because December in Honolulu is memorable for the Japanese attack on Pearl Harbor in 1941, the newsletter featured accounts of incidents dating back to World War II. He related how his Boston-born wife and sister-in-law left Hong Kong during the Japanese occupation and found their way to the American forces in Kunming. He described his feelings for General Stilwell, for whom he had boundless admiration, and who gave the commencement address at his army language school.

These efforts to preserve family bonds, to share historical experiences, and to impart advice from a distance (see below for the case of Mr. Chiang) recall the example of Mr. Lam and his nearly one hundred young pen pals. What this phenomenon suggests is that at least some men are struggling to find an acceptable outlet for their wisdom and experience. With children gone and employment over, they have few opportunities to display their knowledge or to have a direct impact on the lives of younger people. No women were involved in similar activities—partly because fewer of them are literate, but also because they do not see advice in worldly as opposed to familial matters as part of their responsibility.

Many of the children who grew up in Sze Yap had absentee fathers working in the United States. They met their fathers for the first time in their late teens when they joined them in America and lived under their watchful eyes. Wayward boys were sometimes sent back to China. In fact, parents were so fearful of losing children to American ways that even some American-born children were sent back with their mothers to the village, to be raised in a more wholesome environment. Other sons of absentee fathers fled with their mothers and sisters to Hong Kong following World War II. Instead of working in paternal laundries, groceries, or restaurants, they took advantage of the expanding economy of Hong Kong by investing in commercial and construction enterprises.

Sometimes, however, fathers and sons had major disagreements on the uses to which the remittances were put. Fathers who had labored long and hard in a foreign land and who had lived extremely frugal lives in order to be able to provide for their family members occasionally learned that their sons were not as careful about money as they themselves had been. Mr. Kwok, for example, had worked several jobs in the western part of the United States before finally buying his own one-man restaurant in a mountain state. His oldest son in Hong Kong invested the money in real estate. In the 1950s, old Mr. Kwok turned his restaurant over to a son-in-law and retired to Hong Kong. In 1959, his oldest son, having made a handsome profit on his investments, purchased a house in the Yau Yat Chuen district of Kowloon, a high status area of single-family homes on tree-lined streets. To celebrate the purchase and move, the younger Mr. Kwok (then about 30 years old) organized a lavish banquet for many people. Old Mr. Kwok thought both ventures were an extravagant waste of money. He lost his temper at the banquet and embarrassed his son in front of all his friends. He complained loudly about the unnecessary expenditures. He wondered aloud whose money had been used to pay for all this and answered his own question "Mine, of course!"

After this incident, it became extremely difficult for father and son to continue in the investment business together. Not long thereafter young Mr. Kwok came to the United States, where he took over the tiny restaurant from his brother-in-law. His father remained in Hong Kong until the time of the Cultural Revolution, when he became anxious about the security of his funds. Then, without any mention to his son, he decided to liquidate his assets. He sold all their Hong Kong properties and moved back to the United States. Now nearly fifteen years later, the two Kwoks are reconciled. Their finances and households are separate, but they live in the same large West Coast city. Mr. Kwok has shown himself to be a filial son; he arranges birthday banquets for his parents, spends holidays with them, and every few days brings a load of groceries from his own store to them.

The Kwans had a similar arrangement—a father working in the United States and a son making investments in Hong Kong. Mr. Kwan operated on a much smaller scale than Mr. Kwok, owning only a single large apartment. He had to supplement his father's remittances by renting out some of the rooms, and he himself held a job with a transportation company. Life in Hong Kong seemed good, and Mr. Kwan did not feel driven to have outstanding achievements. With reluctance, he uprooted his family from Hong Kong in 1971 and moved to Boston at old Mr. Kwan's insistence. At first the Kwans lived together, but soon found the situation overwhelming. There were eight young grandchildren sharing space with the four adults.

Old Mrs. Kwan was very superstitious and imposed restrictions on hair washing and other activities which the grandchildren could not understand.

Young Mr. Kwan did not have the best work habits. A relative who had been his first employer refused to keep him. Furthermore, Mr. Kwan enjoyed gambling. His wife worked in a garment factory to ensure that there would be a steady source of income with which she could run the household. One day, I ran into Mr. Kwan while he was having a cup of coffee and waiting for the van which would take him to his restaurant job out in the suburbs. He volunteered his view as to why there are disagreements between the generations.

The major problem between the generations is in spending habits. The older people have no work and, therefore, no steady source of income. Their limited income causes them to be very careful about spending money. They can scarcely bear to part with any! The younger people, however, are still working. They like to spend money, and they know that more money will be coming in in the next week. Thus, there is a major difference of opinion in how money should be spent. For this reason it is sometimes difficut for younger people to live together with the older ones.

In order to bring his son and his family to the United States, old Mr. Kwan had borrowed over $3,000 from relatives. These relatives pressed very hard for repayment. As Mr. Kwan senior was withdrawing from the work force, he was understandably concerned about his son's casual attitude. Unfortunately, the two men continued to have a strained relationship until Mr. Kwan senior's death in 1981.

Although the relationship between father and son is usually considered central to the organization of the Chinese family, this male-centered orientation conflicts with American values that parents should love and treat their children equally. Chinese prescriptions call for sons to take primary responsibility for elderly parents whereas American prescriptions call for children of both sexes to take responsibility. An American-born daughter-in-law can make a good case for taking in her own parents rather than her parents-in-law, but the voluntary assumption of this responsibility is not necessarily recognized by the parents. Daughters who contrary to traditional requirements cared for their parents sometimes found that they were left nothing or very trivial amounts compared to their brothers.

Girls frequently resent the preferential treatment that they perceive their brothers receiving. They do not always agree that they are peripheral members of the family and should be willing to accept a lesser share of the family's resources. Daughters have also expressed resentment on learning that their mothers were not considered full members of the families into which they had married. One American-born woman felt that her own mother had in some ways been victimized by her in-laws.

> I would hear that blood is thicker than water. My aunt, the one I stayed with in California for a year, forced on me the idea that she was closer to me than my mother because she was my father's sister. That was not a good year. They were always concerned about my father's health, afraid that he would have a heart attack because of working so hard. They never worried about my mother's health. They never stopped to wonder if the reason she was tired all the time might not have had a health basis. My mother had two myocardial infarctions though we did not realize it at the time. . . . We have been a close extended family, but we all feel that we are our mother's child too. We kids are closer to our mother.

Different notions of the proper relationship between the sexes also generate mistrust between husbands and wives and across generations. One woman who came from Hong Kong in her mid-30s had to deal with men in the course of running her business. Traditionalists could not believe that these encounters were sexually innocent. Someone reported her to her husband for improper behavior, and he had her followed until convinced that there was no basis to the accusation. She now has a window in her office wall so that should a man come on an errand, he is visible to everyone else in the company, and rumors can be easily denounced by scores of witnesses.

Another potential source of misunderstanding in Chinese families is the meaning to attach to the expression of emotions or more likely the relative lack of such expression. Chinese often view American middle class families as composed of people who go around saying "I love you" to each other—husbands to wives, parents to children, siblings to siblings. This is not ordinarily characteristic of their own family lives, and young people sometimes wonder what this lack means. One third-generation Chinese-American came to his older sister with this problem.

He came to me and said, "Sara, I think there's something

wrong with our family." Of course, he didn't state it in such a direct way. He really hemmed and hawed. He said "We don't touch or kiss or anything as a family." I remember everytime I left home (on a long trip) I would give my mother a peck. She didn't exactly force me away, but she didn't really encourage me either. . . . In our family, love was based more on respect and understanding. For example, last year my younger brother took off five days of his vacation to go to California to help my older brother pack up a U-Haul and move to Michigan. But we don't have any great demonstrations of affection or talks between us. It is all low-key. You read a lot through actions. . . . Once I went for a long time with a Jewish fellow. He was very expressive. Every time he saw you, he would extend his arms and embrace you and ask how you've been. It took me a long time to get used to that.

I asked a Hong Kong-raised college-educated woman of 30 who worked in Chinatown how Chinese would talk among themselves about relations between husband and wife.

Well, they would not say they loved each other. To tell this to other Chinese would be to invite ridicule. For example, one of my (Chinese) co-workers brought in a pile of photos taken when she and her husband had been on vacation. In many of the pictures the couple were holding hands. People made all kinds of remarks. "Oh, so you are still dating?" "Oh, are you such a little child that someone has to hold your hand?" 'You already have a son, and you're still holding hands? Aren't you afraid he will laugh at you?"

She added that a Chinese parent would not say "I love you" straight out to a child, but would indicate that love through behavior. "They would touch them a lot, pat them." Another woman from Hong Kong concurred. She rejected the word love and replaced it with concern. "You show your feelings through your actions, not through words. You say 'You'd better wear your coat—it's cold out,' or 'Come and have something to eat' when the person comes in. You ask about their health. You show that you care about them." Still another Hong Kong born, American-educated young woman told me that she would rather use English than Cantonese to talk with me: "Chinese do not sit around and talk directly about their feelings, so I find it difficult to articulate feelings in Cantonese because I don't have an adequate vocabulary. . . . I never saw my mother kiss my father. My mother never said 'I love you' to me until after we moved to the States, and she said it in English!"

Such reticence is even greater among males. One man who spent most of his life in the Chinatown-South End area stated:

> Most kids never see their families express affection. Ninety eight percent probably were never hugged by their fathers. Ninety eight percent probably never saw their fathers kiss their mothers. I was only hugged as an adult. . . . I'm in a Chinese men's group. It is the only one of its kind in the United States. I'm proud to be able to say that I was able to kiss my father, say that I loved him, and have him do the same and say that he was proud of me. Out of one hundred guys, you would get a positive answer on these things from very few—mostly from the human service types. There is no confidential sharing.

Another dimension to this reticence is that one is not supposed to state one's needs directly. Family members should be able to realize what one's needs are and to act on them before any requests are made. Parents expressed tremendous disappointment when children failed to attend to their various needs. This disappointment has a double edge to it. First, a parental need is going unmet, but more importantly the parent has to ask why he or she has apparently unfilial children. If the children are not filial, where can one place the blame? Some children, while feeling strongly about their parents, are unaware that initiatives are supposed to come from them. Nor do they realize that any filial act which they perform affirms to the parents (and to whomever else witnesses the filial behavior) their success in raising their children. American-raised children are additionally handicapped by often not having had the opportunity to observe their own parents' behavior to the grandparent generation. They have no model other than the American one of apparent distance between the generations in old age.

Goals of Marriage

Traditionally, marriage was viewed as a family affair and not simply an individual's affair. Family goals for a marriage included the provision of the next generation, the services of an adult worker (a daughter-in-law), and the extension of family influence through ties established with families from outside the village. If the young couple got along well, so much the better, though companionship was not viewed as an important or worthy goal in its own right. Especially important to most Chinese was the durability of the marriage. As one informant put it, "Fate brought you together, and together you must stay even if the marriage is not a good one."

Most Chinese older people were convinced that Chinese marriages were more stable than American marriages. Stability, however, should not be equated with satisfaction. Chinese had other ways than divorce for dealing with unhappy marriages. First of all, a couple could have a covert separation. They would continue to live in the same household though for all intents and purposes leading separate lives. The husband would busy himself with work and public functions and the wife with children and household management. Emotional estrangement was not considered an adequate cause for breaking up a family. Informants believed that a shortsighted concern or emphasis on the character of one's partner generates unnecessary discontent. Mrs. Choi explained:

> When you love someone, you can't just love their good points. Suppose someone is six points good and four points bad. You have to love the bad points as well as the good; otherwise when people find just one point no good, they will want to leave the other person. If you think you are perfect, maybe you can think that way. But we ought to look at ourselves first to see how perfect we are. Then when you consider that the other person has forgiven many of your imperfections, you are more willing to be tolerant of theirs.

A couple could also have an overt separation with the wife remaining in her husband's village, often with his parents, while he sought a job in a distant location. A man also had the option of bringing additional wives into his household. Women understandably had mixed responses to such a turn of events and did not themselves have the option of bringing in additional husbands. The most acceptable reason for bringing in an additional wife was to provide a male heir. If a first wife had not borne any children or had only borne daughters, a husband could acquire a secondary wife to provide a son. Theoretically, the first wife retained her status as the manager of the household and might even play a role in the selection of her co-wife. In contemporary Hong Kong, women becoming secondary wives now have no recognized legal status, and do not move in with their husbands' first wives. When a Chinese man in the United States has more than one wife, the first is usually in China or Hong Kong and the second in the United States. As long as he continues to support the first wife and she has no desire to emigrate to the United States, people do not become very upset about this. After all, the first wife is only rearing the children and is not providing him with any other wifely services. She should be concerned that he have someone to look after him. If anything happens to him, she would lose his remittances. Traditionally, the ability to support two families indicated a financially successful man.

Most younger women do not view additional spouses philosophically. They would seek a divorce before they would tolerate such a situation. Nor are they willing to tolerate domineering mothers-in-law. They have learned from their own mothers' suffering.

> My mother was twenty five when she married. She always emphasized to me that I should have an independent life and not get married young. I grew up in a marital situation characterized by ambivalence. My mother was considered "the fast woman from Shanghai," and people speculated on how she had snared my father. . . . It was quite a shock for my mother to go from that independent and romantic life in victorious Shanghai to the traditional family of my father with that matriarchal mother-in-law right next door. I would not put up with the stress that my mother did.

The major concrete difficulty that different goals for marriage present to Chinese families is the relative emphasis the different generations place on the parent child tie compared to the husband wife. The mother mentioned above described her situation to her daughter: "Your father is not an independent man. He is married to two women (wife and mother), and I'm not sure I hold the upper hand." Given the potential conflict between mothers-in-law and daughters-in-law, it is no surprise that young couples establish their own residences apart from the parents.

Another major difficulty is the view of marriage as a family rather than an individual matter. Family members frequently feel that they have the right and sometimes the responsibility to intervene in the marital relationship of relatives. Usually they want to play a mediating role, but in the United States such mediation is often taken as meddling. When the marriage of Mrs. Lim's daughter began to fail, Mrs. Lim was not kept closely informed, but she was certain that if she had been allowed to play a part other options besides divorce could have been considered. "With a third person around, they might have been able to work out their marriage. I was not living near them. Maybe I could have talked with them, seen what the problem was, brought them together. But young people are not like that, not like the Chinese way."

Chinese parents in America face a problem seldom faced by Chinese parents in Hong Kong—the marriage of a child to someone not of Chinese ancestry. Most parents fear that the partners in such marriages will not have a shared understanding of what marriage is all about. Many Chinese parents have knowledge of the American lifestyle only from the mass media. Such sources would suggest that Americans view marriage as something temporary, lasting only as long as romantic or sexual love. These parents do not want to see their children frustrated when their partners walk out. They also fear that a non-Chinese spouse will alienate the Chinese partner from his or her natal family and that the grandchildren will be raised as English-speakers unable to communicate with the grandparents.

When parents and children have different ideas about the purpose of marriage or the qualities which make for a good spouse, tension over spouse selection can be great. Parents who force these issues take great risks, and children under pressure sometimes suffer terribly. One young man, the only son of a well-educated couple, drew his parents' wrath when he began to share an apartment with a non-Chinese girl. He and his sisters had been raised in the United States, and his sisters had all made acceptable decisions on spouses. All their husbands were Ph.D.'s of Chinese descent. His parents made it clear that his continuing with this girlfriend would result in his loss of membership in the family. When he visited the parental home, his parents got up from the table whenever he sat down. They also told his siblings not to talk with him. In great distress, he eventually broke up with his girlfriend. He then went into a depression during which time he became a ski bum and thought about driving his car into a telephone pole. Finally, he redirected his energy into his career, and by the time he was in his mid-30s, he was telling his friends that he was interested in meeting some nice Chinese girls.

Many parents, however, are philosophical. Like the Huas they realize that the children are exposed primarily to non-Chinese, and they are not surprised when the children date non-Chinese and announce their plans to marry. One well-educated mother explained how she dealt with her only child's decision to marry a Westerner.

TABLE 3.
Sex and Generation Status of Out-Marrying Chinese N = 41

GENERATION STATUS	SEX		Total	Divorces
	Males	Females		
Foreign-Born	6	5	11	4
U.S.-Born (2nd Generation)	4	8	12	3
U.S.-Born (3rd or Later Gen.)	5	7	12	0
U.S.-Born (Gen. Status Unknown)	4	2	6	1
Total	19	22	41	8

I would have liked to have had a Chinese son-in-law. But then I decided that all people are God's people no matter what country they come from—so I changed my mind. I did this before she made the decision to get married. Already they were friends, so why should I be against it? I didn't want to have conflict with her. The best thing is that they love each other. If I'm against it and cause conflict, I may feel sorry. I knew they would get married so I changed my mind. I talked with my husband about it, and he agreed with me. We did not make it a problem.

In an attempt to determine how realistic parental fears of the instability of cross-ethnic marriages are, I examined the genealogies provided by my informants and added a few cases of non-relatives with whose marital situations they were familiar. I located 41 instances of persons of Chinese ancestry marrying persons of non-Chinese ancestry (see table 3). In nearly all cases the non-Chinese partner was of European ancestry (a very few were of Asian or Hispanic ancestry). Immigrant Chinese who took non-Chinese partners were usually highly educated and married classmates or people met in their professional lives. Jewish partners were disproportionately represented as marriage partners largely because they too tend to be highly educated and in the professions.

Of the 41 marriages 8 have ended in divorce, and likelihood of divorce correlates closely with generation status. None of the marriages of third (or later) generation Chinese-Americans have ended in divorce. The absence of divorces could be due partly to the relative youth of the marriage partners in the third category, but more likely it reflects the importance of a common background to marital durability.

When one spouse is foreign-born and the other is American-born, the partners generally have a substantial cultural gap of which they are not fully aware until they are already married and have switched from dating roles to marital roles. Roles in dating, are relatively easily learned from movies or through observations of one's peers. Conceptions of marital roles, however, are much more likely to derive from one's observations of one's own family. Consequently, a seemingly Westernized Chinese may suddenly appear very traditional following the wedding. A young woman with an interest in Chinese culture married a professional man from Taiwan who has many relatives in the Boston area. She admitted:

> You know my husband and his family and friends don't realize that there is a Western side to me. When I am with them, I speak Chinese, and we do Chinese things together. They don't want to acknowledge that there are other dimensions to my personality. In the first year of marriage it has taken a lot of work. I knew a lot of things—I mean I had read a lot of things, but I didn't have to confront these things in any personal way. It took a lot of adjusting, but at least I could go into work (she has many Chinese co-workers) and say "My husband said such and such to me. Why would he say such a thing?" They would tell me "That is a compliment," and I would be very surprised. It took a lot of getting used to. Like he will simply ignore me, act as if I'm not even there, especially if there are other people around. If I ask him something, he won't even look at me when he replies. He'll just look straight ahead and answer. Now I am able to say "Look, now I'm being Western" and get him to understand that I have other needs.

She is fortunate in having people around who can do cultural translation. Not everyone is so lucky.

As we have seen, there are numerous situations in which cultural and cohort differences in child-care practices, role definitions, and goals of marriage can contribute to disagreements and misunderstandings between the generations. When a disinterested third party is available to provide cultural translation or mediation services, many of these problems evaporate. In the absence of a trusted third party, however, many older people have no acceptable way to interpret their children's apparent rejection of them or their advice. They fear that they themselves may be at fault and realize that in the United States the cards are stacked on the side of the younger generation. As in Hong Kong, differences of opinion do not automatically result in disputes. Members of both generations have learned to avoid topics likely to cause arguments. In the United States though it is more acceptable to "resolve issues" by bringing them into the open, and in some circles it is a touchstone of maturity to stand up to an "unreasonable" older person. Consequently co-residence of parents and adult children is less frequent in the United States than in Hong Kong, and elderly housing holds special attractions for immigrant parents.

Household Composition and Residence Patterns

An examination of the living arrangements of elderly Chinese reveals that intact couples continue to live in their own homes and seldom live with a married child's family. Of the 9 cases in which an unmarried child lives with a parent, all occur in the parental home. In some of these cases, the children have been continuously co-resident; in a few cases, they went away to college and returned while still in their 20s or early 30s. All of these children are American-born.

The 3 cases of married couples living with a married child's family are all different in background. In one case, a couple in their 70s came to the United States from Taiwan following retirement. As they are not in good health, they prefer the security of living with a child. They have alternated residence between their younger and older sons. They first lived with their younger son, but he had a non-Chinese

TABLE 4.
Living Arrangements of Noninstitutionalized Elderly Chinese N = 65

LIVING ARRANGEMENTS	SEX		Couples	Total
	Male	Female★		
Spouse Only	–	–	27	27
Unmarried Child(ren)	1	3	5	9
Married Child(ren) (or Child-in-Law)	2	13	3	18
Alone	0	5	–	5
Other	4	1	1	6
Total	7	22	36	65

★Three females are counted twice: first as part of a couple and later as widows.

spouse, and there was family friction, so the couple joined their older son whose wife was still in Taiwan. By the time the senior daughter-in-law was about to join her husband in the United States, the younger son had divorced his Caucasian wife and married a Chinese woman. His parents moved back with him. Another couple, the Ais (Mrs. Hua's relatives), had moved into their daughter's home in the United States while trying to decide whether or not to move permanently from Taiwan. While they were in Taiwan, their daughter's marriage broke up. When they returned to the United States, their daughter had remarried, and they settled near but not with her. At last report, their younger son who has just married a girl his father helped him meet had moved in with them. The final case, that of a couple living with their married daughter's family, has turned out to be a temporary situation. This couple had moved out of state, but the husband re-turned when the company from which he had retired appeared to have a need of his services again (new contracts with the People's Republic of China). The wife did not want to quit her out-of-state job or sell their house until they were sure of the length of his employment, so they moved in with the only child in the Boston area who had a house large enough to accommodate everyone. When the employment proved short-term, the couple again left the state.

All but one of the remaining 15 cases of a parent living with a married child's family involve a widowed parent. The 1 married parent lives with a married daughter out of state while his wife lives with their unmarried son. She felt her son would benefit by parental su-pervision while he worked on his graduate degree. He had been a diffident student in Taiwan, and his adviser had written him a re-commendation only after a lengthy conversation with his mother. Of these 15 cases of parents residing with married children, 3 are contin-uous, the parent and child having never lived separately. These are all cases of sons, such as Mrs. Chin's youngest son, who have never left their widowed mothers. Twelve cases are discontinuous in na-ture, and in all but 1, the parent has moved in with the child. The primary reasons for joining a married child's household were: illness or disability (5 cases), widowhood (4), retirement and relocation from Taiwan (1), and loss of residence (1). The child who moved in with a parent was actually a son-in-law who moved into his mother-in-law's home when he came East for an advanced degree. Upon com-pletion of his degree, he decided to remain in the area, so his wife returned from the West Coast and moved in with her mother also until they were able to purchase their own home.

Most cases of intergenerational living were of parents and sons (17 instances) rather than of parents and daughters (10 instances). Although several parents expressed a preference for living with daughters, most of them currently live either with a spouse only or alone. Whether or not they will act on these preferences remains to be seen. In 3 cases, daughters were living in the parental home. In 3 other cases, parents had no other children living in the United States so joined their daughters. In 1 of these 3 cases, there is an adopted son, but the widowed mother has long been closely involved with her daughter's family. The daughter was abandoned by her husband, and the mother helped to raise the daughter's children. One mother simply gets along better with her son-in-law than with her daughter-in-law. She has other children living out of state and stays with them for visits of several weeks duration. The remaining 3 cases have already been discussed above: the couple who moved in with a daughter because of their uncertain employment situation, a man whose wife had gone to check up on their student son, and a woman whose son-in-law and daughter moved in with her.

Wu (1975:273) declared it is false to assume that the majority of the elderly Chinese are living with their sons and daughters. In her sample, almost two-thirds of Mandarin-speaking aged in the Los Angeles area were living independently. She also found that Chinese people seem to have a more positive view of intergenerational living when they have less experience with it. When she asked 50 aged and 50 middle-aged Chinese (all but one of whom were foreign-born) about their preferences towards living arrangements, she obtained the following results (Wu 1974:132-140):

	Aged	Middle-Aged
Together	6	29
Separately	39	14
Depends on Situation	5	7

As she points out, most of the aged in her study have had the experience of living with an adult child, whereas most of the middle-aged have not. Most of her sample had lived with children when first arriving in the United States but then came to prefer separate living. When she asked about elderly housing, 37 out of 50 elderly indicated an interest in it. The aged who favored separate living arrangements used such phrases as generation gap, differences in lifestyle, inconvenience, personal freedom, intergenerational conflicts. The aged who favored co-residence emphasized parental needs for care or companionship. One 74-year-old male insisted that the parents should live with their adult children in order to provide guidance for the children and grandchildren. These responses are very similar to those made by elderly Chinese in the Boston area.

There are advantages to elderly housing that attract people to it even when the co-residence with children has been a good experience. One 67-year-old well-educated widow from Taiwan who has spent time living with both of her married children and who remains on good terms with them explained the advantages of her living arrangement.

> When the children are grown up, you feel like a guest in their home. With friends it is different. You have more interests in common, more activities to share, and so you get along better. Also you can leave each other if you want to go to your own place. This is not possible when living with your own children. Old people are not like young people, not always the same, not always sharing the same interests. This makes getting along sometimes difficult. It is important to feel comfortable—especially on a day to day basis, otherwise you have to worry about hurting other people's feelings. If I want to eat meat, take a nap, watch TV, I can do it when I want.

This woman is active in a Mandarin-speaking church group. She enjoys painting and calligraphy, keeping one set of pens and brushes in her apartment and another set in her daughter's home for use during weekend visits. She shares her meals with a close relative who lives in the same elderly housing facility.

A disproportionate number of the Chinese who come from Taiwan are Christian. This is in contrast to most of the Sze Yap immigrants who either are not Christians at all or became Christians only in old age. Many of the Chinese Christians were converted in China by evangelical missionaries and express their religious beliefs in ways that sometimes embarrass their American-educated children. Although Christians themselves, the children prefer a less emotional approach to religion and try to tone down their parents' emphasis on sin and damnation. An elderly family member who preaches to relatives and exhorts them to save their souls is not easily endured.

Mrs. Mao, an 80-year-old widow, has had family problems for many years. She suffered an abusive stepmother, lost her husband while she was very young, and had to face a son and daughter-in-law who did not want her to come to the United States. She felt powerless to change her family relationships, but she did have the satisfaction of seeing God punish her tormentors. Her stepmother, who died during World War II, suffered greatly from edema. Her legs were so swollen that people could actually see the water trapped inside. Mrs. Mao believed that this was God's way of showing her the end of a bad person. God surely knew her stepmother's deeds and her heart. "God can see through a man's heart. One should not do evil deeds or one will be punished." Later in Taiwan Mrs. Mao underwent a conversion experience and began to preach. After her son's family moved to the United States, she waited for them to apply to bring her over, but they did not take any action. They, especially her daughter-in-law, did not want her to come.

> Nevertheless God knew what was in her heart as he does with everyone's heart. He punished her by letting her fall from a high place. Her back was injured and some of her fingers were broken. Her spinal cord was in such terrible shape that she had to rest in bed for several months.

After this, Mrs. Mao began working on a way to come to the United States without her son's assistance and did so. Needless to say, she was not welcomed into her son's household, and she eventually found her way to elderly housing. Now she spends most of her time reading the Bible or in the company of another member of her church who shares her beliefs and speaks English.

All of the residents of elderly housing whom we encountered were foreign-born, as were their children. Of the 18 cases, 14 had had experience living with their adult children in the United States, although this was not necessarily the arrangement from which they moved directly into elderly housing.

In 10 of the cases of intergenerational living, parents lived with sons and in 4 cases with daughters. One couple had different living arrangements from each other because the husband was living in Boston while the wife lived first in Toisan and then in Hong Kong with her son and his family before joining her husband in elderly housing. None of the married couples had previously lived with daughters, though 3 widows and one widower did.

Family Interaction and Mobilization

For Chinese parents in the United States dispersal of children is a more expected event than it is in Hong Kong. Furthermore, because there are many governmental programs to assist older people, they can usually manage on their own even when retired. Consequently, the moving out of children is not as stressful for Chinese parents in the United States. Widowhood, disability, and illness, however, remain major events requiring the attention of the whole family. Examples of how four families dealt with such crises are detailed below.

Mrs. Choi was confronted first by a widowed father-in-law in Boston and a few years later by her mother's widowhood in Hong Kong. Her father-in-law had been working in the United States for many years. Although he was able to bring his wife over, they never had any children, and Mrs. Choi's husband became their paper son. When the Choi family first moved to Boston, they settled near the old couple. In 1974, old Mrs. Choi died, and he could no longer operate his laundry.

> He was forced to give up the work because his mind was failing. He could no longer remember what went with what and mixed up batches of clothes, giving the wrong things to the customers. When he moved in with us, he just sat alone all day with nothing to do. In the past, old people did not suffer such isolation or feel so useless because they were surrounded by other people and because there were many little tasks they could be given around the house. This is no longer the case, and they have nothing to occupy their minds. If they were to go to elderly housing at least things are available for them to do.

Mrs. Choi and her husband suggested to the old man that he move into newly opened elderly housing in Chinatown (from Brookline) and had, in fact, paid two months rent on the apartment that they expected him to take. But he refused to move in. He would not even go for a look at the place because, he insisted, it was more fitting to live in his son's household. When he ran his laundry, he had enjoyed regular social interaction, but he became increasingly confused at his son's home where he had no one to talk to most of the day. He died in 1978 following a stroke.

That same year Mrs. Choi's own father in Hong Kong died. Although one of Mrs. Choi's brothers had remained in Hong Kong, the parents did not live with him. He is a physician and claimed that he needed a quiet environment because of the nature of his work. His parents and a maternal aunt liked to play mah-jong, an activity which he found disturbing. In early 1979, Mrs. Choi's widowed mother came to live with her for three months. Mrs. Choi's aunt remained in Hong Kong with a servant obtained by Mrs. Choi to look after the two women following the death of her father. Mrs. Choi's mother was unusual in that she could speak and read English. Although both she and her husband had been born in Guangdong, they had spent much of their childhood and early adulthood in Singapore and learned English there. Thus, when she came to Brookline, she was able to read newspapers and keep in touch (she did not like to watch television). Nevertheless, at age 82, she could not get around on her own, and she felt quite isolated. Shortly after her arrival, she developed a hay-fever-like allergy. Then her sister in Hong Kong, who had been ailing, died, and she and Mrs. Choi returned together to take care of her affairs. Mrs. Choi's mother decided to stay on in Hong Kong with the servant, a distant cousin brought up from Singapore who served as a companion. She does not want to spend her final days in Boston. These two experiences have convinced Mrs. Choi that living in the United States is a less desirable option for the elderly than living in Hong Kong.

Another elderly widow, 78-year-old Mrs. Tu, also came in 1979 from Taiwan to spend her last years with her daughter's family in Greater Boston. Born and reared in Shanghai, Mrs. Tu spoke English well. She had attended a Southern Baptist mission school for girls, and following her graduation (she was not allowed to go on to college), she taught piano in a lower middle school. She married in 1923 and bore five children, two of whom died in infancy. During the Sino-Japanese War, she and her husband retreated with the Nationalists to southern China and ultimately followed them to Taiwan. They were able to take only their youngest child, Mrs. Wen, with them. Their two older sons remain in China to this day.

In the summer of 1969, Mr. Tu retired from his position with a major Taiwan bank, and at the suggestion of their daughter, the Tus came for a several months visit with her family in Washington, D.C. In 1977, by which time Mrs. Wen's family had moved to the Greater Boston area, the Tus were scheduled to emigrate permanently. They planned to move into the same building as their daughter "to take care of each other," but Mr. Tu died shortly before they were to depart. Mrs. Tu came alone. She found the pace of life in America too hectic; she missed her friends in Taiwan, her church activities, and her freedom to travel about, so decided to return to Taiwan.

In the spring of 1979, Mrs. Tu learned that she had cancer and needed an operation. She called her daughter long distance. Her daugh-

ter and son-in-law urged her to come to the United States immediately. Since she already had a "green card," she did not have to worry
about immigration procedures. Mrs. Wen would not have been able
to stay with her in Taiwan any longer than three months without
sacrificing the rest of the family (she had two young sons). Within a
week of her diagnosis and conversation, Mrs. Tu arrived in the United
States and went directly to a Boston hospital for treatment. Fortunately, she had enrolled in a medical insurance plan during her previous
stay. She did not require surgery after all and was treated instead with
radiation. Her daughter accompanied her daily for this therapy. After
several months, Mrs. Tu seemed to recover her health. A year after
her treatment she felt well enough to take a trip to China to visit her
two sons, whom she had not seen in more than thirty years.

Mrs. Tu's son-in-law Mr. Wen welcomed her into the family.
His own mother had died in their household fifteen years earlier after
a year long stay. Mrs. Tu felt comfortable in her daughter's house
though there were some disagreements. Mrs. Tu had extremely high
standards of cleanliness and neatness and meeting these standards was
a part of every day.

My daughter thinks I am lonesome; she is afraid that I don't
have enough friends. But for me twenty-four hours is too
short a day. I am a quiet person. I like to read, write letters,
make sure that everything is in good order, tidy up the house.
. . . When everything is ordered, then I can do all these other
things. When it is a mess, I can't do anything.

Mrs. Wen's house was, in fact, one of the best kept of all those we
visited. Mrs. Wen, for her part, was sometimes annoyed by her mother's religious fervor.

I don't agree with the way she approaches God. This is a
real area of friction—at times I cannot talk about it in a calm
way (with her). I get upset and speak my mind, and Mother
withdraws from confrontation. The more she withdraws,
the more I want to talk and convince her. I should be more
tolerant. The difference is that Mother thinks that God is in
control of every detail of life. My life is determined by God,
but not in everyday activity. Mother attributes much more
to God than I am willing to. Sometimes I need to bite my
tongue.

Despite this disagreement, Mrs. Wen encourages her mother's involvement in a Chinese language church that embodies the same spirit because she believes that the social interaction is valuable for her. Mrs. Wen is studying for an advanced degree, and although she spends a great deal of time at home, she can't really be available for socializing. She encourages Mrs. Tu's friends to come and visit.

Mr. Soohoo, in his 80s, had been in the United States for more than sixty years. He first came over at the age of 16 to work in a laundry. He later went back to Toisan for five years, during which time his parents arranged his marriage, and he fathered a son. When he returned to the United States, he did so on a false birth certificate and lived in constant fear of being found out. He settled in Ohio, where his real father worked, and where he thought he would be less likely to come to the attention of the immigration officials.

Mrs. Soohoo remained in China, first with her son and later with her daughter-in-law when her son came to the United States. They suffered greatly during land reform, and shortly thereafter, her daughter-in-law fled to Hong Kong. A few years later, Mrs. Soohoo was able to obtain a medical exit visa and followed her to Hong Kong. When her daughter-in-law moved to the United States, Mrs. Soohoo stayed on in Hong Kong with other relatives, expecting her husband to apply to bring her over. Mr. Soohoo, however, was reluctant to involve himself with the immigration authorities. He feared exposure of his illegal status. In the meantime their son died, and Mrs. Soohoo had to rely on a younger brother to act as her sponsor. In 1971, after a separation of forty-five years, she joined her husband in his Cleveland laundry.

The Soohoos' only descendants in the United States were their son's two sons living with their widowed mother in Boston. Their older grandson urged them to come to Boston. Their laundry was failing, Mrs. Soohoo's health was poor, and there were scarcely any other Chinese in Cleveland. Relocation seemed the only possible course of action, but they did not want to move in with the grandsons and their mother. Instead, the grandson arranged their entrance to elderly housing.

In 1979, Mrs. Soohoo was suffering from circulatory problems, diabetes, and high blood pressure. The medication that she took made her legs feel so rubbery that she could scarcely get around. She was admitted to the hospital because her hands were turning black. When she was discharged, she could do little more than sit on the sofa all day. The Soohoo's daughter-in-law, a woman already in her 50s, stayed with them overnight for two weeks attending to their needs.

The Soohoos soon realized this was too great a burden for her as she worked all day in a garment factory. They told her to go home, and Mr. Soohoo attempted to meet their needs. After nearly two months, a social worker became aware of their situation and arranged for a homemaker to visit them. It took a while to locate a bilingual worker, so for several weeks Mrs. Soohoo was unable to communicate with her helper.

The Soohoos developed an extensive support network. Their older grandson (by then married) took care of their bills, and he and his wife brought groceries every couple of weeks. The grandson's wife, who was usually tied down with two pre-school-aged children, came by on weekends to prepare their meals. The grandchildren also listened to their grandparents' complaints and relayed them to the social worker, who was employed by the organization which ran their elderly housing facility. Fellow residents also helped by relaying messages, doing occasional translation work, and even watering their neighborhood vegetable plot. They were also heavily dependent on public programs—Social Security and Medicare, Supplemental Security Income and Medicaid, as well as subsidized housing. They also had the option of taking their lunch in the common room of their building and of buying groceries at the weekly food co-op which was held there.

In January of 1981, Mrs. Soohoo entered the hospital to undergo an arterial bypass operation on her legs, which were receiving so little oxygen that they were turning black. She suffered a heart attack during the surgery and died a week later. Mr. Soohoo seemed to adjust well to the fact of her death. Perhaps her death relieved him of a great strain. They had lived apart for forty-five years, and he had never quite figured out how best to deal with his very assertive wife. She had always dominated the conversation during our visits, and Mr. Soohoo had stood quietly by.

Mrs. Wong was one of the few American-born older people living in Chinatown. She was born in New York in 1900; at the age of 16, following her marriage to a man from Toisan, she moved to the Boston area. After spending one year in a community north of Boston, Mrs. Wong settled in Chinatown, while Mr. Wong accepted a job in a restaurant across the state line in New Hampshire. At first he commuted back to Chinatown once a month, but as transportation improved, he was able to come home every weekend.

Four out of the five Wong children are college graduates, and four out of five of the children remained in the Greater Boston area.

The oldest boy moved out of the parental home at marriage, and shortly thereafter, in 1954, he purchased a two-family house in a suburb north of Boston. The Wongs' older daughter lives in the South End with her husband. Their next son and his family live only a fifteen minute walk away from the oldest son's family. Their younger daughter married a man employed by the federal government, and his job assignments have taken them out of state. Their youngest son lived with them up until Mr. Wong's death in 1975, at the age of 81. Up until that time, old Mr. Wong had been in good health and walked the two flights of stairs to their apartment several times daily.

At the time of Mr. Wong's death, his son was about to be married, and the wedding was held two weeks later in California, the home of the bride. Mrs. Wong and a representative from each of her other children's families attended the wedding. Some family members thought that the wedding should have been postponed. In Hong Kong, I knew of families which had delayed weddings until after the first anniversary of a parent's death. Mrs. Wong's relatives would have been satisfied with a delay of a month, but Mrs. Wong herself was not disturbed by what others thought a breach of form.

Following the wedding, her son and his bride moved to the Back Bay district of Boston while old Mrs. Wong remained in her apartment. She was well acquainted with another family in the building, distant relatives from her husband's home village. Mrs. Wong continued to pay her own rent. Her children brought her groceries and paid for her dental expenses, but they did not make regular financial contributions. In 1980, the building in which she had lived for sixty years was sold, and the new owner wanted to renovate it. Mrs. Wong, like the other tenants, had no choice but to relocate. Her children thought she would be happiest in another apartment in the same area, but she no longer wanted to be alone. She rejected elderly housing on the edge of Chinatown, complaining that it was too far from the shops—a walk of several blocks each way across heavily trafficked streets would have been a formidable task for a woman of her years. In the end, she moved in with her oldest son's family. One daughter-in-law explained: "I think she just wanted to move in with one of her children. Whatever else we suggested, she didn't want."

The main reason for joining the oldest son was the fact that he had the most room. His house had been converted from a two-family into a one-family, and two of his three children had already left home. Also, Mrs. Wong's senior daughter-in-law works only a short distance away from her home and can return every day for lunch to keep her company. Mrs. Wong occupies a room on the ground floor, but she seldom gets out. She has yet to walk around the block and has said that she is afraid that she will get lost. She goes grocery shopping by car with her son; last year, she went down to New York to attend a relative's twenty-fifth wedding anniversary party.

As can be seen from these cases (and also from the cases of the Moys and the Huas discussed earlier), intact elderly couples are likely to spend at least part of their later years without any children in their households. Reunification of the family in the United States means, as it does in Hong Kong, the moving of an older family member into the household of a younger. This fact alone is often enough to discourage a parent from attempting to assert authority, but age itself is also a factor. Most people do not move in with their children until they are physically or emotionally exhausted and no longer prepared to manage on their own. They seldom want to cause trouble; they are much more likely to want to rest. Intergenerational conflicts are more likely to occur when the parent moving in is still relatively young and vigorous. Recently retired parents, for example, are usually in their 60s and in the process of redefining their roles. When they find that intergenerational living is too stressful, they are able to move out to independent living. Given the many government programs in the United States, this is a realistic resolution of their problems in family living. In Hong Kong or Taiwan, such a rupture would be difficult unless the parents were financially independent.

Extended Kin Relations

Obtaining accurate information about collateral kin was an extremely difficult undertaking, particularly in the case of the older people in the study. Many of the older informants did not appear to have any surviving siblings either in China or in the United States. Others mentioned siblings, but failed to indicate their whereabouts when asked. Many older people, while happy to talk about their descendants, were reluctant to talk about siblings. The reasons for this reticence are several. Some informants were not really sure who was still alive or whether they had gone back to China, Hong Kong, or Taiwan. Some people did not know whether certain individuals were truly blood relatives or whether they were "paper" relatives. One widow identified a Chinatown businessman as a brother of her husband, but that same man never mentioned her husband as his sibling, though both had been living in Boston for many years. Several people explained that many men in Chinatown go by two names—their "real" name within the community, and their "paper" name in official records so that all documents are consistent with their immigration records. The children of such men frequently don't know the true reason why they call certain people cousin. Too great an interest in this topic did not enhance rapport.

Also, some families had strained relationships with their siblings and seldom mentioned them. Some of this was a result of having been asked one too many times to send money, to sponsor someone's immigration visa, or to perform some other favor. It was one thing to send money back to a parent or a spouse, but quite another to contribute to the wedding or education of a sibling's child. Many immigrants felt that people in China did not understand how hard they had to work to send them money or how expensive it is to live in the United States. Such people routinely disregard letters from relatives whose motives they distrust.

In China, the custom of village exogamy meant that sisters married out to other villages while their brothers remained in their natal village. In the United States, particularly in the case of the Toisan immigrants, males were the primary immigrants and tended to locate near their relatives. Women came later, brought over by husbands and children, without regard to the location of their siblings. I examined the sibling sets of 29 older people in the Greater Boston area and found precisely this kind of clustering. Of 13 elderly males in Greater Boston, 10 had surviving siblings located in the United States, and 9 of these had siblings in the Boston area. Two men had brothers and sisters living at about the same distance, but 7 lived much closer to a brother. Only 1 man lived closer to a sister. Of the 16 elderly women whose sibling sets I examined, only 8 had a surviving sibling in the United States, and only 4 of these were located in Greater Boston. Four women had brothers and sisters living at about the same distance, 3 lived closer to a sister, and only 1 lived closer to a brother.

Most older people seem to have very infrequent contact with their siblings. We encountered only one instance in which a pair of siblings were both geographically and emotionally close, and this was a pair of sisters. The younger sister, Mrs. Liao, and her two children had settled in Taiwan while Mr. Liao returned to the mainland for a brief trip. He was never able to return. Mrs. Liao's older sister, Mrs. Guo, and her family settled very close to Mrs. Liao, and they were in constant contact. In the middle 1970s, both sisters, by then widowed and with most of their children living in the United States, moved independently to the United States. Both tried living with their children for a time, but they felt lonely and isolated (the children were employed and lived in the suburbs). In 1977, Mrs. Liao moved into housing for the elderly which she had learned about through her church. Several Mandarin-speaking elderly from her church moved into this renovated apartment building at the same time. Two years later, Mrs. Guo moved from her daughter's house in New York to Mrs. Liao's building. The two sisters live on different floors, one just above the other. They have lunch and dinner together and share a variety of interests and hobbies. When asked to speculate about possible living arrangements in old age, another older woman thought that she would rather live with a sister than with a child—but only if the sister were already widowed; "otherwise it might cause trouble."

Care of parents is an issue that frequently causes friction among siblings. Mrs. Kwan, a 47-year-old woman who is the only member of her sibling set in the United States, found herself bearing complete financial responsibility for her mother while a younger sister provided the day-to-day care. Unlike most of the Chinatown-South End Chinese, Mrs. Kwan was not originally from the Sze Yap area, though she met and married in Hong Kong a man from Toisan and has Toisan parents-in-law living in Boston. Her father had operated a successful business in Hong Kong, but a few years before the Japanese take over he returned to his native county north of Guangzhou and invested in land. When the Communists appeared on the verge of victory, Mrs. Kwan, her father, and an older sister went to Hong Kong to wait things out. Her mother, an adopted brother, and a younger sister remained behind. Just before land reform, Mrs. Kwan's father made the mistake of returning to his home village for a brief visit and was caught in China when the border was closed. As a member of the landlord class, he was forced to kneel and walk on his knees across broken glass, and in the end, he was "struggled to death." His widow, too, was tortured.

Mrs. Kwan learned all this only in 1957 when she returned to visit her mother. She stayed in a hotel specially provided for Overseas Chinese, and her mother came to visit her. After bolting the door and examining the room for bugging devices, her mother explained the sad events in the village. In an effort to protect himself, Mrs. Kwan's adopted brother had renounced his family ties, so only the mother and younger sister remained. She and Mrs. Kwan agreed that Mrs. Kwan would send money to help provide for their mother, and that when the sister married, she would take the mother along to her husband's village. Mrs. Kwan's older sister in Hong Kong assumed no responsibility whatsoever. She was a habitual gambler and even told Mrs. Kwan to tell their mother "to cease considering me her daughter. She should act as if I am dead."

For nearly twenty years, Mrs. Kwan sent money back to her younger sister, which was no easy feat as she raised eight children and worked in a garment factory. In 1978, Mrs. Kwan became an American citizen and wanted to begin the process of bringing her mother to the United States. Her sister, however, wrote that their mother was too old to undertake such a trip and preferred to stay in China. Mrs. Kwan wanted to hear this from her mother's own lips and requested her sister to escort the mother to Guangzhou where she could make a long distance phone call to Boston. When her sister declined to do so, Mrs. Kwan became suspicious. She began to think that perhaps her mother was dead and that her sister had not told her because she did not want to lose the remittances to which she had become accustomed.

When she learned that an acquaintance was going to Guangzhou in the summer of 1980, she requested her to stop off at her sister's village to learn the condition of the mother. Mrs. Kwan supplied the visitor with a photograph of her mother and sister because she feared that her sister might produce any old woman as the mother in order to continue the deception. When the visitor went unannounced to the village and brought out the photograph, Mrs. Kwan's sister burst into tears. She volunteered immediately that her mother had had a heart attack about two years before and had died shortly thereafter. She added that she had hesitated to tell Mrs. Kwan about the death because "My sister's health has not been good, and I was afraid that she would not be able to tolerate the news." In short, the situation was as Mrs. Kwan had suspected. When she received the letter with the news, she showed it all around her workplace. The other women were greatly impressed by her ability to find out the true facts.

Another set of siblings had a terrible argument about who would take the responsibility for bringing their mother to the United States. Mrs. Chow had looked after her mother in Hong Kong for nearly twenty years, but when her husband applied for her to come to Boston in the mid-1970s, the mother had to go and stay with another relative. This other relative did not look after the old woman at all, locking her out of the house during the day. Mrs. Chow secretly sent money to another relative to buy food for her mother. She was afraid to accuse the first relative directly lest her mother bear the consequences.

In the meantime, she requested her brother who lived on the West Coast to bring their mother over. Mrs. Chow saw this as properly his responsibility since he was the only son. The West Coast location was also that of another sister, who could look after the mother if their brother tired of his responsibility. Mrs. Chow did not feel that she could bring her mother over as she had less space, was less well-off than either of her siblings, and had already done more than her share.

The argument among the siblings started when their mother was about to come to the United States. Mrs. Chow's own son had agreed to sponsor his grandmother, though she would not live with him. When everything was nearly ready, Mrs. Chow's sister called her brother to confirm his commitment to keep their mother on the weekends and to share her expenses. He hesitated and told her on the phone that he needed to talk to his wife first and would call her back. When he called back, he still seemed unsure and had his wife talk to the sister. An argument between his wife and his sister ensued regarding the mother's medical and funeral expenses. Another relative who had been helping out with visa application procedures attempted to mediate by suggesting that the children could split the costs, but the fact was that the brother's family really did not want the mother to come to the United States. They thought it would be too much for them and for the mother. Mrs. Chow's sister was so angry, that she announced that she would have no more contact with his family even though they lived only a few blocks apart.

Mrs. Chow wishes that her sister and brother had been able to forgive each other before his death in 1980. As for Mrs. Chow's mother—she died in the late 1970s without ever coming to the United States. To everyone's surprise she had accumulated several thousand (Hong Kong) dollars in a bank and left a will favoring her son. Mrs. Chow could not understand how her mother could leave her less than one thousand dollars and even less to Mrs. Chow's son who had offered to be her sponsor. The old lady left Mrs. Chow's brother's family several thousand dollars.

Another delicate issue is the sponsorship of siblings, especially siblings from the People's Republic of China, by other siblings. When I first began interviewing people in Chinatown, I frequently heard that immigrants from China do not know how to work, that they are not as industrious as immigrants from Hong Kong. At first I dismissed these remarks as conservative thinking characteristic of a population long allied with the anti-Communist regime on Taiwan.

But I had also heard such comments in Hong Kong, and finally had the opportunity to spend a few months in the People's Republic of China where I could observe the situation at first hand. People working in state enterprises hold their jobs for life. In fact, such jobs are referred to as "iron rice bowls" because they assure a permanent and regular source of income. Even when production slows down because of a shortage of materials, the workers are kept. Security of tenure is more or less independent of the individual worker's performance. The Chinese government has recently indicated concern about the lack of worker motivation and is developing ways to stimulate it.

Mr. Ho's sisters, Mrs. Chen and Mrs. Tse, exemplify the different adjustments of immigrants from Hong Kong and from the People's Republic of China. In 1979, 58-year-old Mrs. Chen, a native of Hunan province, was brought to the United States by her younger brother. She had lived in Hong Kong for more than twenty years, spoke English, and obtained a position in the state bureaucracy shortly after her arrival in Boston. She moved in with her older son who was already a student in the area. Two years later, Mr. Ho agreed somewhat reluctantly to sponsor his younger sister, Mrs. Tse, and her teenage daughter, who were living in the People's Republic. At first, the two Tses lived with Mr. Ho, but according to Mrs. Chen's son, he very quickly lost patience with them. One day he put their bags out by the front door with the clear message that they should move elsewhere. They moved in with the Chens, and Mrs. Chen's son managed to locate a job for his aunt washing dishes in a Chinese restaurant. Then he enrolled his cousin in an English language program. He and his uncle, Mr. Ho, agreed to split the costs of the tuition ($900 a semester). They hoped that after learning enough English, the girl would go on to college. The Tses then moved into an apartment of their own.

The Chens thought that everything had been resolved until one day they received a call from the language school that the girl had not been attending her classes. They were very surprised and tried to reach Mrs. Tse at the restaurant, but she was no longer there, having been fired because of "too much talking on the job." The phone at their apartment had been disconnected. When they finally reached the landlord, they learned that the pair had moved out without leaving a forwarding address. They asked the landlord to contact them should he have any news. A week later the landlord received a letter requesting him to forward mail to the Midwest. The Chens had no idea that the Tses even knew anyone out there. Mrs. Chen's son fears that the move was a mistake—even dangerous. He wonders how his aunt will obtain work and frets that if his cousin is not studying in a school, it will be easy for her to *hohk waaih* ("learn how to be bad"). He attributes their unsuccessful adjustment to the fact that they were full of illusions about the United States. They thought of it as a land of plenty and had no notion that you have to work hard to get what you want.

As these examples indicate, differences in values, conflicts of interest, and misunderstandings are a predictable part of immigrant family life in the United States. The focus on problems and conflicts, however, should not obscure the fact that many, many individuals did and do live up to very high ideals of family solidarity and support. Despite tremendous personal hardship, individuals like Mr. Soohoo and Mrs. Kwan managed for decades to be the supporters of their families in China. More affluent individuals, especially now that the People's Republic of China has received official recognition by the American government, are supporting their nieces and nephews in their efforts to obtain university educations.

10   Community Support Systems

As demonstrated, Chinese in Hong Kong are largely dependent on their immediate families. In the absence of family members, older people are often isolated unless, like Mrs. Wun, they have managed to locate others from their home communities and gradually to build up a network of supporters. Few old people participate in formal organizations, and in Hong Kong, the mere fact of being Chinese is not sufficient cause for association.

In Boston and other American Chinatowns, historical factors such as discrimination in employment and in the right to immigrate heightened the sense of being a foreigner. On the other hand, dialect similarity and the narrow geographical base from which most of the pre-World War II immigrants came served to draw them together. The small size of the Chinese population meant that a sense of community was possible in Chinatown. Even those individuals living near their suburban laundries remained oriented to Chinatown. On weekends, news was shared at family associations or during chance encounters in grocery stores.

When problems were encountered, most people turned, of course, to family members or traditional organizations for help, but when these were not accessible, people sometimes came to rely on the good offices of what I shall call natural helpers. These are people who, although not actually employed in the human service professions, have voluntarily chosen to spend part of their time helping others. Before the great expansion in programs for the elderly, natural helpers functioned as indigenous social workers. Now their tasks are more likely to include information, referral and emotional support rather than the provision of direct services. All the same, their activities constitute highly valued and necessary supplements to the formal programs currently in operation.

Informal Support: Natural Helpers

Mrs. Ng

Word of Mrs. Ng came to me first from someone who was not among her admirers, but who stated that Mrs. Ng was "very influential with other old people." Unlike many other old women who are usually hesitant to express their opinions, 75-year-old Mrs. Ng stands ready, able, and willing to express her views on a wide range of topics. One day I encountered her holding forth at a federally sponsored nutrition program for the elderly where she was seated at a table with several Toisan-speaking women. She herself lives in a private apartment building owned by her son (to whom she pays rent), but since she lives alone, she frequently takes her noon meal at one or another of the nutrition sites located within a few blocks of her South End home. On this particular day Mrs. Ng was agitated and angry.

> You know this state is supposed to have the best educated people in the country, the smartest professors. That's a pile of junk! That's my opinion. I was watching a TV program last night, and they were talking about a special device for women to wear so that the men can have their pleasure. Abortion! No matter what they say, you plant a seed and it starts to grow. Like a little worm, it struggles to grow. You put poison or something in it to kill it, and you're going to have babies that can't see or hear. No arms. No legs. Awful!

In fact, she was fed up with the state of society in general and contrasted today's easy living with the hardship that served as an incentive to work in her day.

> The unions have ruined everything. When I was young, we had to go and gather up discarded boxes to use for the fire. The kids would go down to the railroad tracks with a bucket to pick up the pieces of coal that had fallen from the coal cars. After school and during the weekends, kids would go to other people's houses and help clean up. A boy could go and help sweep up the bank floor, but now the unions have ruined all that (presumably because of the institution of the minimum wage) . . . No one works anymore. Everyone wants a handout. They use the money for drugs and drink.

. . . The streets are dirty, and money is being given away instead of putting people to work. The Government is in debt. It owes each of us four or five thousand dollars.

She expressed herself primarily in English with occasional summaries of her views in Toisanese for the benefit of the other women at the table, but her opinions were sometimes too extreme for them. While nearly all the women were scandalized to hear of sex education in the schools, Mrs. Ng's forceful denunciation of such programs was stated too coarsely for most of them. The oldest woman present (Mrs. Yeung) demanded that she stop carrying on as "the others (non-Chinese) will laugh at us." The next oldest woman rose to leave saying as she did so that people would not behave as crudely as Mrs. Ng suggested.

I wondered how such a woman, so atypical in her style, could possibly be "very influential." Mrs. Ng does possess certain characteristics which set her apart from most of the other old women who come to this nutrition site. The only one who was American-born, she has spent her entire life in the United States, and is bilingual, speaking both Toisanese and English. She is regarded as a woman of wealth; she owned her own restaurant for many years, and her son owns an apartment building. She is also highly mobile, traveling freely outside of the Greater Boston area. These objective characteristics, however, are only a small part of the story. On top of them, Mrs. Ng is *yauh sam* ("possessing a heart," kind and considerate). This term sometimes is employed as a ritual response to any small act and functions almost as a thank you. If someone notices that you didn't get any dessert, for example, she might quietly return to the line to fetch a dessert for you. An appropriate response would be to say *Neih hou yauh sam* ("You're very kind"). The phrase also has a more intense connotation, implying a person whose heart is good, who takes it upon her or himself to perform some inconvenient or unpleasant task on behalf of someone else without any calculation of advantage and without even being asked. Mrs. Ng is one of these people.

I sometimes noticed people hanging on the fringes of the group with which Mrs. Ng usually took her lunch. I wondered why these people sat so quietly by yet suddenly rose when Mrs. Ng made motions that she was about to leave. I eventually learned that these people were seeking her help. One day, for example, I found Mrs. Ng talking with two residents from elderly housing about another man, Mr. Chu, who lived out in the community. Mr. Chu had had a stroke from which he had not yet recovered, and one of the men knew that Mr. Chu needed assistance in getting his phone location changed since he could no longer easily reach it. He hoped that Mrs. Ng would accompany him to Mr. Chu's house where they could wait for the phone man, and Mrs. Ng could serve as a translator. She agreed to do this. Another day I noticed that Mrs. Ng was quite dressed up. She was wearing an attractive sweater, makeup, and had had her hair curled. I asked whether she had any special engagement. Yes, she was meeting a man in Chinatown after lunch. He had called her up, insisting that he wanted to give her a present—"just a little bottle of liquor." He had recently been discharged from a hospital where Mrs. Ng had helped him out with some translation. She had also mobilized his grandchildren to write to him. A nurse at the hospital who knew Mrs. Ng had informed her of his needs. Mrs. Ng has also helped people gain admittance to elderly housing and taken them around to meet the other residents.

When I came to know Mrs. Ng better, I realized that these were not new activities for her. Before moving to the South End from the southeastern part of the state six years ago, where she had owned and operated a large restaurant serving both Chinese and American food, she had been an active fund raiser for both local and international causes. In addition to fund-raising, she also came up to Boston to visit the sick. Once she was awarded the title Citizen of the Year by the local chapter of the Elks for her contributions to the community. Among these contributions was having allowed the Elks to use her restaurant as a meeting place when their own building burned down. She had sponsored a collection center to send clothing to China and donated money to a man known as "the Noodle Priest" who was based in Hong Kong and who distributed wholesome noodles to refugees who had little to eat otherwise. She once sent him money and a note that should he ever be in her area, he should drop by her restaurant. To her amazement, she one day received a letter from him saying that he would, indeed, be stopping by. When word of his coming spread, the whole town wanted to attend the dinner Mrs. Ng was giving for him at the restaurant. She quickly organized a raffle which netted the priest $1,300.

Mrs. Ng knew how to set limits on the amount of help she would give. She quickly terminated phone calls from people "who would otherwise talk your ear off," and her gruff facade and outspokenness also limited the number of people who dared approach her. After showing me her plaque from the Elks, Mrs. Ng said "I've done my share helping people." Mrs. Ng never gave any reason for her generous behavior, but she clearly derives satisfaction from the act of helping. She has several times indicated her belief that evil acts sooner or later have evil consequences even if several generations further down the line. Similarly good acts have good consequences. She managed to pull through two very difficult experiences in her earlier life because of the help of others.

Mrs. Ng's mother died unexpectedly, leaving behind a husband and seven children under the age of 14. The oldest girl quit school to look after the others, and the residents of the small town in which the family lived (a former mining town in California that most of the earlier Chinese miners had left) tried to make things easier for them. Her father rented a farm, so they had enough to eat, and the woman who owned the farm came around only in the summer to collect the rent. She accepted whatever Mrs. Ng's father was able to give and eventually sold the farm to the family. Other neighbors donated clothes to them.

Mrs. Ng left her town when her older brother arranged her marriage to a man from China who lived in southeastern Massachusetts. Mrs. Ng's husband worked in restaurants in different locations throughout the state and was not always available when family crises occurred. One weekend, she realized that her 17-year-old daughter was ill and didn't want her to go to school.

> It was all like a terrible dream. She was sick and gone within a week. She had influenza or something on top of typhus. The day she died I passed out. When I came to, she had been buried and everything. I was in the hospital for a week. I was in a daze. . . . I took to my bed for months. I couldn't get over it. It was if I had died myself.

It was primarily through the encouragement of a certain Mrs. Wong that Mrs. Ng was finally able to put her life back together again. This woman came down from Chinatown to visit her and later introduced Mrs. Ng's son to a nice girl who would fit in to the Ng family. Just before his high school graduation, he and the girl were married. He was then drafted and sent overseas while his wife stayed on with Mrs. Ng.

After the war, the Ngs started their big restaurant. After it was sold in the 1970s, Mr. and Mrs. Ng senior moved up to Boston where both were receiving medical treatment. Mrs. Ng has since regretted selling the restaurant because without it she no longer has a rich social life. "I used to have it (social interaction) in the restaurant naturally. We had people coming and going all the time. Once I left the restaurant and came up here, I had to find something to do. If you're not active . . ."

Mrs. Ng has seen two sisters suffer paralyzing strokes, and she is intent on avoiding this fate for herself. In her mid-70s she became a very active dancer, attending classes in ballroom dancing twice a week. The people at the dance studio are very proud of her. She also sews and crochets many things, giving them to friends, including those at the dance studio. Her other major activity is her informal social work.

Mrs. Choi

Mrs. Choi first came to my attention through a group interested in developing a nursing home for elderly Chinese. While she thoroughly accepted the need for such an institution, she had become discouraged and had withdrawn from the group because of community infighting concerning who would build and operate the facility.

> The government (from whom two rival groups were seeking a Certificate of Need which would authorize the construction) will say "How can you run a nursing home if you can't even work together on setting it up?" The government will just throw out the idea. I began to wonder what was more important—the nursing home or who would run it. Do you know what I mean? Now I just come to work (in Chinatown) and go home. I don't pay attention to what is going on out there. When somebody calls me up to find out what is happening, I just tell them I don't know anything.

When Mrs. Choi and her husband lived in Hong Kong, they managed very well on her father-in-law's remittances. With his money, they had managed to purchase eight apartments. Although she had five children, she had three servants to do most of her work: one to cook, one to take care of the children, and one to take care of the house. She herself spent all her time shopping and visiting her friends; but she did not, in fact, find these activities very rewarding. She was plagued by a variety of mysterious aches and pains for which she sought treatment from many doctors, to no avail. She finally concluded that she needed to spend her time pursuing something more worthwhile and began visiting people in the hospital.

When she arrived in Boston in the late 1960s, she was surprised to discover that her church did not have an active visiting program. At her suggestion the church started an association whose members would visit the sick and the depressed; currently the group consists of seven members. Mrs. Choi receives two or three referrals a month to do this kind of work. Their mission is to demonstrate to the individual that even though he is alone, he is still loved. They do not simply express concern but attempt to assure him that God's love is transmitted to him. If anyone is helped through their visits, she explained, it is not because of their efforts but because of God's love. Generally, they do not provide direct services but will refer the individual to a social worker, physician, or the Department of Social Welfare. Sometimes they will escort someone to a doctor or perform some household task, but not on a regular basis.

Mrs. Choi runs an unusually humane business; she does so partly because of her own bitter experience as a stitcher in the garment industry. When she first came to the United States, her children were still young and required attention, but she had no one to help her. Mrs. Choi described the move from Hong Kong to the United States as a change of 180 degrees in lifestyle. One day, one of her children was sick, and she had to take him to a doctor, so informing her boss in the morning. When she returned in the afternoon, her boss, instead of being sympathetic, told her to finish the bundle she had been working on and go home for good. At that time, Mrs. Choi's English was not adequate for her to deal with the situation. That kind of experience made her want to be independent and to be able to help people like herself.

She began working at another garment factory and showed such promise that she was rapidly promoted to supervising and doing the books. Shortly thereafter, with support from a merchandising firm, she set up her own factory. She currently employs more than fifty workers, including trainees who are Indochinese refugees. She used to have some one come twice a week to offer English lessons to her workers, but her teacher moved away. She brought someone from one of the adult language programs in Chinatown to the factory to explain about the availability of night classes. Her shop is a refuge from the harsh realities of stitching all day long. There is a modicum of community feeling that is impossible in most of the garment factories that are operated by non-Chinese. One day when I dropped by the factory, I found Mrs. Choi and several of her employees standing around a table on which there were several very deep (as if from a restaurant kitchen) cooking pots. I was pressed into joining the group and sharing the souplike mixture which contained eggs, vinegar, pork, and ginger. This particular dish is a specialty associated with new mothers and had been sent over to the factory by a co-worker who had given birth to a son twelve days earlier. It was her way of inviting her friends to share in her good fortune.

Mrs. Choi is very familiar with Chinese traditional customs and with their Hong Kong adaptations. She is also aware of the problems involved in raising Hong Kong-born youngsters in the United States. She knows the role conflicts that a working mother with elderly relatives in the home inevitably faces, and she knows the kind of gossip that people spread when they are not familiar with American ways. She too has sponsored relatives from Hong Kong and worried about the best way of providing care for a widowed parent remaining in Hong Kong. In short, in her 48 years she has acquired the experience which makes her a valuable resource to other immigrants and their families.

Mr. Chiang

Mr. Chiang, now officially retired at 68, is also a recent immigrant to the United States, but he has had years of international living and is highly educated. As such, he is familiar with a different segment of the population, the Mandarin-speaking immigrants from Taiwan, most of whom were born in China. His children were all educated in the United States and came here long before he and his wife did. When the Chiangs first came to New York in 1975, they lived with their oldest son (their second child) and his family. They soon discovered areas of friction, particularly concerning child-rearing. Mr. Chiang concluded that living together was probably not a good idea. He stated that if you didn't go and live with your children then they would think of you, but if you go, then there is trouble. After a few months they decided to move to the Boston area, where their oldest daughter as well as a friend lived. They moved into the house of their friend, planning to collaborate on a book, but they soon learned that the older man expected their assistance in maintaining the building. After much deliberation, they moved out and back to New York. They contemplated returning to Taiwan where they had many friends. On the other hand, all of their children were living in the United States, though in five different states.

During the time they spent in the Boston area, the Chiangs had been active in a Chinese church; through a social worker there, they learned of subsidized housing for elderly people in Boston. Several other members of their church had moved to this facility. Every Sunday, they were picked up by a van and brought out to the suburban church for services. During the week, they held a Bible study group. Most of the participants were widows who knew little English. The church social worker appealed to Mr. Chiang's helping instincts directly, pointing out that the others needed his assistance.

The Chiangs have been living in elderly housing for the past three years and find it a satisfactory arrangement. They know firsthand the difficulties of intergenerational living and can help to explain to others that living in the United States requires special tact, that parents cannot hold on to old ways of thinking about respect and attention. The Chiangs now think that if they were some day to have to live with a child, they would prefer to live with a daughter. They have already tried to live with their older son without success. Their other son married a Cantonese-speaking girl, and they speak Cantonese with each other (the Chiang children were placed in boarding schools in Hong Kong while their parents worked elsewhere for an international organization as the Chiangs had been afraid to leave them in Taiwan). Both parents feel that the language issue divides them from this couple. Daughters (and sons-in-law) are perceived as easier to get along with. Mr. Chiang does not worry about having to stand on ceremony with his son-in-law. As an educated man himself, he is not self-conscious about the achievements of the younger generation. He is not threatened by their knowledge as is sometimes the case when there is an educational gap between the generations. As another man pointed out, the fact that Chinese men seldom work together anymore (no longer tilling the same land) seriously weakens the argument that co-residence should be determined by sex. He suggests that since women share the household responsibilities in a way that men do not, it is more logical for them to stay together.

Mr. Chiang has also figured out a way to serve as an advisor to his children without having to face the rejection of his advice.

> I write letters to the children very often, maybe one letter per week. I also need to send them articles about healthy food, behavior. I xerox them and send them out. If we have urgent news or messages, then we call. Writing and sending these articles helps them; they see it and say "Thanks." But I don't know if they really use it; I can't tell or worry about it. But this makes me happy—I am a "correspondent consultant." I don't know if I am right—maybe they don't need

these articles or help, but I do it. . . . Right now if they do
things bad, then I tell them. I send them articles and hope
this will persuade them. But my son still smokes because he
works too hard. I don't say anything anymore—they are so
big what can I say? I don't want to cause trouble.

Mr. Chiang does not confine his advice and help to his children; he
also helps out the Chinese residents of his apartment building. He
informs them of various programs, assists them with their travel plans,
and represents their interests in other organizations. He also teaches
tai chi and tutors people in Chinese. He takes a fatherly interest in his
students, providing them with contacts in Taiwan. Providing contacts
for one's associates is an inescapable responsibility of any Chinese, he
feels, but he also acknowledges that this has its bad side. Had they
moved back to Taiwan, for instance, he fears that he would have been
plagued with special requests from his many associates there.

As a youngster in China, Mr. Chiang had taken on adult responsibilities at a very early age. He and a group of classmates had
been selected to teach courses to the army of a rival of General Chiang
Kai-shek. Later the two generals cooperated in the war effort. He felt
that the only way he could win the respect of his classmates (he had
been appointed their leader) was to work even harder than they did.
He firmly believes that motivation is the key to good work performance.

You must protect your staff at work. This is important even
on issues of money. If you have the money, then you give
extra money to them. If someone has a difficult situation,
you help him. If you can give them more, they help you,
especially in spirit. This is my working philosophy. It may
be different in the United States. . . . In China it is just like
a family; we work together. If you sacrifice, then you feel
happy. In the United States the relationships are based on
law; with the Chinese there is no sense of law—it is based
on personality and a family sense.

Mr. Chiang was distressed that other people living in his neighborhood were wasting their lives in gambling and drink. He thought
they should try to help people too. Mr. Chiang sees himself as a man
of considerable personal resources that he should employ for the bet-
terment of others. He has not been able to gain the appreciation of
his children, but he has acquired a broader audience which does appreciate his skills. He is not wasting his old age.

Mrs. Ng, Mrs. Choi, and Mr. Chiang are helpers for diverse reasons; they all clearly value the act of helping. They do not make their livings as social workers, and so they can pick and choose those whom they will help as well as the kinds of help they will offer. Other old people also play this role but less frequently and less self-consciously. From this perspective, one of the great advantages of elderly housing is the opportunity it can present for informal assistance. By helping others, old people can continue to play an important part in everyday life. Even those who cannot speak English or are afraid to travel alone outside of their building can retain a sense of worth by serving those worse off than themselves. If someone is sick, another can pick up his or her mail. If someone has lost a spouse, one can visit the bereaved's room and offer silent company. Those more confident can run errands or pick up groceries on an ad hoc basis.

Elderly housing also provides a setting in which older people can find the support and recognition that they feel is their due for having survived a life of hardship. As 96-year-old Mrs. Yeung explained:

> My life has been very hard. Most people who see me assume that because I am so old and do not complain that I must have had a good life. In fact, I have had a very troubled life, but I have kept it all in. People do not want to hear your troubles, and young people cannot understand them. It is only since coming here that I have had the opportunity to talk about my hardships with the other old people. Other old people can understand what your life has been like.

Mrs. Yeung's list of misfortunes is impressive, including an abusive mother-in-law, a cruel husband, and social isolation. While she spent several weeks each year visiting with her daughters in New York, she did not want to live with them because she felt isolated from her grandchildren who do not speak any Chinese. Despite having been in the United States for nearly sixty years, Mrs. Yeung speaks only fragmented English—a word here and a word there.

She first thought of moving to elderly housing when she learned that a sister-in-law, also in her 90s and living in New York, had moved into elderly housing despite having several children in the United States. Mrs. Yeung was also a long-time acquaintance of Mrs. Ng, who encouraged her to move into elderly housing where there would always be other people around in case something should go wrong. Since moving in, Mrs. Yeung has learned that there are other advantages to elderly housing—for one thing there is always something going on. While too weak to travel alone away from the building, Mrs. Yeung enjoys sitting out in front of the building with other old women watching people come and go. She also participates, largely as an observer, in every activity she knows about in the community room of her building.

The Chinese constitute only about one-quarter of the building's ethnically mixed population, and perhaps because of her many years of living in a non-Chinese community, Mrs. Yeung is very concerned about creating a good impression. She attends many functions, even when she has no idea what they are about, solely to create the impression that the Chinese residents are concerned about community issues. One day, for example, she noticed a crowd in the community room and joined it. Not until nearly two hours later did she realize that she had walked into a religious meeting of the building's Hispanic population.

Even more important than the opportunity to see and participate in activities previously denied her is the comfort she gains from being among people who can understand her. One of the tragedies of the immigration experience, or perhaps of any rapidly changing society, is that of cohort differences. One generation is unable to understand and appreciate the little victories that are so important to the other. What one generation considers a worthy achievement may be deemed stupid by another. Older people find it very disappointing to pour forth tales of great suffering without receiving acknowledgement of their fortitude or courage for having endured such hardship. One young man explained the younger generation's perspective:

> You know Chinese parents don't communicate with their children very much. I really didn't know anything about the village from them. I think part of this is because they had a very hard time back there, and they don't want to burden the younger generation with this sort of thing. Also I guess we weren't all that interested with what was going on in China. We were more interested in what was going on in the United States today. How much was it going to cost to go to a movie and stuff.

Age homogeneity of a neighborhood has long been known to facilitate the development of friendships by older people (e.g. Carp 1966; Rosow 1967). Age by itself, however, is seldom a sufficient basis for a lasting friendship. Most studies of age-homogeneous settings (e.g. Hoyt 1954; Johnson 1971; Hochschild 1973; Winiecke 1973;

Byrne 1974; Shelly 1974; Ross 1977; Fry 1979; and Keith 1980) have found that similarities in education, income, and working life are extremely important variables conditioning the conversion of a physical entity (housing) into a social entity (a community). One of the most powerful of these background variables is, of course, ethnicity. People who are estranged from their neighborhoods not only by age (cohort effects) but also by ethnicity (cultural effects) can logically be expected to find advantages in elderly housing or retirement communities organized around the principle of ethnicity.

Wu (1974) and Chen (1979) found that the elderly Chinese of Los Angeles were very willing to consider such arrangements, and they have already become popular in Boston. Quincy Tower, for example, which opened in 1977 on the southern edge of Chinatown, has 180 units accommodating 260 residents, about three-quarters of whom are Chinese. In 1978, only 12 openings became available for new tenants, and the waiting list by 1979 included 475 applicants. Other subsidized housing units such as Unity Tower and Franklin Housing in the South End also contain substantial minorities of Chinese tenants, and more are currently under construction on the fringes of Chinatown. Private apartment buildings also accommodate large numbers of elderly Chinese in Chinatown, but such buildings accept tenants of any age.

Socialization of newcomers to the United States is another valuable function of elderly housing. Informal instruction by one's peers is helpful in reinterpreting values and family relationships. When a widow learns that no one has a daughter-in-law willing to perform the kinds of services she has asked her own daughter-in-law to perform, she realizes that her daughter-in-law is not unreasonable in refusing to do them. Peers can also help in coping with the stress of everyday life, such as how to shop in a department store when one doesn't speak English, or which Chinese pharmacy carries the best herbs.

Another advantage of many subsidized facilities is the availability of bilingual personnel who can assist the older person with the translation of phone or utility bills, with Medicare and Medicaid problems, and during emergencies. These services are precisely those that older people living at home must obtain from their children. If they do not live with their children, they must wait for them to visit or turn to people like Mrs. Ng or Mrs. Choi if they happen to live in the neighborhood. Parents are reluctant to burden their children with these routine tasks. They would prefer that the visits of children be pleasant occasions during which the children can relax. One woman who was making halfhearted efforts to learn English dismissed my suggestion that she ask her children to assist with pronunciation. "They work all day and are tired when they come to see me. They should rest." The semi-professional services performed by the staff at the subsidized facilities make the relationship between parent and child more pleasant. Children who voluntarily come to their parents, inquire about their welfare, and take them out for entertainment are much more appreciated than children who come only to perform services at the request of the parent. Unlike the elderly in Wah Hong Hostel in Hong Kong, most of the Chinese elderly living in special housing in Boston do have children in the area and continue to interact with them.

Life in elderly housing is not completely rosy. One cannot, for example, select one's neighbors; if they are unpleasant, they must nevertheless be tolerated. If they belong to a different ethnic group, it is difficult to communicate one's needs or displeasures. People are understandably angry when they walk into a community room and find a person who is drunk and disorderly. They wonder about the motives of people who push open their doors only to retreat when they find that the apartment is, in fact, occupied. They worry about bizarre behavior and are annoyed by people who want to save their souls. Relatively little interaction seems to take place outside of the public space of the community room. Most of the people we knew who came for lunch ate their breakfasts and dinners alone. Least involved of all in the social life of these buildings are the men.

In one of the facilities with which we were most familiar, many of the men are for all practical purposes single. Some have never married, some brought their wives to the United States only to be widowed, and others declined to bring their family members to the United States. There are a few couples in the building, but they do not take their lunch together in the common room. Rather, the wife prepares their meal in their room where they eat it together; or in one case, the husband prepares it for himself as he had done for so many years before his wife's arrival, while she comes downstairs to eat on her own. Most of the male residents are former laundry operators or employees who have long made their way in an almost exclusively male environment. Many of them are bitter about the circumstances that forced them to close their laundries and are angered by the insecurity they feel when they walk around the neighborhood at night. Some men take daily walks to Chinatown where they stop for a cup of coffee or tea during the hours that the restaurant workers congregate in the narrow streets waiting for the vans that will take them to their distant places of employment. They also drop by the various gambling spots to play a little fan tan. Other men stay in their rooms most of the day, and some of them have serious alcohol problems.

This separate social life does not mean that there is no association between the men and the women in the building. The men are more functional in English and more knowledgeable about resources than the more recently arrived women. Some of the men are distant relatives of the women and have news to share of people known in common, but none of these assets seems strong enough to override the general belief that there is little reason for older men and older women to want to spend time together. As in Hong Kong, nearly everyone said that remarriages would not occur between older people, though a man might remarry a younger woman. Most people thought that the reason for such marriages would be male helplessness—that they needed someone to look after them.

Ironically, it was the high proportion of elderly single men which first stimulated activists in Chinatown to set up a drop-in center for older people in a run-down building in 1972. While men did initially drop by, they did not tend to stay. When meals were provided through the nutrition program (Title VII of the Older Americans Act), the men were gradually displaced by women, who did stay on, chatting or playing cards. Male staff was gradually replaced by female staff. When a new facility was constructed adjacent to Quincy Tower, the capacity was greatly increased. Men in small numbers continue to come to the new meal site, but leave it almost immediately after the meal to sit in the foyer of adjacent Quincy Tower. Women seldom sit there.

In general, one gets the impression that living in elderly housing is more rewarding for old people in Boston than it is in Hong Kong. Their satisfaction has less to do with the quality of the housing, private apartments in Boston versus a tiny efficiency shared with three others in Hong Kong, than with the external environment. Chinese in elderly housing in Hong Kong are still sensitive to the possible stigma of being perceived as having poor family relationships, even when many of them have no family living in Hong Kong. Furthermore, though they do gain the security of medical and social supports by living in elderly housing, they are quite capable of taking care of their own needs outside of the hostel as long as they are mobile; no cultural or linguistic barrier separates them from the other segments of the population. In American cities, however, the external environment for non-English speakers is very difficult to negotiate, particularly if they live outside of the ethnic community. Having a place full of familiar-looking faces and familiar-sounding voices makes a tremendous difference to one's sense of well-being. There are in addition many activities to observe or participate in so that one does not have to depend so heavily on one's family members.

Formal Supports: Programs and Agencies

Theoretically, Chinese immigrants and Chinese Americans can participate in public programs for the poor or elderly on the same terms as other residents of the United States. During the 1960s, however, there was a growing awareness that minority group status severely limited individual participation in such programs. Advocates charged and subsequently documented (e.g. Cuellar and Weeks 1980) that elderly members of minority groups did not receive benefits or services on a per capita basis to the same extent as Americans of European ancestry. For example, their Social Security payments were lower, and they were underrepresented in long term care facilities. These facts gave rise to the double jeopardy hypothesis first enunciated by the National Urban League in 1964 (Cuellar and Weeks 1980:2). According to this view, the welfare of minority elders is jeopardized first by racial or ethnic discrimination and secondly by age discrimination. Subsequent writers on this topic added a third burden, sexual discrimination, borne by older women of minority status.

The double or multiple jeopardy hypothesis was originally applied to discrimination suffered by the black population in the United States. Initially, less concern was expressed for possible discrimination against the Asian or Asian-American population in the United States. According to the Pacific/Asian Elderly Research Project (1978:39), the first major surfacing of a concern on the national level for the Pacific and Asian elderly can be traced to the Special Concerns Session of the 1971 White House Conference on Aging. Only through the efforts of a handful of advocates led by the Japanese American Citizens League was this session on the Asian American elderly included at all. Among its recommendations were that:

> Federal funds for research and demonstration projects to determine how older Asian Americans can be effectively assisted, based on their needs, cultural differences, values, and desires, should be expanded and should involve researchers

of Asian background. The findings from such efforts should be disseminated to policy makers, program planners, and service providers.

Advocates wanted to know to what extent the different rates of participation were a function of discrimination, denial of access, lack of information, inappropriateness, or lack of interest. Some advocates offered more positive interpretations of the differential participation rates, arguing, for example, that minority groups place more emphasis on the extended family and are thereby less likely to consign elderly relatives to nursing homes. From this point of view, ethnicity itself could be seen as a valued resource unique to the elderly (e.g. Cool 1980). After *Roots* by Alex Haley had popularized an interest in genealogy and ethnicity, the ethnic elderly were believed by some to have become the essential links between their descendants and the past in ways that could only enhance their self-esteem.

People with firsthand knowledge of the Chinese population and of the characteristics of the various Chinatowns in the United States knew that values which might make agency programs less necessary for Chinese were overwhelmed by the absence of extended families to carry them out. A flurry of studies on Chinese populations (e.g. Chen 1970, 1979 and Wu 1974, 1975 in Los Angeles; Carp and Kataoka 1976 in San Francisco; Cheng 1978 in San Diego; and Nagasawa 1980 in Phoenix) were carried out. Multi-ethnic studies including the Chinese were also carried out (e.g. the Pacific/Asian Elderly Research Project) to determine the service needs of minority elderly. By the end of the 1970s, several final reports were already on the table (e.g. Bell et al. 1976; P/AERP *Final Report* 1978; Human Resources Corporation's *Policy Issues Concerning the Minority Elderly* 1978; and Cuellar and Weeks' *Minority Elderly Americans: A Prototype for Area Agencies on Aging* 1980).

The conclusions of these local and national studies were remarkably in agreement. Again and again the reports emphasized the need for an improved data base on the Pacific and Asian elderly. Planners must be aware not only of the diverse national origins of the elderly of Asian descent, but also of the fact that they are concentrated in cities on the East and West coasts, each offering distinctive environments. Furthermore planners should be alert to cohort differences within the elderly population itself. In the 1960s, males who had many years of experience living in the United States were considered typical of the elderly Chinese population; but by the 1970s, this population was being replaced by females with no prior experience of living in the United States. Obviously, the needs of these two populations are very different. In order to run effective programs, planners also should be sensitive to cultural differences in coping styles. Natural support networks should be studied and, in so far as possible, incorporated into the service delivery system. Finally, programs must be accessible and acceptable to the elderly; specifically, the personnel running service programs should be bilingual and bicultural in order to communicate effectively with clients.

Minority researchers frequently point out the need for a cultural affinity between provider and client, but it is a fallacy to assume that a shared ethnic background automatically grants an understanding of the needs of the elderly. Policy makers and the elderly frequently disagree on the priorities they would assign to various programs and services. Indeed, Cicirelli (1981) found that adult children frequently disagree with their own parents as to which programs would be most beneficial or most desirable for them.

A staggering array of national, state, and local programs for the elderly, both public and private, are operating at any given moment in the United States. These range from national efforts serving millions, such as Social Security and Medicare, to local efforts serving a few thousand such as the Elders Mobile Market and Dial-A-Ride-Transport (DART). Estes (1979) and Gelfand and Olsen (1980) provide a good introduction to the proliferation of programs for the elderly and to the bureaucracies which have come into being in order to run them. Chinese living in Greater Boston participate in many of these programs and have found that they can live independently of their families largely because of them.

Issues in Service Delivery

By the late 1960s, community activists came to realize that some concrete actions had to be taken to meet the needs of an ever increasing elderly Chinese population. Men who were no longer retiring to China were the most visible segment of the needy elderly. The recognition of these needs was not limited to Boston. In San Francisco, for example, the same perceptions led to the opening in 1973 of a senior day health center (Lurie et al. 1976). According to Gaw (1975:333) the idea of a drop in center in Boston began when a Catholic nun who had taken care of several elderly Chinese had to leave the city. She contacted several individuals in the health care field, who then held a series of meetings. One member of the group, a restaurant owner, suggested that providing Chinese meals would be a very acceptable means of helping the elderly. The group served meals including home-delivered meals even before the beginning of the Nutrition Program of the Older Americans Act (Title VII). In its early days the center served an average of 30 Chinese elderly a day; in its new facility it serves over 100.

An early and continuing problem in some programs is defining a proper relationship between staff and participants. On my first visit to a nutrition site, I was taken aback by the behavior of some of the participants. Many received enormous portions of rice which they secreted into plastic containers brought with them for that purpose. They clearly intended to extract both their noon and evening meals from the food which was being served. Leftover food was eagerly accepted even if the individual had no intention of eating it—it could be saved and offered to someone else. When the meal was over, I noticed that many threw away their paper plates, but brought their plastic utensils to one of the diners; her son ran a restaurant, and she was collecting them for his use. In other words, nothing was allowed to go to waste. While this philosophy certainly has a good deal to offer and did so even more back in China where food and goods were more limited, it sometimes led to aggressive and greedy behavior. As one former worker at a meal site observed: "At my place the people were really greedy. I guess that is the way people get if all their lives they've had very little and had to struggle for it." I had seen a similar enthusiastic assault on a table of food at a family association banquet, which the elderly can attend free of charge (probably a carryover from feasts in the village to which elders were traditionally invited without having to provide a fee or gift). Such aggressive behavior does not inspire respect on the part of the personnel charged with dishing out the food. One man grumped that he did not like to eat at one meal site because the food is terrible, and because the staff simply slaps the food on the diner's tray "as if the elderly are pigs."

People performing social work and homemaker services felt that the elderly were difficult clients. For many of the older people such services were traditionally provided either through family members or through hired servants. The phenomenon of professional or voluntary personnel performing tasks formerly deemed the sphere of servants created confusion for some of the elderly and the staff. What were the proper forms of interaction? One young male worker explained the lessons he learned in his work with the elderly.

One thing I learned there was patience. They were always

testing me. It took three or four months before they were willing to talk to me casually. I had to prove myself first. For example, Mrs. Wong would come over to me and ask me to translate a letter for her when she knew that I was busy with other things. She would never come when she knew I was available. If I dropped what I was doing to help her, this meant two things. First it meant that I was interested in helping her personally. Secondly it meant that I was showing proper respect for the elderly. I won her trust. She even had me over to her house one time and invited me to look around. This means a lot if you understand how rare it is to be invited into a Chinese person's house.

An elderly woman employed as a homemaker expressed irritation with her role one day, in a similar vein. Her two clients, she felt, treated her like a servant and asked her to do all sorts of things that were beyond what they were entitled to receive. She complained that all clients were evaluated prior to the assignment of the worker and that the worker performed the tasks for which the client was certified. Another social worker emphasized that the Chinese client seeks concrete or material assistance (Chen 1979:597). They do not feel they have been helped if they are given only emotional support.

Many clients or would-be clients resist the admittance of a worker into their homes. Others disagree with the worker's assessment of their own or a relative's needs. A health worker described one of her most frustrating cases.

Mr. Gee used to come to the clinic, but we hadn't seen him for two years when his wife suddenly turned up wanting one of the physicians to certify that he was ill and needed a relative to come to the United States to care for him. This was for immigration purposes. Since we hadn't seen the man for so long, we insisted on checking him out and found that his condition had deteriorated. He is now completely bedridden and needs assistance even in turning over. His wife, the only caretaker, does not think he needs a home health aide. She feels that she is doing everything necessary. The man has bedsores, but they have not broken through. Instead of rotating his body every four hours, she rubs ointment on them.

Furthermore, the man's wife has restricted the nurse's access to her husband to once a month and had made it clear that from her perspective, even that much outside contact is interference. Mrs. Gee, however, spends much of her time outside of the house, leaving no one to attend to her husband.

The inaccessibility of medical care was also a major issue for the elderly in the early 1970s. In 1969 (Gaw 1974:344), a community Health Task Force was set up to plan more effective ways of meeting the needs of the Chinatown population. Major efforts were directed towards increasing the accessibility of medical services available at Tufts-New England Medical Center, and an evening clinic for Chinese patients was set up in conjunction with the hospital, which is located in Chinatown. It was held on Monday evenings, a time when many of the restaurant workers are free. In March 1973 the Boston Chinese Community Health Center (now known as the South Cove Community Health Center, *SCCHC*) was opened. The staff is bilingual, trained in Western medicine, and convinced of its efficacy. However, because many staff members are also bicultural, they are at least familiar with traditional health concepts and react supportively when a patient asks about the dangers of combining traditional treatments with Western ones. They are also alert to the special fears of Chinese patients such as loss of blood or the dangers of surgery. The SCCHC also has a mental health unit which is physically indistinguishable from the rest of the center. Patients waiting to see a psychiatrist need not suffer the potentially humiliating experience of being seen by their neighbors while they do so. Many Chinese do not share Western definitions of the cause of mental illness. Disturbed individuals are often perceived as behaving willfully or, alternatively, as being possessed and in need of exorcism (see, for example, Lin et al. 1978).

As in Hong Kong, many people believe that the responsibility for medical treatment lies first with the individual. Many of the older people brew their own tonics and pay careful attention to their diet, particularly when they have already developed symptoms. At the nutrition site, for example, women routinely omitted boiled vegetables from their plates when they felt that they were suffering from an excess of "cold." Furthermore there are diseases which Western practitioners are unable to identify and therefore unable to treat. Mrs. Gan, an immigrant in her 50s, suffered from a chronic circulatory disorder in her leg. No Western doctor seemed able to diagnose her problem, which was so severe that she was sometimes unable to walk. As her oldest son explained: "It is a disease that only the Chinese get, so Western doctors are not familiar with it and can't treat it. There are a lot of diseases associated with tropical living." Unfortunately there is no longer any local practitioner who can treat Mrs. Gan. She had to go to New York to obtain treatment from a doctor who had immigrated from Hong Kong. Unfortunately, the treatment is effective only for a few days at a time, and the family cannot afford to drive her down to New York every weekend because it hurts their business to close down on the weekends; so her trips are limited to once a month. Of course, as in Hong Kong, such treatments are not covered by any health plan.

In addition to the SCCHC, Chinatown also boasts an Adult Day Care Center located in Quincy Tower. It has a capacity of 30 people, and it is almost always full. There is also a homemaker and home health agency operating on the outskirts of Chinatown serving a very mixed clientele including the Chinese. However, a severe shortage of bilingual staff limits its usefulness. The major need of the elderly in Chinatown now is widely believed to be a nursing home. Placement in a nursing home is dreaded by most older people, but the fear and inconvenience it causes non-English speakers is considerably greater. The nursing home resident cannot make clear his or her needs and cannot understand the reasons for various treatments. The food is entirely Western in style, and for a population accustomed to linking health with particular foods, the notion of eating potentially "unbalanced" Western foods is appalling.

For several years, groups within the community have recognized this need, and land on the outskirts of Chinatown has been allocated for this purpose; but as of 1982 construction still remained in the future. Nursing homes are not enthusiastic about accepting Chinese patients with language difficulties, so Chinese who are already in them are scattered about the metropolitan area. One nursing home in the Brighton-Allston area has a small concentration of Chinese patients—maybe 7 at any given time—but they do not necessarily speak the same dialect, and there is no permanent bilingual staff member who can interpret for them. Usually, the relatively healthy patients help out the sicker ones with translation. In this context the casual visits of a Mrs. Ng or a Mrs. Choi take on considerable importance.

Most income maintenance programs are easily accepted by the elderly. Newcomers learn that these programs are their right, that in the United States the government supports the elderly. One long-time Chinatown resident explained the new point of view:

People who have grown up or lived here for a long time do

not have the same expectations for themselves in terms of care in old age that perhaps their own parents had. They are aware of the economy and the system here. In the first place they know that their kids will probably scatter to find good jobs. In the second place they know that there is Social Security and housing for the elderly. These men used to send money back to their families every year.

When I asked him whether older parents in Boston were likely to receive money from children living in other states, he exclaimed:

Well, I've never heard of it! . . . If your family was in China, you knew that if you didn't send the money back, they would probably starve. They were counting on you. This is not the situation for the elderly in the United States. They are not going to starve if the children do not send them money.

Other elderly have expressed gratitude for the generosity of the American government which allows them to relieve their children of a heavy financial burden.

While a monthly income of three or four hundred dollars may not seem like a great fortune, many of the elderly regard it as a princely sum, particularly if they are living in elderly housing where their rent is limited to 25 percent of their income. Considering their frugal eating habits, there is ample money available for discretionary spending. So people often feel that this is a good time of life financially speaking. On the other hand, they always face the threat of certain kinds of medical expenses, and they are frequently unaware or fail to make use of some programs which could help them save additional money. Few older people knew, for example, of the Mayor's shuttle bus service, and once learning of it, many still declined to use it because they couldn't speak with the driver. One woman who was unfamiliar with public transportation had to take a taxi to visit her husband in the hospital. She spent $25 a day on roundtrips until someone offered to accompany her by public transport. Once she learned the way she was able to go on her own.

Because of language barriers and high rates of illiteracy, especially among women, many older people cannot learn of the availability of special programs for the elderly through printed materials such as advertisements. Their great dependence on the spoken word means that family members, friends, neighbors, and other natural helpers continue to play critical roles in bringing information and services to the elderly.

PART IV
Conclusions

11 Aging and Adaptation

The process of aging is lifelong requiring the individual to adapt constantly to the fact of his or her changing capabilities. In a stable society, most people have acquired by early adulthood a reasonably clear idea of what they should be able to expect of themselves and of others as they move into or out of their productive years. Most of the elderly whom we have met in the preceding pages are now aged in societies very different from the ones in which they spent their formative years. For many people the mere passage of time has served to estrange them from contemporary society. For others, particularly immigrants, drastic relocations in space have complicated their adjustments.

It is a truism that the adaptation of any individual is conditioned for better or worse by the wider society in which he or she lives. The majority of the older Chinese in Hong Kong and in Greater Boston grew up in a still traditional China. As we saw (Chap. 1), all seven of the conditions which Rosow (1965) found contributing to favorable status of the elderly could be found in traditional China. To grow old in a society in which the contributions of the older members are valued and whose official ideology praises the old is a relatively easy task. To age gracefully in a society in which the contributions of the elderly are devalued and in which the old are regarded collectively though not necessarily individually as pathetic creatures is a much more demanding task.

A review of Rosow's variables can help to illuminate the differing circumstances to which the elderly Chinese of Hong Kong and of Greater Boston must adapt.

1. The extent to which the old own or control property on which the young are dependent:
In both Hong Kong and Greater Boston, the vast majority of children obtain their jobs and their housing on their own. Parental withholding

of funds can delay marriage or house purchases and can cut short educational pursuits, but children can with relative ease support themselves. Furthermore, the scarcity in Hong Kong of pensions and the limited income maintenance programs mean that the old are increasingly dependent on the young at the same time that their abilities to apply sanctions to a child are much weaker. In Boston older people are less dependent on children because they are eligible by virtue of age to participate in a wide variety of programs that allow them to lead independent though not affluent lives.

2. The extent to which the old have a vital command or monopoly of strategic knowledge of the culture:

In both Hong Kong and Greater Boston, the knowledge and the skills of the elderly have been severely devalued. The greater the educational gap between the generations, the less immediate utility the knowledge and skills of the older generation appear to have. Since most young people in Hong Kong have parents or grandparents who are old-fashioned, children are not particularly embarrassed by their elders beliefs and attitudes, however inconvenient they might be. In Greater Boston, however, the majority of non-Chinese children encountered in school or on the street are unlikely to understand the limitations that Chinese parents or grandparents try to put on their children. In this context, the young people frequently have to decide whether they will live up to family or to peer expectations. Children also often find themselves playing responsible roles in the outside community at a young age because of their greater English language competency.

3. The extent to which the elderly are links with the past:

By and large, neither community places much emphasis on the past. Ancestral rites are fading in Hong Kong and are almost nonexistent in Greater Boston. Separation from the past is often valued, particularly when delving into the past may reveal unresolved family conflicts associated with decisions to immigrate and responsibilities to those left behind. The current efforts of some younger Chinese Americans to recover their heritage may have a slight positive effect on the status of the elderly in their communities.

4. The extent to which kinship and the extended family are central to social organization:

Kinship remains extremely important in both Hong Kong and in Greater Boston. It is, however, a kinship that is contracted to the stem family. Both older populations are composed primarily of migrants who, as such, have split kinship networks. While migrants are willing to support parents, spouses, and children, they are less inclined to support their collateral relatives and may decrease the amount of contact they maintain with them. Future cohorts of the elderly in both locations may have more collaterals available for interaction, but in the absence of some common economic motivations for cooperation, it is unlikely that the extended family will come to prevail. At the same time that the family has contracted, the burdens imposed upon it have greatly increased. The greater financial dependency of older people in Hong Kong and the need to rely on family members in cases of long-term illness or disability cause them considerable anxiety because there are few resources outside the family to which they or their families can turn. In Greater Boston, there has been greater recognition of the problems care-giving can impose, and a variety of programs are being developed to assist care-givers with their tasks. In Boston also, the greater acceptability of housing for the elderly means that peers and in some cases professionals are available to reduce the amount of services family members would otherwise have to provide to non-English-speaking kin.

5. The size, stability, and homogeneity of the community:
During the past decade, Hong Kong has been undergoing a massive relocation of its population from the densely inhabited districts of Hong Kong Island and Kowloon to the satellite towns of the New Territories. These relocations have caused considerable hardship for older people whose support systems were external to the family. Until the 1960s, Boston Chinatown could perhaps have been described as a "gemeinschaft" society; people were drawn from a relatively narrow population base in Sze Yap and tended to live within a few blocks of the Chinatown shopping district. Business transactions often took place in a personalized context, with buyer and seller discussing home village affiliations. The major population shifts to the South End, Brookline, and Brighton-Allston beginning in the 1960s, along with the wider emigration base, changed the nature of the community. Elderly housing represents an attempt to reconstruct a small, stable, and homogeneous community.

6. The degree of economic productivity:
The per capita productivity of both Hong Kong and Greater Boston produce standards of living well above that experienced by the typical Chinese peasant in the past or the present. The fact that this productivity occurs in a cash economy makes nearly invisible the non-cash contributions that older people can make to their families while at the same time inflating the financial burdens their disability can bring to their families. When older family members have pensions or Social

Security payments to share, these cash contributions are more visible and easily appreciated. Forced retirement and the decline in unskilled jobs reduce the opportunities available to those elderly who wish to continue working.

7. The degree of mutual dependence among the members of a group:

The larger the scale of public programs for the needy the less the inclination of individuals to go to the assistance of needy neighbors. (A reverse cause and effect is possible for this relationship, of course). Both Hong Kong and Greater Boston are characterized by a very narrow circle of individuals to whom others feel they have any personal obligations.

As this review should make clear, aging in Hong Kong and Greater Boston requires adapting to societies very different from traditional or contemporary China. The mere existence of an urban rather than a rural environment in itself poses unique problems to former villagers. Traffic courtesy in Hong Kong (to say nothing of traffic courtesy in Boston) leaves a great deal to be desired, and pedestrians take many unnecessary risks. In Hong Kong, an older person's life is in danger any time he or she attempts to cross the street. Hearing and vision deficits impede the perception of danger, and slower reaction time makes it difficult for an older person to respond when danger is perceived. At present, older people constitute about one-third of Hong Kong's annual traffic fatalities. Worries about injury frequently lead families to restrict the older person's mobility. They are either accompanied on excursions or do not go out at all. In Boston an older person who does not speak any English is similarly handicapped.

The lessened mobility of the elderly frequently means a diminished social life. Yet given the value differences between the generations, there is probably a high need for peers with whom to share experiences. Unless the older person lives in one of the more stable neighborhoods, it may be difficult to operate in a social arena beyond the family. This contracted sphere of social interaction can make the older person's constant presence in the home a source of frustration, and in overcrowded quarters it renders privacy difficult.

Most older people remain capable of making major contributions to the running of the household, such as doing marketing, laundry, cooking, or otherwise freeing other household members to engage in money-making activities. The problems of reduced social networks and dependency are most acute in time of incapacitating illness. A major difference between Hong Kong and Boston, however, is the degree to which the older person can function independently. In Hong Kong, an elderly person can manage most activities without assistance. He or she can easily go to the market, find appropriate entertainment in the park or on television, select the preferred mode of medical treatment, and meet others who share the same world view. This ease of everyday living is possible because of the absence of language barriers (except for the few minority language speakers) and the presence of a large population sharing the same heritage and interests. This independence is jeopardized by financial constraints and leads to much doubling up of families. The possible inconveniences of living arrangements are made tolerable by the very fact of the scarcity of acceptable alternatives and by conventions that require people to keep their suffering to themselves and to avoid burdening others.

In the United States, doubling up is a culturally less acceptable alternative, even though in extreme old age, it is still a fairly common practice. Other alternatives are available, and the psychological advantages of elderly housing are increasingly recognized. Young people born or raised in America may be less tolerant of an older family member's attempts to influence family practices or decisions. To save everyone's feelings, separate residences are frequently seen as the best solution. In discussions of intergenerational living, older Chinese, like older Americans, prefer their children to move in with them rather than vice versa. Moving into a child's home confuses the lines of authority, particularly when the older person is still healthy and active and deprived of other means of making his or her personality felt. An increasingly common method of dealing with these problems is for the generations to maintain separate residences until frailty or disability make co-residence the most viable alternative to institutionalization. This is the same solution elderly of other backgrounds have reached, though for other reasons. The value emphasis on independence is still not that attractive to most older Chinese. They have chosen separate residences more to avoid potential conflicts over family roles than because of a genuine preference for independent living. As more and more older Chinese live independently of their children, the not yet old will become more familiar with the concept and view it as a likely arrangement for themselves. They may even come to value it for reasons of independence.

As to whether it is preferable to age in Hong Kong or Boston, there is a consensus. Most middle-aged residents in Greater Boston whose parents have spent most of their lives living in China or Hong Kong recognize that their parents can enjoy life more in Hong Kong (or Taiwan) than in the United States. Many of these parents come to the United States for visits of several months and often agree that they are more comfortable among their peers abroad. Consequently, they retain their Hong Kong or Taiwan bases until they can no longer manage on their own. Then they are likely to move permanently to the United States to be with or near a child. This way of coping with the later stages of the family life cycle is shared by many non-Chinese families in America, and it is at the same time an adaptation of traditional solutions to a new environment.

Glossary of Cantonese Terms

abaak 阿伯 "Father's older brother" = a common address term for old men
apoh 阿婆 "Mother's mother" = a common address term for old women
dim sam 點心 "Little hearts" = small pastries stuffed with meat or sweets
fung sap 風濕 "Wind-wet" = rheumatism
gaaifong 街坊 Neighbor
gam laahn jimui 金蘭姊妹 "Golden orchid sisters" = sworn sisters
git baai hingdaih 結拜兄弟 Sworn brothers
hei 氣 Air, breath
hei gung 氣功 A therapeutic technique practiced by Taoists
hohk waaih 學壞 "Learn (how to be) bad"
hou pahngyauh 好朋友 Good friend
huhng baau 紅包 "Red packet" = red envelopes containing gifts of cash
jaai tohng 齋堂 A residence in which only vegetarian meals are served
jauyuhk pahngyauh 酒肉朋友 "Wine and meat" friend = fair weather friend
jigeige pahngyauh 知己嘅朋友 Friend who knows myself
jing 精 Vital essence
jisamge pahngyauh 知心嘅朋友 Friend who knows my heart
jung yi 中醫 "Chinese" doctor = a doctor trained in Chinese medicine
kai 契 Various kinds of fictive kin relationships
keui fung yauh 驅風油 "Drive out the wind oil"
louh pahngyauh 老朋友 Old friend
louhsi 老師 Teacher, a respectful address term
mouh cho 冇錯 "You said it" or "No mistake about that"
neih hou yauh sam 你好有心 You are very kind, thoughtful
neih mouh yuhngge 你冇用嘅 You good-for-nothing
poutung pahngyauh 普通朋友 Common or ordinary friend
sai geuk seuhng syuhn 洗脚上船 "Wash the feet and get into the boat" = stop laboring and relax
sai yi 西醫 "Western" doctor = a doctor trained in Western medicine

247

sei jai 死仔 "Dead boy" = implication of wishing the child dead

siht bun fo 蝕本貨 "Goods on which money is lost" = daughters

tit da yisang 跌打醫生 "Fall-hit" doctor = "bone-setter"

yauh sam 有心 To possess a heart = to be kind, considerate, thoughtful

Bibliography

Achenbaum, W. Andrew. 1978. *Old age in the new land.* Baltimore: Johns Hopkins University Press.

Agassi, Joseph, and I. C. Jarvie. 1969. A study in Westernization. In *Hong Kong: A society in transition,* ed. I. C. Jarvie in consultation with Joseph Agassi, 129-63. London: Routledge and Kegan Paul.

Ahern, Emily. 1973. *The cult of the dead in a Chinese village.* Stanford: Stanford University Press.

Anderson, E.N., and Marja L. Anderson. 1973. A preliminary note on fictive kinship in Chinese society. In *Mountains and water: Essays on the cultural ecology of South Coastal China,* ed. E.N. Anderson and Marja L. Anderson, 77-97. Taipei: The Orient Cultural Service.

Baker, Hugh D.R. 1977. Extended kinship in the traditional city. In *The city in Late Imperial China,* ed. G. William Skinner, 499-520. Stanford: Stanford University Press.

Bell, Duran, Patricia Kasschau, and Gail Zellman. 1976. *Delivering services to elderly members of minority groups: A critical review of the literature.* Santa Monica, Calif: Rand Corporation.

Bernstein, Richard. 1982. *From the center of the Earth: The search for the truth about China.* Boston: Little, Brown and Co.

Biegel, David E., and Wendy R. Sherman. 1979. Neighborhood capacity building and the ethnic aged. In *Ethnicity and aging: Theory, research, and policy,* ed. Donald E. Gelfand and Alfred J. Kutzik, 320-40. New York: Springer Publishing Co.

Blau, Zena Smith. 1973. *Old age in a changing society.* New York: New Viewpoints.

Boston 200 Corporation. 1976. *Chinatown.* Boston: Boston 200 Neighborhood History Series.

Bott, Elizabeth. 1971. Family and social network: Summary and general discussion. In *Readings in kinship and social structure,* ed. Nelson Graburn, 389-91. New York: Harper and Row.

Brody, Elaine. 1981. 'Women in the middle' and family help to older people. *The Gerontologist* 21(5):471-80.

Bruner, Edward M. 1970. Medan: The role of kinship in an Indonesian city. In *Peasants in cities: Readings in the anthropology of urbanization*, ed. William Mangin, 122-34. Boston: Houghton Mifflin.

Bulatao, Rodolfo A. 1980. The transition in the value of children and the fertility transition. Paper prepared for a seminar on Determinants of Fertility Trends: Major Theories and New Directions for Research in Bad Homburg, F.R. Germany.

Burgess, Ernest W. 1960. Resume and implications. In *Aging in Western societies*, ed. Ernest W. Burgess, 377-88. Chicago: University of Chicago Press.

Butler, Robert N. 1975. *Why survive? Being old in America*. New York: Harper and Row.

Byrne, Susan W. 1974. Arden, an adult community. In *Anthropologists in cities*, ed. George Foster and Robert Kemper, 123-52. Boston: Little, Brown and Co.

Carp, Frances M. 1966. *A future for the aged: Victoria Plaza and its residents*. Austin: University of Texas Press.

Carp, Frances M., and Eunice Kataoka. 1976. Health care problems of the elderly of San Francisco's Chinatown. *The Gerontologist* 16(1): 30-38.

Carter, Margaret J. 1976. *Community nursing in Hong Kong*. Hong Kong: Hong Kong Council of Social Service.

Chan, Wing-tsit. 1953. *Religious trends in modern China*. New York: Columbia University Press.

Chang Chih-tung, [1898] 1960, Exhortation to learn. Excerpted in *Sources of Chinese Tradition*, ed. Wm. Theodore de Bary, pp. 743-49. New York: Columbia University Press.

Chen, Han-seng. 1936. *Landlord and peasant in China*. New York: International Publishers.

Chen, Jack. 1981. *The Chinese of America*. San Francisco: Harper and Row.

Chen, John T.S. 1973. *1001 Chinese sayings*. Hong Kong: Chung Chi College, Chinese University.

Chen, Pei-ngor. 1970. The Chinese community in Los Angeles. *Social Casework* 51:591-98.

——— 1979. A study of Chinese-American elderly residing in hotel rooms. *Social Casework* 60:89-95.

Chen, Pi-chao. 1972. Overurbanization, rustication of urban-educated youths, and politics of rural transformation: The case of China. *Comparative Politics* 4(3):361-86.

Chen, Theodore H.E., and Wen-hui C. Chen. 1959. Changing attitudes towards parents in Communist China. *Sociology and Social Research* 43:175-82.

Cheng, Eva. 1978. *The elder Chinese.* San Diego: The Campanile Press.

Chow, Tse-tung. 1967. *The May Fourth Movement: Intellectual revolution in modern China.* Stanford: Stanford University Press.

Chu, Louis. 1979. *Eat a bowl of tea.* Seattle: University of Washington Press. (Originally published 1961).

Cicirelli, Victor G. 1981. *Helping elderly parents: The role of adult children.* Boston: Auburn House Publishing Co.

Clark, Margaret, and Barbara Anderson. 1967. *Culture and aging: An anthropological study of older Americans.* Springfield: Charles C. Thomas.

Cohen, Myron. 1976. *House united, house divided: The Chinese family in Taiwan.* New York: Columbia University Press.

Cool, Linda. 1980. Ethnicity and aging: Continuity through change for elderly Corsicans. In *Aging in culture and society: Comparative viewpoints and strategies,* ed. Christine L. Fry and Contributors, 149-69. New York: J.F. Bergin Publishers.

Cooper, Eugene. 1980. *The wood-carvers of Hong Kong.* Cambridge: Cambridge University Press.

Crissman, Lawrence W. 1967. The segmentary structure of urban overseas Chinese communities. *Man* 2(2):185-204.

Crossman, Linda, Cecilia London, and Clemmie Barry. 1981. Older women caring for disabled spouses: A model for supportive services. *The Gerontologist* 21(5):464-80.

Cuellar, Jose B., and John Weeks. 1980. *Minority elderly Americans: A prototype for area agencies on aging.* San Diego: Allied Home Health Association.

Davis-Friedmann, Deborah. 1977. Strategies for aging: Interdependence between generations in the transition to socialism. *Contemporary China* 1(6):34-42.

————1981. Retirement and social welfare programs for Chinese elderly: A minimal role for the state. In *the situation of the Asian/Pacific elderly,* ed. Charlotte Nusberg and Masako Osako, 52-65. Washington, D.C.: International Federation on Aging.

Diamond, Norma. 1969. *K'un Shen: A Taiwan village.* New York: Holt, Rinehart and Winston.

Doolittle, Rev. Justus. 1966. *Social life of the Chinese.* Taipei: Ch'eng-wen Publishing Co. (Originally published 1865).

Estes, Carroll L. 1979. *The aging enterprise.* San Francisco: Jossey Bass.

Fei, Hsiao-tung. 1946. *Peasant life in China.* New York: Oxford University Press.

Fengler, Alfred P., and Nancy Goodrich. 1979. Wives of elderly disabled men: The hidden patients. *The Gerontologist* 19(2):175-83.

Fessler, Loren. 1976. Women in Hong Kong. *East Asia Series* 33(1). Hanover, N.H.: American Universities Field Staff.

Fischer, David Hackett. 1978. *Growing old in America.* Oxford: Oxford University Press.

Freedman, Maurice. 1967. Ancestor worship: Two facets of the Chinese case. In *Social organization: Essays presented to Raymond Firth,* ed. Maurice Freedman, 85-103. Chicago: Aldine.

————1970. *Lineage organization in Southeastern China.* London: The Athlone Press.

Fried, Morton H. 1953. *Fabric of Chinese society.* New York: Praeger.

Frolic, B. Michael. 1980. *Mao's people.* Cambridge: Harvard University Press.

Fry, Christine L. 1979. Structural conditions affecting community formation among the aged: Two examples from Arizona. *Anthropology Quarterly* 52(1):7-18.

Gallin,. Bernard. 1966. *Hsin Hsing, Taiwan: A Chinese village in change.* Berkeley: University of California Press.

Gaw, Albert C. 1975. An integrated approach in the delivery of health care to a Chinese community in America: The Boston experience. In *Medicine in Chinese cultures: Comparative studies of health care in Chinese and other societies,* ed. Arthur Kleinman et al., 327-49. Washington, D.C.: U.S. Department of Health, Education, and Welfare.

Gelfand, Donald E., and Jody K. Olsen. 1980. *The aging network: Programs and services.* New York: Springer Publishing Co.

Gold, Thomas B. 1980. Back to the city: The return of Shanghai's educated youth. *China Quarterly* 84:755-70.

Green Paper. See Hong Kong Government Publications.

Gruman, Gerald J. 1977. *A history of ideas about the prolongation of life.* New York: Arno Press.

Guttmann, David. 1979. Use of informal and formal supports by white ethnic aged. In *Ethnicity and aging: Theory, research, and policy,* ed. Donald E. Gelfand and Alfred J. Kutzik, 246-62. New York: Springer Publishing Co.

Hareven, Tamara K. 1976. The last stage: Historical Adulthood and old age. *Daedalus* 105(4):13-28.

Harrell, Stevan. 1981. Growing old in Taiwan. In *Other ways of growing old: Anthropological perspectives*, ed. Pamela T. Amoss and Stevan Harrell, 193-210. Stanford: Stanford University Press.

Harris, Louis, and Associates. 1975. *The myth and reality of aging in America*. Washington, D.C.: The National Council on the Aging, Inc.

———1981. *Aging in the eighties: America in transition*. Washington, D.C.: The National Council on the Aging, Inc.

Hochschild, Arlie Russell. 1973. *The unexpected community*. Englewood Cliffs, N.J.: Prentice-Hall.

Hodge, Peter. 1981. The politics of welfare. In *The Common Welfare: Hong Kong's Social Services*, ed. John F. Jones, 1-20. Hong Kong: The Chinese University Press.

Holzberg, Carol S. 1982. Ethnicity and aging: Anthropological perspectives on more than just the minority elderly. *The Gerontologist* 22(3):249-57.

Hong, Lawrence K. 1970. *The Chinese family in a modern industrial setting: Its structure and functions*. Ph.D. diss., University of Notre Dame.

Hong Kong Government Publications:
Census and Statistics Department. 1972. *Hong Kong population and housing census: 1971 main report*.
———1982. *Hong Kong 1981 Census: Basic Tables*.
Director of Medical and Health Services. 1976. *Annual department report 1975-1976*.
Government Information Services. 1979. *Hong Kong 1979, report for the year 1978*.
———1982. *Hong Kong 1982, a review of 1981*.
Government Secretariat. 1977. *Services for the elderly*. (Also referred to as the Green Paper).
Interdepartmental Working Party on the Future Needs of the Elderly. 1973. *Report of the Interdepartmental Working Party on the Future Needs of the Elderly*. (Unpublished report also referred to as the *Working Party Report*).
Social Welfare Department. 1972. *Study of members of three selected aged clubs*. (Unpublished report by the Research and Evaluation Unit).

Hoyt, G.C. 1954. The life of the retired in a trailer park. *American Journal of Sociology* 59(4):361-70.

Hsu, Francis L.K. 1940. Incest tabu in a North China village. *American Anthropologist* 42:122-35.

———1953. *Americans and Chinese: Two ways of life.* New York: Henry Schuman, Inc.

———1971a. *The challenge of the American dream: The Chinese in the United States.* Belmont, Calif.: Wadsworth Publishing Co.

———1971b. *Under the ancestors' shadow.* Stanford: Stanford University Press. (Originally published in 1948).

Huang, Parker Po-fei. 1970. *Cantonese dictionary.* New Haven and London: Yale University Press.

Human Resources Corporation. 1978. *Policy issues concerning the minority elderly: Final report executive summary.* Submitted to the Federal Council on the Aging, San Francisco.

Ikels, Charlotte. 1975. Old age in Hong Kong. *The Gerontologist* 15(3):230-35.

———1983. The process of care-taker selection. *Research on Aging* forthcoming.

Johnson, Sheila K. 1971. *Idle Haven: Community building among the working class retired.* Los Angeles: University of California Press.

Joint Hong Kong Council of Social Service Social Welfare Department Working Group on Social Service Needs of the Elderly. 1977. *Report of the study on the social service needs of the elderly in Hong Kong.* (Also referred to as the Social Service Needs Study).

Jordan, David K. 1972. *Gods, ghosts, and ancestors.* Berkeley and Los Angeles: University of California Press.

Kallgren, Joyce K. 1968. *Aspects of 'Social Security' in China.* Ph.D. diss., Harvard University.

Kan, Angela. 1974. *A study of neighborly interaction in public housing: The case of Hong Kong.* Hong Kong: The Social Research Centre of Chinese University.

Keith, Jennie. 1980. Old age and community creation. In *Aging in culture and society: Comparative viewpoints and strategies,* ed. Christine L. Fry and Contributors, 170-97. New York: J.F. Bergin Publishers, Inc.

Kendis, Kaoru Oguri, and Randall Jay Kendis. 1976. The street boy identity: An alternate strategy of Boston's Chinese-Americans. *Urban Anthropology* 5:1-18.

Kessen, William, ed. 1975. *Childhood in China.* New Haven: Yale University Press.

Kiefer, Christie W. 1974. *Changing cultures, changing lives.* San Francisco: Jossey Bass.

Kingston, Maxine Hong. 1977. *The woman warrior.* New York: Alfred Knopf.

———1981. *Chinamen.* New York: Ballantine Books.

Kivett, Vira R., and R. Max Learner. 1982. Situational influences on the morale of older rural adults in child-shared housing: A comparative analysis. *The Gerontologist* 22(1):100-06.

Kung, S.W. 1962. *Chinese in American life.* Seattle: University of Washington Press.

Lai, T.C. 1970. *Selected Chinese sayings.* rev. ed. Hong Kong: University of Hong Kong. (Original edition published 1960).

Lamson, Herbert Day. 1934. *Social pathology in China.* Shanghai: The Commercial Press.

Lang, Olga. 1946. *Chinese family and society.* New Haven: Yale University Press.

Laslett, Peter, ed. 1972. *Household and family in past time.* Cambridge: Cambridge University Press.

Lee, Rance P.L. 1975. Interaction between Chinese and Western medicine in Hong Kong: Modernization and professional inequality. In *Medicine in Chinese cultures: Comparative studies of health care in Chinese and other societies,* ed. Arthur Kleinman et al., 219-40. Washington, D.C.: Department of Health, Education, and Welfare.

Lee, Rose Hum. 1958. The stranded Chinese in the United States. *Phylon* 19(2):180-94.

———1960. *The Chinese in the United States of America.* Hong Kong: Hong Kong University Press.

Lee, Shu-ching. 1953. China's traditional family, its characteristics and disintegration. *American Sociological Review* 18:272-80.

Lethbridge, Henry J. 1969. Hong Kong under Japanese occupation: Changes in social structure. In *Hong Kong: A society in transition,* ed. I.C. Jarvie in consultation with Joseph Agassi, 77-127. London: Routledge and Kegan Paul.

Leung, Basil. 1971. Preliminary report on a survey into the social needs of old people in Wong Tai Sin resettlement estate. Hong Kong: Wong Tai Sin Community Centre.

Levy, Marion. 1949. *The family revolution in Modern China.* Cambridge: Harvard University Press.

Light, Ivan H. 1972. *Ethnic enterprise in America.* Berkeley: University of California Press.

Lin, Tsung-yi, et al. 1978. Ethnicity and patterns of help-seeking. *Culture, Medicine, and Psychiatry* 2:3-13.

Little, Virginia, C. 1979. Hong Kong in transition: Policy and services for the elderly. Paper presented at the Western Gerontological Society annual meeting, San Francisco.

Litwak, Eugene. 1965. Extended kin relations in an industrial democratic society. In *Social Structure and the Family*, ed. Ethel Shanas and Gordon Streib, 290-323. Englewood Cliffs, N.J.: Prentice-Hall.

Liu, Yung-huo. 1976. Older people in new China: Rights and obligations. In *Aging with dignity: An examination of local, national and international concerns for the elderly, Hawaii Governor's Bicentennial conference on aging, conference proceedings June 7-14, 1976*. Honolulu: State of Hawaii Commission on Aging.

Loewen, James W. 1971. *The Mississippi Chinese: Between black and white*. Cambridge: Harvard University Press.

Lopata, Helena Znaniecki. 1973. *Widowhood in an american city*. Cambridge, Mass.: Schenkman.

Lowenthal, Marjorie Fiske and Clayton Haven. 1968. Interaction and adaptation: Intimacy as a critical variable. *American Sociological Review* 22:20-30.

Lurie, Eleanor, et al. 1976. On Lok Senior Day Health Center. *The Gerontologist* 16(1):39-46.

Lyman, Stanford. 1974. *Chinese Americans*. New York: Random House.

McCunn, Ruthanne Lum. 1979. *An illustrated history of the Chinese in America*. San Francisco: Design Enterprises of San Francisco.

————1981. *Thousand pieces of gold*. San Francisco: Design Enterprises of San Francisco.

Miller, Stuart Creighton. 1969. *The unwelcome immigrant: The American image of the Chinese, 1785-1882*. Berkeley: University of California Press.

Mindel, Charles H. 1979. Multigenerational family households: Recent trends and implications for the future. *The Gerontologist* 19(5):456-63.

Mitchell, Robert Edward. 1972a. *Family life in urban Hong Kong*. Taipei: The Orient Cultural Service.

————1972b. *Levels of emotional strain in Southeast Asian Cities*. Taipei: The Orient Cultural Service.

Mote, Frederick W. 1977. Yuan and Ming. In *Food in Chinese culture: Anthropological and historical perspectives*, ed. K.C. Chang, 193-257. New Haven: Yale University Press.

Munro, Donald J. 1977. *The concept of man in contemporary China*. Ann Arbor: University of Michigan Press.

Myerhoff, Barbara. 1978. *Number our days*. New York: Dutton.

Nagasawa, Richard, et al. 1980. *The elderly Chinese: A forgotten minority.* Tempe: Arizona State University.

Nee, Victor G., and Brett DeBary. 1972. *Longtime californ': A documentary study of an American Chinatown.* New York: Pantheon.

Niebanck, Paul. 1965. *The elderly in older urban areas: Problems of adaptation and the effects of relocation.* Philadelphia: University of Pennsylvania.

Osako, Masako M. 1979. Aging and family among Japanese Americans: The role of ethnic tradition in the adjustment to old age. *The Gerontologist* 19(5):448-55.

Osgood, Cornelius. 1975. *The Chinese: A study of a Hong Kong community.* Tucson: University of Arizona Press.

Pacific/Asian Elderly Research Project. 1978. *Final report.* Los Angeles.

Palinkas, Lawrence A. 1980. Rhetoric and social change in a Chinese Christian community. Paper presented at the annual meeting of the American Anthropological Association, Washington, D.C.

Palmore, Erdman. 1975. *The honorable elders: A cross-cultural analysis of aging in Japan.* Durham, N.C.: Duke University Press.

Parish, William L., and Martin King Whyte. 1978. *Village and family in contemporary China.* Chicago: University of Chicago Press.

Pasternak, Burton. 1972. *Kinship and community in two Chinese villages.* Stanford: Stanford University Press.

Podmore, David. 1971. The population of Hong Kong. In *Hong Kong: The industrial colony,* ed. Keith Hopkins, 21-54. Hong Kong: Oxford University Press.

Rhoads, Edward J.M. 1974. Merchant associations in Canton. In *The Chinese city between two worlds,* ed. Mark Elvin and G. William Skinner, 97-118. Stanford: Stanford University Press.

Robinson, Betsy, and Majda Thurnher. 1979. Taking care of aged parents: A family life cycle transition. *The Gerontologist* 19(6): 586-93.

Rosen, Sherry. 1976. Sibling and in-law relationships in Hong Kong. Paper presented at the annual meeting of the National Council on Family Relations, New York.

Rosow, Irving. 1965. And then we were old. *Transaction* 2(2):20-26.

———1967. *Social integration of the aged.* New York: Free Press.

Ross, Jennie-Keith. 1977. *Old people, new lives: Community creation in a retirement residence.* Chicago: Chicago University Press.

Salaff, Janet W. 1971. Urban residential communities in the wake of the Cultural Revolution. In *The city in Communist China,* ed. John W. Lewis, 289-324. Stanford: Stanford University Press.

———1974. The Hong Kong Chinese family as enterprise: An anachronism in the industrial setting? Unpublished paper. Toronto: Department of Sociology, University of Toronto.

———1981. *Working daughters of Hong Kong: Filial piety or power in the family.* Cambridge: Cambridge University Press.

Sankar, Andrea. 1978. *The evolution of the sisterhood in traditional Chinese society: From village girls' houses to chai t'angs in Hong Kong.* Ph.D. diss., University of Michigan.

Schorr, Alvin 1980. "*. . . thy father and thy mother . . .*" *A second look at filial responsibility and family policy.* Washington, D.C.: Social Security Administration.

Scott, Janet Lee. 1980 *Action and meaning: Women's participation in the Mutual Aid Committees, Kowloon.* Ph.D. diss., Cornell University.

Seelbach, Wayne C. 1977. Gender differences in expectations for filial responsibility. *The Gerontologist* 17(5):421-25.

Shanas, Ethel. 1979. The family as a social support system in old age. *The Gerontologist* 19(2):169-74.

Shanas, Ethel, and Marvin B. Sussman eds. 1977. *Family, bureaucracy and the elderly.* Durham, N.C.: Duke University Press.

Shelly, Joseph F. 1974. Mutuality and retirement community success: An interactionist perspective in gerontological research. *International Journal of Aging and Human Development* 5(1):71-80.

Simmons, Leo. W. 1945. *The role of the aged in primitive society.* New Haven: Yale University Press.

Siu, Paul C. 1952. The Sojourner. *American Journal of Sociology* 58:34-44.

———1953. *The Chinese laundryman: A study of social isolation.* Ph.D. diss., University of Chicago.

Skinner, G. William. 1977. Introduction: Urban social structure in Ch'ing China." In *The city in Late Imperial China,* ed. G. William Skinner, 521-54. Stanford: Stanford University Press.

Smith, Arthur H. 1965. *Proverbs and common sayings from the Chinese.* New York: Paragon Book Reprint Corp. and Dover Publications. (Originally published in 1914).

———1970. *Village life in China.* Boston: Little, Brown and Co. (Originally published in 1899).

Social Service Needs Study-See Joint Hong Kong Council.

Sullivan, Charles, and Kathlyn Hatch. 1970. *The Chinese in Boston, 1970.* Boston: Action for Boston Community Development.

Sung, Betty Lee. 1967. *The story of the Chinese in America.* New York: Collier Books.

Sussman, Marvin B. 1977. The family life of old people. In *Handbook of aging and the social sciences*, ed. Robert H. Binstock and Ethel Shanas, 218-43. New York: Van Nostrand Reinhold Co.

———1979. *Social and economic supports and family environments for the elderly*. Final Report submitted to the Administration on Aging, Washington, D.C.

Topley, Marjorie. 1975. Chinese and Western medicine in Hong Kong: Some social and cultural determinants of variation, interaction and change. In *Medicine in Chinese cultures: Comparative studies of health care in Chinese and other societies*, ed. Arthur Kleinman et al., 241-71. Washington, D.C.: Department of Health, Education, and Welfare.

———1975. Marriage resistance in rural Kwangtung. In *Women in Chinese Society*, ed. Margery Wolf and Roxane Witke, 67-88, Stanford: Stanford University Press.

Topley, Marjorie, and James Hayes. 1968. Notes on some vegetarian halls in Hong Kong belonging to the sect of Hsien-T'ien Tao. *Journal of the Hong Kong Branch of the Royal Asiatic Society* 8:135-48.

Trela, James E., and Jay H. Sokolovsky. 1979. Culture, ethnicity, and policy for the aged. In *Ethnicity and aging: Theory, research, and policy*, ed. Donald E. Gelfand and Alfred J. Kutzik, 117-36. New York: Springer Publishing Co.

Turnbull, Colin M. 1972. *The mountain people*. New York: Simon and Schuster.

United States Government:

U.S. Commission on Civil Rights. 1980. *Success of Asian Americans: Fact or fiction*. Clearinghouse Publication 64. Washington, D.C.

Vogel, Ezra F. 1971. *Canton under Communism: Programs and politics in a provincial capital, 1949-1968*. New York: Harper and Row.

Watson, James L. 1975. *Emigration and the Chinese lineage: The Mans in Hong Kong and London*. Berkeley: University of California Press.

Weeks, John R., and Jose B. Cuellar. 1981. The role of family members in the helping networks of older people. *The Gerontologist* 21 (4):388-94.

Winiecke, Linda. 1973. The appeal of age-segregated housing to the elderly poor. *International Journal of Aging and Human Development* 4(4):293-306.

Woehrer, Carol E. 1978. Cultural pluralism in American families: The influence of ethnicity on social aspects of aging. *The Family Coordinator* 27 (4):329-39.

Wolf, Margery. 1975. Women and suicide in China. In *Women in Chinese society*, ed. Margery Wolf and Roxane Witke, 111-41. Stanford: Stanford University Press.

Wong, Aline K. 1972. *The Kaifong associations and the society of Hong Kong*. Taipei: The Orient Cultural Service.

Wong, Fai-ming. 1969. *Modern ideology, industrialization, and the Chinese family in Hong Kong*. Ph.D. diss., University of California at Santa Barbara.

————1979. Family structure and processes in Hong Kong. In *Hong Kong: economic, social and political studies in development*, ed. Tzong-biau Lin et al., 95-121. New York: M.E. Sharpe, Inc.

Working Party Report. See Hong Kong Government Publications.

Wu, Frances Y.T. 1974. *Mandarin-speaking aged Chinese in the Los Angeles area: Needs and services*. Ph.D. diss., University of California at Los Angeles.

————1975. Mandarin-speaking aged Chinese in the Los Angeles area. *The Gerontologist* 15(3):271-75.

Yang, Chin-kun. 1959. The Chinese family in the Communist Revolution. In *Chinese Communist Society: The family and the village*, C. K. Yang. Cambridge, Mass.:MIT Press.

Yap, P.M. 1962. Aging in underdeveloped Asian countries. In *Sociological and psychological aspects of aging*, ed. Clark Tibbitts and Wilma Donahue, 442-53. New York: Columbia University Press.

Index

Advocates, 5, 231–32
Ancestor worship, 12, 22–24, 32, 99. *See also* Lineages; Filial piety

Boston Chinatown: history of, 143–44, 147–49; organizations and services in, 144–46, 152; sources of disunity in, 149–52
Burial societies, 26–27, 66, 100, 112

Child-rearing practices: discipline, 20, 144, 175, 182; modeling, 182–83; paternal role, 165–66, 185–87
Chinese language churches, 155
Clans. *See* Family associations; Lineages
Cohort differences, 180, 227, 232–33
Collateral kin, 95, 100. *See also* Siblings; Family structure
Cultural conflicts, 189–92
Cultural Revolution, 29, 32, 69, 188

Daughters-in-law, 61–62, 86, 163
District associations, 26–27
Double jeopardy hypothesis, 231

Elderly housing, 202, 226–31. *See also* Homes for the aged; Hostels for the elderly
Employment, 45–48, 82, 84
Ethnicity, 10, 228, 231–33

Family associations (surname associations), 26–27, 99–100, 145, 162
Family life cycle, 74, 86, 246
Family structure: extended family, 12, 95, 242; stem family, 79, 100, 242; traditional structure, 107. *See also* Lineages

Fictive kinship: kai relationships, 21, 28, 33, 66–67, 92; sworn sibling relationships, 20–21, 105–6
Filial piety: in Hong Kong, 82–83, 112; among immigrants, 139; in traditional China, 16–20. *See also* Ancestor worship
Five Guarantees, 33
Friends, 104–8, 110. *See also* Peer relationships

Gaaifong associations, 111–12
Generation gap, 179, 200; coping with, 82; examples of, 79, 80–82. *See also* Cohort differences; Intergenerational relations
Gray Panthers, 6
Green card, 93

Homes for the aged, 79, 108, 119–22. *See also* Elderly housing; Hostels for the elderly
Hostels for the elderly, 108–9
Household division, 23, 96, 99

Illness, causes of, 63, 132
Immigration of Chinese to United States, 137–42
Income maintenance programs, 123–24; Infirmity Allowance (Old Age Allowance), xiii, 46, 55, 83, 123–24. *See also* Five Guarantees
Intergenerational relations: communication problems, 192, 226–27; financial contributions, 8, 82–84, 238; sources of tension, 181, 187–89, 201, 205–6, 209. *See also* Generation gap
Intermarriage, 167, 195–97. *See also* Marriage

Jaai-tong (chai-tong), 28, 122–23

Kai relationships. *See* Fictive kinship
Knowledge of elderly: educational attainments, 44, 70–71, 142, 153; experience, 11, 16–17, 23, 183–84; limitations, 18, 29, 242

Language differences: as barriers, 110, 147–48, 237; in Hong Kong, 41
Lineages: absence of, in urban areas, 96, 98–100; in village life, 21, 24, 102; weakening of, in People's Republic of China, 29, 32
Living arrangements of elderly: historical trends, 6–8; multigenerational households, 9, 79–80, 200. *See also* Elderly housing
Longevity, 16–17

Marriage: blind marriage, 28, 43; marital status of older people, 71; matchmaking, 60, 157–58, 168–69; remarriage, 74–75, 107–8; traditional marriage, 191–94. *See also* Intermarriage
Medical services: in Boston Chinatown, 152, 235–37; in Hong Kong, 126–32; in the People's Republic of China, 32
Methodology, xi–xiv, xv–xvi
Modernization, 10–11
Mortality, 125
Mutual Aid Committees (MACs), 111–12

Organizations of Chinese in Greater Boston, 154–55

Peer relationships, 102–4, 228. *See also* Friends
Pensions, 27; in Hong Kong, 46, 49, 83; in the People's Republic of China, 31, 34
Population data: Hong Kong, 39–42, 68; United States, 152–53
Proverbs, 17–18
Public housing in Hong Kong, 41–43, 86–87, 90–91

Reciprocity, 19
Research goals, xi, xv
Residence patterns of Chinese parents, 74–79, 198–200. *See also* Living arrangements
Residents' Committees, 112
Rosow's variables, 11–12, 23–25, 241–44

Sample, xi–xiv, xv–xvii
Service delivery in Boston Chinatown, 233–38
Siblings, 95–96, 210–15
Social services in Hong Kong, 118–20, 124–25
Sources of income of elderly in Hong Kong, 83. *See also* Intergenerational relations
Status of the elderly: power and authority, 3, 14–15, 30; status markers, 13–16, 22, 32
Suicide, 4
Support systems: alternatives to sons, 20–22; co-workers, 27–28; examples, 116, 207; family caregivers, 9–10; natural helpers, 216–26; in the People's Republic of China, 30, 33
Surname associations. *See* Family associations
Sworn sibling relationships. *See* Fictive kinship

Taoism: beliefs and practices, 16, 53, 54, 57; halls and associations, 56–58; Wong Tai Sin, 57, 91–93

Value changes, 11, 28, 29
Visiting patterns, 85–86